"I'm delighted to hear that the Adney biography is reaching publication, news that is as promising and welcome as it is overdue."

—John McPhee, author of *The Survival of the Bark Canoe*, quoted with permission from correspondence with Keith Helmuth

TAPPAN ADNEY

From Birchbark Canoes to Indigenous Rights

C. Ted Behne
and
James W. Wheaton

with
Keith Helmuth
Daryl Hunter
and
Nicholas N. Smith

Keith Helmuth, Editor

Chapel Street Editions
and
Goose Lane Editions

Edited by Clarissa Hurley.
Copy edited by Jill Ainsley.
Cover and page design by Brendan Helmuth, Chapel Street Editions.
Cover image and frontispiece courtesy of the Carleton County Historical Society.
Printed in Canada.
10 9 8 7 6 5 4 3 2 1

Goose Lane Editions and Chapel Street Editions acknowledge the generous support of the Government of Canada, the Canada Council for the Arts, and the Government of New Brunswick.

Goose Lane Editions
500 Beaverbrook Court, Suite 330
Fredericton, New Brunswick
CANADA E3B 5X4
gooselane.com

Library and Archives Canada Cataloguing in Publication

Title: Tappan Adney : from birchbark canoes to Indigenous rights / James W. Wheaton and C. Ted Behne ; with Daryl Hunter, Nicholas N. Smith, and Keith Helmuth ; edited by Keith Helmuth.
Names: Wheaton, James W., author. | Behne, C. Ted, 1942-2014, author. | Helmuth, Keith, 1937- author, editor.
Description: Includes bibliographical references and index.
Identifiers: Canadiana (print) 2024034605X | Canadiana (ebook) 20240351142 | ISBN 9781773103143 (softcover) | ISBN 9781773103150 (EPUB)
Subjects: LCSH: Adney, Tappan, 1868-1950. | LCSH: Artists—United States—Biography. | LCSH: Photographers—United States—Biography. | LCSH: Illustrators—United States—Biography. | LCSH: Ethnologists—United States—Biography. | LCGFT: Biographies.
Classification: LCC N6537.A36 W44 2024 | DDC 700.92—dc23

Goose Lane Editions and Chapel Street Editions are located on the unceded territory of the Wəlastəkokewiyik whose ancestors along with the Mi'kmaq and Peskotomuhkati Nations signed Peace and Friendship Treaties with the British Crown in the 1700s.

Chapel Street Editions
150 Chapel Street
Woodstock, New Brunswick
CANADA E7M 1H4
chapelstreeteditions.com

Contents

Preface

The ancient Egyptians tell us a person dies twice, once when they take their last breath and again the last time their name is spoken. This biography of Tappan Adney is the collective effort of a group of people moved to ensure his name continues to be spoken.

Adney is best known for a singular achievement. He was the artist, writer, and craftsman who preserved the knowledge of how to build birchbark canoes when they were on the verge of extinction.

But that is only part of the Adney story. He was also the researcher and activist who in 1947 presented the legal case in a Canadian court for Indigenous rights to land and resources based on the Peace and Friendship Treaty of 1725. Adney lost his case, but a later discovery and subsequent court decisions have confirmed that he was right; the Wəlastəkokewiyik did indeed have both treaty and Aboriginal rights to hunt, fish, and access forest resources. A new era in the reclamation of Indigenous rights now prevails in Canada.

Along with saving the birchbark canoe and the defence of Indigenous rights, Adney's life included vocational engagements with art and design, wilderness adventure and natural history journalism, graphic illustration and photography, pomology and orchard management, anthropology and archaeology, and ethnography and linguistics.

Any one of these disciplines can be the basis for a life's work. Adney's vocation was to combine serious work in all these fields into one life. His passion for the birchbark canoe at nineteen and his devotion to Indigenous rights at eighty bookend his vocational paths. His love for the birchbark canoe and its preservation was lifelong. The ground for his fierce defence of Indigenous rights late in life lay in his continuing relationships with his Wəlastəkwi friends and his appreciation of their material, linguistic, and material culture. The preservation of culture is the thread consistently woven throughout his life's work.

Adney was an artist. He sketched, drew, and painted wherever he travelled. He was at the same time an avid student of the living world and natural history. Ornithology was his special passion. He packed an artist's kit, complete with drawing board, on his expeditions into the far reaches of New Brunswick's forested watersheds. Sometimes he also carried a camera.

As an artist, his spontaneous reaction to experience was aesthetic and relational. His intuitive response to the natural world was awe, keen interest, and appreciation. In the same way, his openness to learning from new experience drew him into ethnography as a participant-observer, from which he gained a high regard for the social, linguistic, and material forms of traditional Indigenous cultures.

Tappan Adney's early education was a program of home schooling conducted by his father, who was a university professor of agriculture and natural sciences. This education combined rigorous academics, practical work experience, and direct study of the natural world. At the age of twelve, Adney was admitted to the University of North Carolina as a provisional student. One year later, he was granted regular student status.

At fourteen he enrolled in Trinity School in New York City, where he was immersed in the academic study of classical disciplines. During his four years at Trinity, he also took classes at the Art Students League that equipped him to later become an illustrator of publications associated with the American Museum of Natural History. This put him in touch with prominent natural history scientists of the time and led to membership in several newly founded scientific organizations. He later created a series of large oil paintings for the headquarters of the Explorers Club in New York, of which he was a founding member. These paintings continue to be so highly prized that the club has declined recent requests to photograph them.

At eighteen, he was an accomplished ornithologist, researching the nesting habitats of birds in New York's Central Park and publishing his reports in the proceedings of the American Ornithologists' Union. He was on track to enter Columbia College (later Columbia University), but in the summer after graduation from Trinity his life took an adventurous turn. He never looked back. With this rich mixture of academics, experiential learning, and creativity well in hand, Adney's sense of intellectual ability and artistic talent made him a supremely self-confident young man.

He was insatiably curious. With notable powers of retention, he became well informed about every subject he pursued. His studies ranged from archaeology to zoology, from poetry to petroglyphs, from ornithology to

Jim Wheaton (left) and Ted Behne (right) at the Wooden Canoe Heritage Association Assembly, 2003. (photo: Elizabeth Behne)

canoe building, from medieval heraldic art to the scientific hybridization of apples, from botany to bookbinding, and more. He was knowledgeable about human and natural history, linguistics, photography, fine art, craftwork, hunting and fishing, wilderness living, and myriad other interests.

In the chapters that follow, Adney's vocational paths are treated in detail, but the larger goal has been to braid them into the story of his overarching activist ethnographic vocation: the preservation of Wəlastəkwey material and linguistic culture, and the restoration of their Indigenous rights to land and resources.

How This Book Came to Be

James W. Wheaton initiated the Adney biography in the mid-1980s. As the husband of Joan Adney Dragon, he became fascinated with the life and multi-faceted accomplishments of her grandfather, Edwin Tappan Adney. Jim started researching the Adney story with the idea of writing a complete biography. He worked steadily on this project and by 2003 had completed drafts of fourteen chapters.

Jim Wheaton met Ted Behne at a birchbark canoe workshop. Ted began working with him on the biography in an editing capacity. For the last two years of their collaboration, Jim was in treatment for an illness that took his life in 2005. Before he died, he asked Ted to complete the book. Ted picked up the project and embarked on additional research and writing. By 2007, he had prepared a new version of the manuscript but continued his research, determined to pull in everything he could find that would help complete the story of Adney's remarkable life and legacy.

When the opportunity came to transcribe and edit Adney's travel journals for publication by Goose Lane Editions, Ted turned his attention to that important project. Volume 1 was published in 2010. Ted completed his work on volume 2 but became ill and died prior to its publication in 2014.

Ted expected the Adney biography would also be of interest to Goose Lane Editions, but some key aspects of the story were yet to be included at the time of his death. His wife, Elizabeth Behne, whom Ted described as "my first and best reader and editor," continued working with Goose Lane toward publication of the biography, but the manuscript remained to be completed and already stood at over 115,000 words.

Fortunately, publishers in the province of New Brunswick know each other. In the course of conversations between Susanne Alexander, publisher at Goose Lane Editions, and Keith Helmuth, publisher at Chapel Street Editions (CSE), and with the approval of Joan Adney Dragon and Liz Behne, the Adney biography migrated to CSE. As a not-for-profit, cultural heritage publisher, CSE could invest the time required to complete, edit, and prepare the manuscript for publication without incurring unsupportable costs. As the manuscript neared completion, further conversations between Keith Helmuth and Susanne Alexander led to an agreement for co-publication.

Daryl Hunter has been ever-present over the entire span of the biography's gestation, working with Jim Wheaton, Ted Behne, Liz Behne, and Keith Helmuth, providing research, information, editing, writing assistance, and crucial advice. Daryl is the primary archivist of the Tappan Adney story as well as that of Francis Peabody Sharp (Adney's father-in-law) and is the author of chapter 8, "The Orchard Business in New Brunswick."

Nicholas N. Smith, an ethnographic scholar who worked with Adney's language research papers at the Peabody Essex Museum, is the primary author of chapter 12, "Maliseet (Wəlastəkwey) Linguistics and the Preservation of Culture." Daryl Hunter assisted Nick Smith with the organization and writing of this chapter.

Keith Helmuth, the book's general editor, composed chapters 9 and 13 from the research of Jim Wheaton and Ted Behne. He is also the author of the preface and epilogue. As a contributing author and general editor, he is responsible for the final assembly and thematic structure of the book. He composed text that threads the overarching themes of Adney's life and work from chapter to chapter and throughout the body of the narrative. Clarissa Hurley provided significant supplementary editing in the final stages of preparation that greatly improved the book's overall presentation. Alan Sheppard, managing editor at Goose Lane Editions, contributed in a similar way.

Without the initial work by Jim Wheaton and the continued devotion of Ted Behne to the development of the manuscript, this biography would not exist. Liz Behne picked up work on the manuscript at a personally difficult time and kept it from stalling. Susanne Alexander at Goose Lane Editions played a crucial role in fielding the manuscript and keeping the project alive. But were it not for Daryl Hunter's decades-long support in facilitating communication among the parties and for tirelessly supplying crucial information from his archive or finding it elsewhere, it's unlikely this book would have made it to publication.

Editor's Addendum: A Personal Note

I first became aware of Tappan Adney and the significance of his legacy in 1967, three years after his book *The Bark Canoes and Skin Boats of North America* was published. Tom Findley, a fellow faculty member at Friends World College, had the book open on his seminar table. He and a group of students were developing an experiential education project that included building five canoes and an expedition from their boatyard on the north shore of Long Island, New York, up the Hudson River into Canada and then west and north following the old canoe routes. They built fibreglass canoes, but the Adney book was their inspiration and a guide to design and framing.

My family moved to New Brunswick in 1971 and established North Hill Farm at Speerville. Soon thereafter, John and Lois Thompson of Woodstock introduced us to Joan Adney Dragon with the thought that my wife, Ellen, and I might be interested in acting as caretakers and rental managers of the Adney cottage at Skiff Lake in return for its use in spring and fall seasons. We were glad to do so. Thus began our association and friendship with Joan and her husband, Jim Wheaton.

The first time I entered the Adney cottage, original oil painting portraits of Tappan and his wife, Minnie Bell Sharp, were hanging on the wall by the stairs to the second floor. Examples of Adney's artwork were also on display. On reaching the large open room of the second floor, I saw an Adney model canoe on the table against the south wall. A vintage typewriter was on the desk next to the table. I did not realize, at the time, I was looking at Tappan Adney's typewriter. We later met Glenn Adney, Tappan and Minnie Bell's son and Joan's father, when R. Vaughan Thompson loaded a piano on the back of a flatbed truck and had it driven to the outdoor Woodstock Farm Market so Glenn could add his rendition of Broadway show tunes and popular jazz numbers to the festivities of the day.

Jim Wheaton shared early drafts of the Tappan Adney biography with me. I had a previous career in the book business and college library management, so Jim's biography project was of special interest to me. Although I later wrote and published a short, illustrated book on Tappan Adney, I had no inkling I would become involved in the long saga of producing the full biography. It now appears the stars have been aligning in this way for a long time.

My affinity for the Adney story is connected to both my academic background and the cultural milieu in which I grew up. My university studies focused on European intellectual history and the European invasion and colonization of North America. My post-graduate studies included anthropology, geography, and social ecology. I have been particularly interested in the way anthropology as a discipline grew out of the study of history, and the way ethnography as a discipline emerged from the development of the social sciences. Adney's work contributed to the emergence of these new disciplines.

I grew up in a family setting of rural skills and self-provisioning that included the woodland culture of hunting, trapping, and fishing. Some of my earliest reading included adventure novels of wilderness living set in the "north country" of Canada. My older brother and I were both taken by the same wilderness mystique that repeatedly drew Adney back to New Brunswick. We simulated a version of this lifestyle in the still forested areas around our northeast Ohio home.

And when I became a teacher, it was with a new college that was developing the core of its academic program around the progressive innovation of experiential education—learning from engagement with real-world relationships and hands-on work experience. Friends World

College extended this approach to education into various cultural settings around the world. It pioneered a systematic approach to cross-cultural experience at the undergraduate level that is now a regular feature of many college and university programs.

Tappan Adney was primed from childhood for experiential learning, a disposition he consistently deployed in each of his vocational trajectories. My affinity with this orientation enabled me to integrate this fundamental theme into the overarching narrative of his life and accomplishments.

Keith Helmuth
Chapel Street Editions
Woodstock, New Brunswick

Note on Language, Names, Spelling, Quotations, and Chronology

During Tappan Adney's life, and for much of the composition of this biography, Maliseet was the commonly used name for the Indigenous People who live in what was called the Saint John River region of New Brunswick. But this was a nickname European invaders picked up from the neighbouring Mi'kmaq. The correct name for this First Nation is Wəlastəkwiyik or Wəlastəkokewiyik. Since the latter is considered more accurate, it will be used in this book. In the early twenty-first century, members of this community mounted a concerted effort to establish usage of the correct names for their nation, language, and the river of their home region, along with its surrounding environment.

The transition has been accomplished and this book was edited accordingly. *Wəlastəkw* is the name for the river and its watershed region. *Wəlastəkokewiyik* is the name for the People, meaning literally the People living on the *Wəlastəkw* (the Saint John River). *Wəlastəkwew* is a noun for a single person. *Wəlastəkwi* is an adjective for a person or persons. *Wəlastəkwey* is an adjective for most things, communities of people, and the language.

This restoration of original names is accompanied by the use of a spelling system that promotes accurate pronunciation. Readers familiar with English dictionaries and the branch of linguistics concerned with phonetics and phonology — the pronunciation of words and their representation in alphabetic script — will recognize the upside-down letter *e*. Others may be puzzled by its appearance. A few words of explanation will be helpful.

This spelling (orthography) used for these Indigenous names is known as the schwa system. This system, used first by English dictionaries to assist correct pronunciation in English, has been used by linguists to represent the unaccented vowel sound that occurs in many Indigenous languages and is not accurately represented when they are transcribed into the Latin script of conventional English spelling. The term schwa — from the Hebrew *shva* — was used to name this sound and the practise of its use. This sound was given the alphabetic symbol of an upside-down letter *e* to indicate its pronunciation.

This unaccented vowel sound is a regular feature of the family of languages indigenous to northeast North America. Linguists and teachers of these languages have found the *schwa* system helpful in preserving accurate pronunciation, and they encourage its use. Our decision to use the *schwa* system of spelling in this book has been guided by Andrea Bear Nicholas, former chair of Indigenous Studies at St. Thomas University, and Carole Polchies, a teacher of Wəlastəkwey.

Indeed, it was Carole's father, Dr. Peter Paul, who, on working with the linguist Karl Teeter in the 1960s, was among the first Wəlastəkwi speakers to opt for the schwa system.

It is important to note, however, that the schwa system of spelling exists along side a system of conventional spelling for Wəlastəkwey names and words now widely used in media and government communications. This usage is known as the Passamaquoddy system since it was developed by linguists and Passamaquoddy speakers for children's books in the 1970s, a time when most Passamaquoddy children were still fluent speakers of their language. It has been advanced by the creation of the Passamaquoddy-Maliseet Dictionary, which is a feature of the Passamaquoddy-Maliseet Language Portal (https://pmportal.org/), a project developed largely by Passamaquoddies but including the participation of some Wəlastəkwi speakers in New Brunswick. This spelling system will usually show *Wolastoq* for the river and its watershed region, *Wolastoqey* for communities of people and language, *Wolastoqiyik* for the People, and *Wolastoqew* for a single person. *Wolastoqey* is an adjective for most things, communities of people, and language. *Wolastoqi* is an adjective for persons. Other variations in spelling are also in use.

In preparing this Adney biography, we made the choice to use the schwa system for spelling names because we want to support and help advance the work of the teachers and scholars devoted to preserving the most accurate pronunciation of the Wəlastəkwey language.

The name *Maliseet* has been retained where it appears in quoted material, and in these cases the spelling varies. We have also retained the use of Maliseet in chapter 12, because this is what the people and language were called at the time of Adney's pioneering work and up to recent times. Nicholas N. Smith, an anthropologist and ethnographer familiar with Adney's linguistic studies, prepared chapter 12. In the context of this chapter, it would have been inappropriate and editorially awkward to shift to a term not used by the author, by Adney, and by others also working with the language during this time.

In general, when the correct names are used for the first time, the old term is shown in parentheses, but not thereafter. The words *Indian* and *Native* have been changed to *Indigenous* except where they appear in quoted material. Grammar, spelling, and punctuation in quoted material appear as written in the original documents.

Finally, the Indigenous People of the southwest region of New Brunswick whose collective name has long been spelled Passamaquoddy, have now established Peskotomuhkati as the appropriate spelling for correct pronunciation. We use this spelling except where the former appears in quoted material or when referring to those living in Maine who still use Passamaquoddy for the spelling of their name.

Chapters 1 through 10 are chronological, matching the trajectory of Adney's life. Chapters 11 and 12 are thematic; they deal with his dedication to the survival of the birchbark canoe and the Wəlastəkwey language and culture — research and vocational activities commanding Adney's attention from the time he arrived in the Canadian province of New Brunswick as a young man to the end of his life. Chapters 13 and 14 return to chronological presentation.

Chapter One

.Family and Early Education

... the book of Nature, rather than the medium of books, affords the most instructive and inviting field to all that would become acquainted with her manifold beauties and her solid and valuable facts. —William Adney

I feel myself fortunate that I grew up with an outstanding educator... my own father. —Tappan Adney

Edwin Tappan Adney was born July 13, 1868, in Athens, Ohio. The American Civil War had ended only three years earlier. The United States was only eighty years old. Ohio had been a state for sixty-five years.

What became the state of Ohio had been under active settlement since the United States Congress passed the Northwest Territory Ordinance in 1787. This large-scale appropriation of territory for expanded settlement included all the land west of Pennsylvania, north of the Ohio River, east of the Mississippi River, and south of the Great Lakes. By 1788, homesteaders from New England, Pennsylvania, Virginia, and North Carolina were moving into the area and establishing settlements. From 1830 on, railroads were constructed farther and farther into the settled areas, and by 1845 two canals connected Lake Erie with the Ohio River. By the time of Adney's birth, large areas of verdant forestland in the Ohio territory had been cleared, giving way to farms, villages, towns, and small cities. The Indigenous nations of the region had been violently defeated, their numbers decimated, and the remnants mostly forced to move beyond the Mississippi. The struggles of the settlers became memories, and the frontier of land grabbing had moved a thousand miles west.

Tappan Adney's father, William Harvey Glenn Adney, had risen to the rank of lieutenant colonel of the 36th Ohio Volunteer Infantry Regiment, a regiment he helped organize when the Civil War began. Tappan's mother, Ruth Clementine Shaw Adney, was the daughter of a prominent farmer and politically active citizen of Washington County, Ohio. The Adneys and the Shaws were both pioneer families. The Adneys came from Pennsylvania, North Carolina, and Virginia, and the Shaws from Massachusetts.

According to the 1908 biography Adney wrote for the *Ohio University Bulletin*, his father was six feet three inches tall and slender "but of unusual physical strength," and had early manifested "a quiet love of nature and a taste for letters as well as the exact sciences." As a young man, William Adney taught at the district school in Vinton, Ohio. Later, he attended Ohio University in Athens, entering in the fall of 1857 with the class of 1860. Tappan Adney wrote:

> In a class of able men he graduated with honors and as
> valedictorian. He manifested rare talent for imparting knowledge
> and arousing enthusiasm among his students. Teaching was
> his profession throughout life, to the aid of which he brought a
> lively interest in a wide range of subjects. His first position after
> graduation was as superintendent of the Harmar schools. The
> year of graduation also witnessed his marriage to Miss Lucy
> Wyatt, of Amesville, Athens County. Her death occurred only
> four months later under "tragic circumstances."[1]

Graduates of the class of 1860 from every college were destined for service in the Civil War. William Adney recruited young men for Company B, 36th Ohio Volunteer Infantry. He was wounded in the right hip at the Battle of Chicakamauga in northwest Georgia on September 19, 1863. After a three-month convalescence he returned to duty until the end of the war and was discharged as a lieutenant colonel. He resumed his studies at Ohio University and received a master of arts degree in the fall of 1865. He joined the university faculty as principal of the Preparatory Department, responsible for ensuring that new students were prepared for the rigors of college-level study.[2]

William Adney and Ruth Shaw were married on November 17, 1865. She was twenty years old; he was thirty-one. Ruth Shaw Adney is a somewhat shadowy figure in the family story. Only a few photos, newspaper clippings, property deeds, and her will document her life. No letters, diaries, or other tangible evidence have been found that reveal her personality, thoughts, and beliefs. What we do know is that at a certain point she exercised an initiative that played a crucial role in her children's lives.

Tappan Adney describes his father as having a "quiet love of nature and a taste for letters," which gives the impression of a low-key, even-tempered man. His son certainly inherited a love of nature and a taste for letters, but his temperament was different. Perhaps his mother endowed her son with the fiery side of his personality as well as the fierce determination that enabled him throughout his life to do what was important to him, and to do it in his own way.

Young Adney got his unusual middle name from one of his father's close friends, Professor Eli T. Tappan. The two men had known each other since 1859, when William Adney was entering his senior year of undergraduate school. When Adney's son was born in July of 1868, he paid his friend the honour of naming the boy after him. When Professor Tappan left Ohio University in December 1868, William Adney took his place as professor of mathematics.

For the first five years of his life, young Adney lived with his family in Athens, Ohio. We get our first visual image of him along with his younger sister, Mary Ruth, and their mother from studio photographs taken in Marietta, Ohio, a forty-five-mile journey from Athens. Tappan appears pensive, almost solemn, but having formal photographs taken may have been an ordeal for a five-year-old and perhaps accounts for his demeanour.

The post–Civil War world was filled with change and uncertainty. Political and social upheaval were everywhere. The military conflict was settled, but people and institutions in the northern and southern states remained in turmoil. Economic depression and runaway monetary inflation made university education an unaffordable luxury for an increasing number of people—a fact that put many university professors out of work.

For Ohio University, the nationwide economic depression, political turmoil at the state level, competition for funds with other institutions, and anemic enrollments created a struggle for survival. Tappan Adney wrote in the biography of his father:

> In 1872, affairs at Athens were at a very low ebb. In these dark
> days he and a few others practically carried along the affairs
> of the college. There wasn't enough money to repair the fence
> to keep the cows out of the campus. Under these conditions,
> Professor Adney reluctantly resolved to leave the institution.[3]

The Adney family archive contains letters from William Adney to and from various friends and acquaintances seeking their help in finding another position. Among those he contacted were Edward D. Noyes, governor of Ohio, and future US presidents Rutherford B. Hayes and James A. Garfield, both of whom had served with him in the Civil War. A letter from Adney's friend Thomas G. Wildes to Hayes, dated July 29, 1872, says in part: "Prof. Adney is too good a man and too good a scholar to be wasting his time in the Ohio University as it now is. He is qualified to fill any Chair in our best Colleges...."[4]

In 1873, when Tappan Adney was five years old, his father took the position of LeMoyne Professor of Agriculture and its Correlative Branches at Washington & Jefferson College in Washington, Pennsylvania. The college catalogue for the academic year 1878–79 lists Adney and describes the Agricultural and Correlative Branches Department as offering studies in "Geology, Mineralogy, and the several branches of Natural History." In a passage likely written by William Adney, the catalogue indicates "the book of Nature, rather than the medium of books, affords the most instructive and inviting field to all that would become acquainted with her manifold beauties and her solid and valuable facts." We can easily imagine his son, Tappan, writing a similarly striking sentence decades later.

From the ages of five to eleven, Tappan lived with his family in Washington, Pennsylvania. There is no documentation of his formal schooling during these formative years. He later wrote that under his father's guidance he was acquiring both an academic and practical education. Considering William Adney's approach to education at the college level, he no doubt provided the same kind of experiential learning situations for his son. Margaret Mead said she spent long stretches being taught at home by her grandmother because "my family deeply disapproved of any school that kept children chained to their desks, indoors, for long hours every day."[5] It appears William Adney took the same approach.

As a child, Tappan was precocious and relentlessly curious. Like most children in those days, Tappan spent a lot of time outdoors playing and exploring the natural world. But being part of a family that placed a high value on education and intellectual life gave him a special advantage. Looking back in July 1944, he wrote:

> I feel myself fortunate that I grew up with an outstanding
> educator... my own father, and had an outstanding teacher,

Left to right: William Harvey Glenn Adney, Ruth Clementine Shaw Adney,
Edwin Tappan Adney, undated (Adney family collection)

Dr. Holden, at Trinity School, NY. Though I entered college,
I did not complete a college course and hold no college degree.
But outside, encouraged by my father, I acquired a very broad
foundation education. I did get through Xenophon in Greek, and
Caesar, Livy, Cicero, the *Aeneid* and the *Ecologues* in Latin, much
further than some who decide on special scientific courses now.[6]

In his biographical notes, Adney relates that his father's war wound began
to undermine his "remarkably robust constitution." William and Ruth
Adney decided to move to North Carolina, hoping a warmer climate would
result in improved health for both.

In 1879 Ruth Adney purchased Gum Spring Plantation, located four
miles northwest of Pittsboro, North Carolina. The property comprised 331
acres of land, a farmhouse, a barn, and other small cabins formerly used
to house slaves. She purchased the land in her own name with no reference
to her husband on the deed, a transaction that had become legal in North
Carolina only with the social and governmental reforms that followed the
Civil War. She paid $1,000 for the farm.

The term *plantation* may suggest antebellum mansions and cotton
farming, but in the Pittsboro area plantations were relatively small farms
that grew tobacco. Houses and barns were modest and functional. It was
an area of working farms owned and operated by working people. The
Adneys moved their household to Pittsboro during the summer of 1879.
William Adney returned to Washington, Pennsylvania, to complete his

teaching contract for the 1879–80 school year and rejoined his family in July 1880.

It must have long been evident to William and Mary Adney that their son had an extraordinary capacity for learning that a local rural school would not satisfy. In response, they took the unusual step of arranging for his enrollment at the age of twelve in the University of North Carolina (UNC) at Chapel Hill. Although there is no evidence of how this happened, we can imagine that Professor Adney had an influential conversation with an administrative figure — perhaps the university president — and an arrangement was made. For the academic year 1880–81, Tappan was enrolled as an "optional" or provisional student at the university, and because Pittsboro was twenty miles from Chapel Hill with no train service available, he was undoubtedly a boarding student. That would be Tappan's first experience with a high level of formal schooling and a test of how well his father had tutored him. Both Tappan and his father passed the test with ease. At the age of thirteen, young Adney was granted regular student status for the 1881–82 school year at the University of North Carolina.

He attended classes in Latin, geology, mathematics, and history. In his second year he was a member of the Philanthropic Society, one of two debating societies at UNC, in which membership was mandatory for all students. The debating societies, although not part of the formal curriculum, were considered an integral part of a university education because they provided practical training in public speaking and debate. Such skills were basic in the pre-electronics age for anyone destined for a professional or academic career. This association with college students and professors must have been a heady experience for a boy of thirteen.[7]

Tappan's artistic skills were also blossoming. In 1881, both he and his mother won first prizes at the North Carolina State Fair in Raleigh. Mrs. Adney won first prize for her collection of marine plants. Her son won two blue ribbons: one for an oil painting and one for a pencil drawing. He was awarded cash prizes of three dollars for each.[8] Unfortunately, these prize-winning works have not been found.

Despite the move south, William Adney's health continued to deteriorate. Promised teaching posts at UNC did not materialize, so he taught lower grades in the new public school in Goldsboro, eighty miles from Pittsboro. The job required him to live at the school as a resident monitor for boarding students, apart from his family, while school was in session. Professor Adney later taught at Pittsboro Academy, the leading private prep school in North Carolina at the time, whose graduates include two governors, a US senator, an associate justice of the US Supreme Court, university presidents, and numerous doctors, lawyers, and scholars.

Ruth Adney moved with fifteen-year-old Tappan and fourteen-year-old Mary Ruth to New York City in 1883. It was a move that gave her children access to the superior educational opportunities of the nation's leading metropolis.

New York was the commercial and financial capital of the United States and, like Boston and Philadelphia, boasted some of the finest academic and cultural institutions in the country. Ruth Adney ran a boarding house in central Manhattan but continued to own Gum Spring Plantation, sharecropping the use of the land with local farmers. William Adney remained in North Carolina to manage the farm and continue teaching at Pittsboro Academy.

Life in New York City was good for Tappan. By day he attended to his studies at Trinity School, where he was now enrolled. In the evenings and on weekends he developed his artistic talent at the Art Students League, a venue in which he associated with aspiring artists and practising professionals — again, a rich and stimulating environment for a person in his mid-teens. But in June 1885, he received what must have been a crushing blow: his father, at the age of fifty-one, died in Pittsboro, a week after a young bull on the farm attacked and badly injured him. The *Chatham Record* published news of the death on June 25, 1885:

COL. ADNEY DEAD

It is with deep regret that we announce the death of
Col. W.H.G. Adney.... He was buried in the Episcopal
churchyard.... and his funeral was more largely attended than
any...held here in a long time. His death has thrown a gloom
over this entire community...because of the sorrow felt by
everyone at the untimely loss of so esteemed a gentleman and
popular a citizen. During his sickness every attention was paid
him by his many friends, indeed we do not know of any citizen
in this community ever having received such general attention

in sickness. All this sympathy extended by Southern democrats to a Northern republican, by ex-Confederate soldiers to one who had gallantly "worn the blue" during the war.

For many years after his death, every tenth of May, when the Daughters of the Confederacy decorated the graves of Confederate soldiers, they also placed flowers on Adney's grave, the one Union officer in the cemetery.

Tappan was, above all, his father's son. His admiration and respect for his father are crystal clear in everything he wrote about him. His rich and broad intellectual life, his love of books and of nature, and his independent, self-reliant spirit all originated with his father. Now, suddenly, his first teacher, his role model, his father, was gone. With this loss, the direct, formative influence of William Adney on his son's life came to an end, although the foundation of academic study combined with experiential education and a love of the natural world his father had provided continued to serve Tappan well.

Chapter Two

Trinity School and the Art Students League

I had three years…learning to observe and draw accurately at the Art Students League, NY, under French-taught masters…the value of their instruction was in assisting how to observe as well as record. —Tappan Adney

When Ruth Adney and her two children arrived in New York in 1883, it was the fastest-growing city in the world, with a population exceeding one million. Changing constantly and reinventing itself, the city promised rewards to those willing to seize its opportunities. Employment in thousands of city factories, warehouses, and shops drew immigrants from Europe hoping to improve their economic circumstances.

New York City was a study in contrasts. It could be easy living for those wealthy enough to access its amenities and afford its luxuries, but for those of lesser means, it could be an unhealthy, foul-smelling cauldron of noise and dirt. During the winter months, buildings heated with coal or wood fires belched constant clouds of chimney smoke and soot. In the summer, factories' coal-fired power plants and ovens polluted the air. Horse manure was everywhere in the streets. Garbage collection and street cleaning were unreliable. The sewer system was ancient and inadequate.

By the early 1880s both telephones and electricity were available in New York City but only as high-cost luxuries for wealthy individuals and businesses. The elevated railway system had been operating for more than a decade, using small steam-powered locomotives and providing service on four separate uptown–downtown lines. The fact that the trains were fast, reliable, and affordable made them popular and overcrowded. The Sixth Avenue line, for example, ran 420 trains a day—a train approximately every six minutes.

By the middle of the 1880s, when Tappan Adney would have been a frequent passenger, traffic had increased to such an extent that many viewed the elevated lines as no better and no more comfortable than travel by horse-drawn streetcar in the streets below. In addition, the coal-fired locomotives on the elevated lines were a major source of noise and air pollution throughout the city. Although these "els" made it possible for Adney to reach any corner of the city, getting there would not have been pleasant.

Ruth Adney established a residence suitable for taking in boarders three blocks from the Art Students League in Lower Manhattan. She later relocated to a similar residence that could accommodate borders in Midtown, a short walk from Trinity School. The Art Students League remained easily accessible via a short ride on the el. Young Adney adapted well to life in New York. His mother had provided him with a rich, stimulating environment at a critical time of his life, and he made the most of it. New York City was a living laboratory in which he tested himself and learned the importance of social networks and influential friends. The oasis of Central Park, situated on the eastern flyway of migrating birds, provided a natural sanctuary for him and the birds he loved.

The years between 1883 and 1887 were an intense period of academic training and artistic development for Tappan Adney. They marked the end of his formal schooling and his first steps on the road to enterprising self-reliance he would travel for the rest of his life. Attending Trinity School by day and the Art Students League by night, Adney honed the intellectual and artistic skills on which he relied thereafter to develop his multi-faceted vocation and secure a livelihood.

Founded in 1709 in the old Trinity Church at Broadway and Wall Street, Trinity School is the fifth-oldest educational institution of its kind in the United States and the oldest continually operating school in New York City. Fifty years later, Columbia University, first called Kings College and then Columbia College, was founded on the first floor of Trinity School's new building adjoining Trinity Church. Over the years, Columbia College and Trinity School retained close ties, and although most Trinity School graduates did not go on to college, many who did went to Columbia.

When Adney attended Trinity School, it was an Episcopal boys' school in which most of the approximately seventy students were given a free private school education funded by scholarship donations from Episcopal parishes throughout the city. There were also a small number of tuition students, the children of parents who could afford to pay. By funding scholarships, the Episcopal Church of New York hoped both to educate the children of loyal congregants and to entice a few to take up the priesthood.

Daily class routine at Trinity School included prayers and religious education. To be eligible for scholarships, students had to be baptized in the Episcopal Church, have parents who were Episcopal Church members, and be of "good moral and religious habits." Preference was given to children of deceased clergymen, widows, and church members. There are no records as to whether Adney was a scholarship or tuition student, but he could have easily qualified as a scholarship student, especially after his father died in 1885.

The school frequently changed locations in Manhattan and struggled for financial survival. When Adney attended, it was located in a rented four-storey building at 648 Seventh Avenue, a few blocks from Times Square and a ten-block walk from his residence at 29 West Thirty-Sixth Street. Trinity was composed of upper and lower schools, encompassing grades one to twelve. The Classics Department of the upper school, in which Adney was enrolled, was designed to prepare students for admission to Columbia College. This required a working knowledge of at least one classical language such as Latin or Greek and at least one modern language other than English. French was the modern language taught at Trinity. For admission, Columbia also required students to pass exams in mathematics, geometry, algebra, geography, history, English grammar, and composition. After Adney's father died, Reverend Dr. Robert Holden became his intellectual mentor. Holden was rector of the school and instructor in many of the courses for college-bound students. He was a scholarship graduate of Trinity, a graduate of Columbia, and an Episcopal minister.

Holden was nine years older than William Adney. When Adney became a Trinity student in 1883, Holden had served as Trinity's headmaster for twenty-seven years, guiding the school through the difficult transition following the Civil War and leading it into the modern era. As a bright student and the son of a loyal widow congregant, Adney would have been a prime candidate for the path to the priesthood envisioned for at least a few of the scholarship students at Trinity School. But he didn't share that vision and remained aloof about organized religion throughout his life. He had a scientific outlook even at a young age, and his four years at the school apparently did not alter this worldview. He was preparing for his entrance exams at Columbia when he went to New Brunswick for the summer vacation that transformed his life.

When Adney began his art studies in New York, the art world was in the midst of a revolution. The Impressionist movement had begun in France nearly two decades earlier, and visionary painters were breaking the rules of academic painting. The Impressionists' influence spread as American artists, trained in Europe, returned home to work, teach, and sell their paintings.

Rebellious students of the conservative National Academy of Design founded the Art Students League (ASL) in 1875. Led largely by women, the ASL was launched to protest the academy's restrictive and mandatory art training program for new students. ASL's program, by contrast, provided open enrollment and flexibility and was adapted to the needs and interests of each student. It had no formal curriculum or preset qualifications for graduation. It was perfectly suited for Adney's questioning and self-directed orientation.[1]

ASL's operating principles remain the same today as when Adney attended:

> Students are free to choose from a wide range of modes of
> expression. Instructors develop their own methods and ideas
> without interference from the administration. Open enrollment
> allows students to register in any class they choose and with
> whomever they wish (class size permitting). Class registration is
> for one month at a time, which enables students to easily make
> changes in their chosen course of study.[2]

When Adney began taking classes in 1883, the League had just moved to larger rented quarters in the top three floors of a building only a short walk from the boarding house his mother ran on Fourteenth Street. This move provided ASL with much needed larger rooms and with the opportunity to install skylights on the top floor. After 1884, when the Adneys moved uptown to Thirty-Sixth Street, closer to Trinity School, attending ASL classes required a short ride downtown on an el.

Beginning in 1878, five years before Adney enrolled, the League hired its first full-time faculty members, all successful artists who had trained in Europe. The League's reputation and artistic standing were greatly enhanced when William Merritt Chase became its chief instructor and began teaching drawing and painting. Chase was a colourful and controversial spokesman for the progressive movement in American art. He later became one of the best-known and most highly regarded

American Impressionists. Today, his paintings hang in most major museums.

Chase proved to be a natural teacher. He was widely acknowledged as a master technician who forcefully conveyed his knowledge of materials and technique to his many students, including young Adney. He was considered the League's most important teacher, whose presence made a great contribution to its early success. Georgia O'Keeffe, one of America's most famous modernist artists, recalled her early days as a Chase student at the League. "When he entered the building, a rustle seemed to flow from the ground floor to the top that 'Chase has arrived.'" She added: "Chase...encouraged individuality and gave a sense of style and freedom to his students."

Former ASL student Ella Condie Lamb wrote about a costume ball held by the school in the winter of the first year of Adney's enrollment. "The students, fascinated by color, design and texture, didn't do much dancing," she noted, "but spent most of their time admiring each other's costumes, all either genuine or carefully copied from period or character examples." Describing Chase's instruction methods, Lamb wrote: "as an alternative to live models, he made still-life arrangements from his own collection of draperies, copper and brass...."[3] Adney's earliest surviving artwork is titled *First Sketch from Nature in Watercolor*, dated June 6, 1885. Comparing it with his 1899 painting of the barn at Gum Spring Plantation in Pittsboro, North Carolina, it appears this earlier watercolour also depicts the house and barn on the family farm. A few years after the League was founded, it began requiring sample works for admission to specific classes.

The Art Students League served as the home for Adney's artistic development and as a meeting place to establish friendships with other student artists. Daniel Carter Beard, a fellow student and later writer of books on the "the Great Outdoors," became one of the founders of the American Boy Scouts and published Adney's early work on the construction of birchbark canoes. Frederic Remington, who was already famous for his paintings of the American West, attended a life class in March 1886.[4] Adney also attended this class. It is probable that Adney and Remington at least met.

Life-drawing classes are the traditional cornerstone of art training. Accurately drawing the human form is often the most difficult task an artist encounters. The human body is familiar yet enigmatic because we conceal it with clothing. Life-drawing is challenging because it is so

Adney's *First Sketch from Nature in Watercolor*,
painted June 6, 1885 (CCHS)

unforgiving. We all intuitively understand the proper proportions of the human body and learn to recognize individual faces in the first weeks of our lives, and so even the smallest errors in a drawing will be instantly recognizable to most viewers. In life-drawing classes, the student must master the complexities of line, form, proportion, value, and composition to produce an image — under time pressure — that viewers will accept as an accurate representation. Adney's polished drawings were likely accomplished through multiple posing sessions conducted over several days.

In October 1885, Adney attended the evening antique class and in November, the life class, in which he produced a charcoal drawing of a male nude titled *The Algerian*. It is a basic life drawing, perhaps one of his earliest efforts. He noted in the margins of this sketch: "The Algerian, a former Paris model, caused a near panic in the Ladies Artistic Anatomy Class before he could be made to understand to drape himself. He spoke no English." At that time, the end of the Victorian era, ASL's life-drawing classes with nude models were segregated by gender. Women attended the morning and afternoon classes. Men attended classes in the evening.

Adney placed a high value on his art training in New York. Sixty years later he wrote:

When I first landed in New Brunswick, on a visit, I had three
years of drawing, learning to observe and draw accurately at
the Art Students League, NY, under French-taught masters who
continually advised, "Don't think of making a picture, draw what
you see." And the value of their instruction was in assisting how
to observe as well as record.[5]

In addition to his academic and art studies in New York, Adney spent much
of his free time pursuing his interest in ornithology. He was fascinated with
birds and travelled extensively throughout the city wherever the public
transit system would take him to add sightings of new species to his growing
ornithology journal. During the summer months he would go at dawn to
Central Park to study and sketch the many bird species that inhabited this
magnificent green and wooded oasis in the middle of Manhattan.

The American Museum of Natural History (AMNH), which had
opened its doors just six years before Adney's arrival, was located adjacent
to Central Park and a natural destination for a young birder.[6] It was easily
accessible by a combination of elevated train and horse-drawn streetcar. It
was actively expanding its collections by sponsoring research expeditions
throughout the world conducted by the leading naturalists of the time.
The AMNH's fledgling Anthropology Department had a small collection
of Indigenous American artifacts that would eventually become its largest
and most diverse holding. For young Adney it was his first exposure to the
ethnology of Indigenous cultures, a new science that was soon to absorb
his interest and set the course for much of his life's work.

This interest, however, appears to have been already active when he
was living in North Carolina. In 1885, Adney wrote to Spencer F. Baird,
secretary of the Smithsonian Institution, to ask if the Smithsonian would be
interested in ethnological specimens from central North Carolina. Adney
evidently had a collection of Cherokee archaeological items or perhaps
had inherited it from his father. Baird sent an enthusiastic reply saying that
central North Carolina was a region of special interest to the Smithsonian.
While there is no record of any Smithsonian donations from Adney, the
correspondence documents his early interest in Indigenous history.[7]

Adney was a frequent visitor to the AMNH and made friends with both
amateur and professional naturalists associated with the institution. He
also became a member of the Linnaean Society of New York, the world's

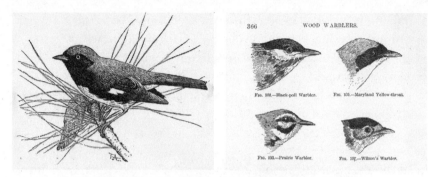

Adney provided 110 illustrations for Frank Chapman's
Handbook of Birds of Eastern North America, 1899 (CCHS)

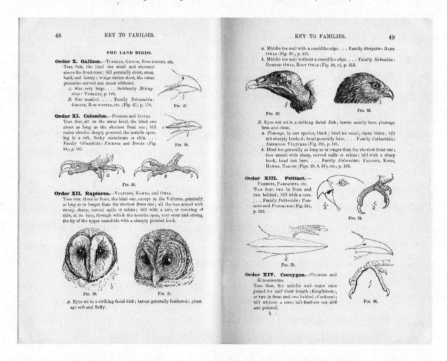

oldest extant biological society. He joined the American Ornithologists'
Union (AOU), founded in 1883, the same year he arrived in New York.
Attending AOU meetings, he met Frank Chapman, a professional
ornithologist and a member of the board of trustees of the American
Museum of Natural History. This association led to Adney becoming an
illustrator of Chapman's 1895 *Handbook of Birds of Eastern North America*,
using specimens from the museum's collection as models. The book
became a best-seller, was reprinted four times in the years immediately

after its release, and was the most popular field guide for East Coast birders well into the next century.

In 1884 and 1886, Adney published reports of bird sightings in the *Auk*, the quarterly journal of the AOU.

> The Cardinal Grosbeak breeding in Brooklyn, N.Y.—June 8, 1884. I found *Cardinalis virginianus* breeding in Prospect Park, Brooklyn. The nest, which contained three eggs, was very loosely constructed, principally of the long, slender leaves of various aquatic plants, and was suspended in a mass of vines drooping over the bed of a small brook.—E.T. Adney, *29 West 36th St., New York City.*[8]

This sighting was notable because the cardinal grosbeak, although common in northern states today, was rare outside southern regions in the 1880s. This report is the earliest known publication by Adney and an indication of how serious he already was as a student of ornithology. It also shows his independence of movement around the city as a teenager. Prospect Park in Brooklyn was a long way from his home in Manhattan. Finally, the article documents that the Adneys had moved from their 1883 address on Fourteenth Street to new quarters at 29 West Thirty-Sixth Street less than a year after arriving in the city.

The 1886 report includes greater context, more detail, and wider institutional association:

> Naturalization of the European Goldfinch in New York City and Vicinity—I am informed by Mr. W.A. Conklin, of the Central Park Menagerie, New York City, that the European Goldfinch (*Cardeulis elegans*) first appeared in the Park in 1879, having probably crossed the Hudson River from Hoboken, N.J., where some birds had been set at liberty the previous year. The species is now common and apparently resident.
>
> On April 20, 1886, I discovered, in precisely similar situations, two nests, one of which, containing five fresh eggs, has been forwarded to the Smithsonian Institution. It was placed in a pine tree, resting among the tufts of long needles near the end of a slender horizontal limb, some twelve feet from the ground.

The species seems to be gradually extending its range, as on May 23, 1886, I met with a pair occupying a clump of pines six or seven miles to the northward. — E.T. Adney, *New York City*.[9]

In the spring of 1887, Adney graduated from Trinity School and, at eighteen, was ready for the next step in what was likely to be an academic career. He had a classic prep school education behind him, he had the solid development of his artistic talent well in hand, he was a member of two significant scientific organizations devoted to the study of natural history, and he was preparing to take the entrance exams for Columbia College. It was at this point Adney and his sister, Mary Ruth, accepted the invitation of Minnie Bell Sharp, who was a resident at their mother's boarding house, to a summer holiday at her home in Upper Woodstock, New Brunswick, Canada.

It would be almost two years before he again walked the streets of New York City, and when he did, his outlook on life would be greatly changed.

Tappan Adney, 1889 (CCHS)

36

Chapter Three

A Fateful Decision and First Encounter
with the Birchbark Canoe

Here was a whole new world thrown open to me, a kind of air I had never breathed before. No woods had ever impressed me as these woods did.
— Tappan Adney

Imagine Ruth Adney watching from her doorstep as her son sets off toward the docks. At six feet two inches, he is clearly visible for some time, a full head taller than most people on the crowded New York street. When she can no longer see him, Mrs. Adney turns back to the chores of running a boarding house. Tappan, who turns nineteen in two weeks, makes his way to the docks below Thirtieth Street along the North River, as the Hudson was called in those days to distinguish it from the East River.

It was Thursday, June 30, 1887, and a hot, humid evening. The docks were jammed with people escaping the sweltering heat of the city, bound for cooler, healthier destinations. Tappan had just graduated from Trinity, the most prestigious prep school in the city. Having booked passage on the night boat to Boston, he was headed for Woodstock, a small town in the Canadian Maritime province of New Brunswick.

Minnie Bell Sharp had invited Tappan and his sister to stay at her home in Upper Woodstock. She was the first-born daughter of Francis Peabody Sharp and Maria Sharp, the proprietors of a prosperous orchard and nursery business. Minnie Bell had come to New York to study music and had taken lodging at Mrs. Adney's boarding house. She and Mary Ruth had departed earlier for New Brunswick, and Tappan now followed, his valise heavy with the books he needed to study in preparation for the entrance examinations for Columbia College. In addition, he brought along the notes he was accumulating from his study of birds, his chief interest at the time, and correspondence for Montague Chamberlain, a New Brunswick ornithologist.

Adney found his berth on the Fall River Line side-wheel steamer unbearably hot. The boat was packed with noisy travellers, so he went out on deck to sleep, curling up in a coil of mooring rope. It was still dark when the boat docked at Fall River, Massachusetts, where passengers boarded a train to Boston, arriving just after first light. He ate breakfast in the Old Colony station, took a cab to the International Steamship Company, and paid for a berth to Saint John, New Brunswick, via Portland and Eastport, Maine.

As the steamer left Boston, Adney noted in his journal, "The sea was like glass except for a long ground swell, and the petrels circled around on the smooth surface like swallows." At Portland he went ashore and noted, among the town's magnificent shade trees, "red-eyed vireos, chipping sparrows, and redstarts, all in full song."[1]

Early the next morning, as his ship steamed northward, the rocky coast of down-east Maine came into view. Later in the day, the cliffs of Grand Manan Island appeared on the starboard side. As the ship entered the waters between Eastport, Maine, and Campobello Island, New Brunswick, the international boundary between Canada and the United States, Adney noted "vast flocks of a small gull larger than terns. In thousands they covered the surface of the water darting hither and thither in pursuit of small fish. Where their white wings cut against the dark shores of Campobello, the air quivered like a swarm of bees."[2]

He spent the two-hour stop at Eastport as far out of town as the boat schedule would allow and was rewarded by adding fourteen new species of birds to his ornithology journal. He saw boys lying flat on the dock catching flounder and pollock in green waters so clear he could see fifteen feet or more into their depths. He watched the foot-long fish take hold of the baited hook. If a bony sculpin came along and tried to seize the bait, the boys would jerk the hook away. When now and then one managed to seize the bait and get hooked, the boys would haul it in and bang it off on a post. The sculpins would appear to be dead, but when thrown back in the water they were lively as ever.

Arriving in Saint John, he delivered letters from friends in New York to Montague Chamberlain, an accomplished amateur ornithologist and author who had published *A Catalogue of Canadian Birds* earlier in 1887. Chamberlain was the co-founder in 1883 of the New York–based American Ornithologists' Union, of which Adney was also a member. Chamberlain repaid Adney's letter-delivery service with an invitation to stay the night.

The next day, he joined a pre-arranged field trip with thirty members of the Linnaean Society, a naturalist group from New York of which he was also a member. The Linnaean group had come to witness the world-famous high tides in the Bay of Fundy and explore the shoreline flora and fauna of the Saint John area. Adney spent a week with the group exploring the city, the coastal environment, and the nearby forests, where he added the sighting and identification of bird species to his journal. He took an early morning walk with Chamberlain and marvelled at his ability to identify birds from a single note.

Chamberlain was also a student of Wəlastəkwey culture and language and later became a professor at Harvard. Adney's contact with a senior figure in both the study of natural history and the culture of the region's Indigenous people foreshadowed the transformative experiences yet to come for this young artist and budding scientist.

On July 8, Adney secured passage aboard a small side-wheel steamer, the *David Weston*, which would take him north up the Wəlastəkw (Saint John River) to Fredericton, the capital of New Brunswick. On this voyage, he met ten-year-old Theodore Goodridge Roberts, later to become one of Canada's most prolific writers of novels for young people. Roberts came from a distinguished family of writers and artists. His older brother, Charles G.D. Roberts, whom Adney would meet several years later in Nova Scotia, is known as the father of Canadian poetry. He inspired other poets of his generation, including his cousin Bliss Carman, with whom Adney would eventually share an apartment in New York in the early 1890s. Every turn of this summer holiday was providing connections that would re-emerge in some aspect of Adney's later life.

The overnight journey on the *David Weston* landed the visitor from New York City in Fredericton on a Saturday morning. The river, as usual for this time of year, was crowded with log booms from the previous winter's timber-cutting in the vast watershed region of the Wəlastəkw. Adney sketched the two-mast schooners, their decks loaded so heavily with sawn lumber that their hulls were submerged nearly to the high nose of the bows. They came downriver with their sails spread on both sides, like butterfly wings, to catch the windward breeze. Adney was so preoccupied with his artwork he missed the Saturday train to Woodstock. Since no trains were available on Sunday to make the sixty-mile journey to his destination, he spent another day exploring the town and adding to his bird journal.

Tappan Adney and Minnie Bell Sharp standing in front of
Francis Peabody Sharp's house, Upper Woodstock, undated (CCHS)

On Monday, July 11, Adney arrived at the Woodstock train station and walked the remaining two miles to Upper Woodstock. On the way, he asked directions to the home of Francis Peabody Sharp and was told to "keep on till I came to the most remarkable house I had ever seen."[3] Indeed, it was a house of dramatically unconventional design for the 1880s. With its crenellated roofline, it looked more like a three-storey stockade with a lookout tower than a family home. The house had been designed by Mr. Sharp as a replacement for a large, elegant Victorian house that had burned to the ground in 1881.

Francis Peabody Sharp was a botanical pioneer and businessman who developed and propagated improved varieties of apples, plums, and other fruits and vegetables. He also developed and used unique cultivation methods to enable the fruit trees, even delicate peaches, to survive New Brunswick winters. The Sharp orchards at one time had tens of thousands of trees producing fruit sold throughout Canada, the New England states, and even England, making the Sharp family relatively affluent.

Tappan received a warm welcome from his sister, Mary Ruth, and the Sharp family. Two days later, they celebrated his nineteenth birthday with a modest family party attended by Maria Sharp; her daughters Minnie Bell,

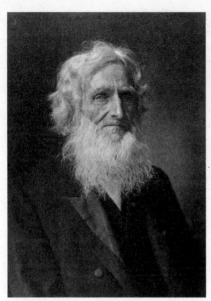

Francis Peabody Sharp, undated (CCHS)   Minnie Bell Sharp, undated
(Adney family collection)

Lizzie, and Jennie; and her son Franklin. Missing were son Humboldt, who was on a year-long visit to western Canada, and Maria's husband, Francis, who was out tending his orchards.

Although it is tempting to assume that Tappan's 1887 visit to Upper Woodstock and sojourn with the Sharp family was partly motivated by an interest in Minnie Bell, there is no evidence for this in his journal of the trip or in his later recollections. Likewise, there is no evidence Minnie Bell included Tappan in her invitation for a summer holiday with a special interest in him. It seems likely the primary invitation was extended to Mary Ruth, with her brother added on. Minnie Bell was three years older than Tappan. At twenty-two and nineteen, the difference was significant. They were both ambitious characters with professional, artistically oriented careers in mind. Only after a long acquaintance did Minnie Bell and Tappan become a couple.

Humboldt Sharp returned to his Upper Woodstock home from travelling in western Canada in early September 1887, two months after Adney's arrival. The two were almost the same age with mutual interests and temperaments. They quickly struck up a close friendship. This association plunged Adney into a life of outdoor adventure and began the independent way of living he would continue to pursue. A few days after

41

Tappan Adney's painting of Peter Jo building a birchbark canoe at Lanes Creek Point. Adney's illustration was published alongside his article, "How to Build a Birchbark Canoe," in *Outing* magazine, May 1900. (CCHS)

his return, Hum, as he was known, rose from the lunch table, took down his shotgun from its rack, called for his dog, Purps, and with Adney in tow, headed out the door to go partridge hunting in the nearby woods.

Hum Sharp was a free spirit who loved the outdoor life. Like his older brother, Franklin, he worked in his father's orchards, but he also spent much time hunting, fishing, camping, and canoeing. He found an eager companion in Adney, who was new to the experience of wilderness living and its sense of freedom. Their first big adventure was a caribou hunt in December 1887 with Peter Jo, an Indigenous man who would become Adney's mentor in a life-altering way. A few months later, in January 1888, Humboldt and Tappan went on another caribou hunt that included camping in -30°F temperatures.

In September 1888, Humboldt and Tappan undertook an extraordinary adventure: a canoe expedition through the Squatook (Squatec) chain of lakes just over the border in Quebec, a territory unmapped and uninhabited by settlers. As Hum said, "Nobody but a few Frenchmen ever goes up there. What do you say we go?" Adney noted: "It was never my policy to differ with Humboldt about matters like this."[4] So off they went, in a leaky birchbark canoe, on a two-week exploration into the unknown that ended up more challenging than they expected.

Adney's illustration *Carrying in the Bark* that accompanied his article "How to Build and Birchbark Canoe," *Outing* magazine, May 1900 (CCHS)

During his second summer in Upper Woodstock, Adney became an apprentice of Peter Jo, who, with his mother, Alice, and a nephew had established their summer residence on the point of land where Lanes Creek flows into the Wəlastəkw. For shelter they had built a traditional summer dwelling framed with poles and covered with birchbark.

Peter Jo was a canoe builder and had a summer worksite on the shore of the Wəlastəkw in front of his dwelling. The whole set-up caught Adney's attention. Having the curiosity of a scientist and the skills of an artist, he was intrigued with the construction methods and cultural significance of the birchbark canoe. He was familiar with boats of various kinds but had never seen anything like this—a small boat of obvious utility and striking beauty, built using only a few simple tools and materials gathered directly from the forest.

We can imagine that when Adney appeared at Peter Jo's worksite on the shore of the Wəlastəkw, the canoe maker might have been as intrigued with this intense young man's interest as Adney was with what Peter Jo was doing. It was a propitious meeting. The fifty-year-old Indigenous canoe maker introduced the nineteen-year-old artist from New York City to the birchbark canoe, which was to become an enduring passion for the rest of his life.

It would not have been typical in those days for someone from the non-Indigenous world to take this kind of interest in the knowledge, skills, and handcrafted equipment of traditional Wəlastəkwey (Maliseet) culture. Peter Jo and Adney struck up a long-term friendship that began as mentor and student.

A pivotal figure in Adney's life, Peter Jo also introduced him to a forest-based way of life that included hunting, trapping, outdoor living, and woodcraft technologies that had deep roots in traditional Indigenous culture. And along with his canoe building apprenticeship, Adney began learning Wəlastəkwey, the language of the Wəlastəkokewiyik. Although Peter Jo grew up in the Peskotomuhkati (Passamaquoddy) community near Princeton, Maine, he and his family were now living in the Wəlastəkw area of New Brunswick. The language of these communities is essentially the same with only slight differences.

Combining his knowledge of ornithology with language instruction from Peter Jo, Adney compiled a list of Wəlastəkwey names for birds and other animals of the region that the Linnaean Society in New York published in 1893—an unusual honour for so young a researcher and author. It was the first such list of Wəlastəkwey names for wildlife professionally published.[5]

Adney was a naturally adept linguist. His years at Trinity School included a thorough introduction to Greek, Latin, and French. In later life he took up the study of the Old Norse language. But it was his encounter with Wəlastəkwey and the window it opened on Wəlastəkwey culture that now absorbed his attention.

During the summer of 1888, Adney worked with Peter Jo to build a full-size birchbark canoe and two one-fifth-scale model canoes, making notes and drawings that documented the construction process. These models were the first of many more to come. In 1890 he published an illustrated feature in the magazine *Harper's Young People* that was the first accurate account of how a birchbark canoe is constructed.[6] This was the beginning of the documentation and writing that eventually became *The Bark Canoes and Skin Boats of North America*, the book that saved the birchbark canoe from oblivion. Over a century later, this book is the workshop guide for those who are again building birchbark canoes.

Adney's encounter with the bark canoe was a pivotal event in his life, though it may not have been immediately clear to him in this way. His journal of that first trip to New Brunswick barely mentions canoes. It is filled instead with notes on his chief interests at the time: ornithology, hunting, camping, and testing his limits in this new world with his new friend, Humboldt Sharp.

> ...nothing had a more positive influence upon my life.... It deter-
> mined the whole manner of my later life, and when [I] set to earn
> a livelihood, it supplied the experience that was of the greatest
> service to me.... But here was a whole new world thrown open, a
> kind of air I had never breathed before.... one had but to go half
> a mile back to find traces of an original forest that are now as
> wild looking as any that one will find in the remotest wilderness.
> No woods had ever impressed [me] as these woods did.[7]

Mary Ruth and Minnie Bell returned to New York in August 1887. Tappan had intended to return to New York at the same time, complete his entrance exams for Columbia College, and begin classes early in September, but he extended his visit at the urging of the Sharps, paying for his keep by tutoring the Sharp sisters in various subjects and working at a variety of jobs in the family orchards. On September 24, he noted in his journal that he had written to his mother, telling her he would not be returning to start college.

Nine months later, on July 26, 1888, while Adney was still in New Brunswick, his mother married Reverend Edward Kenney, a New York Episcopal minister. For the ceremony, they travelled to Pittsboro, North Carolina, where she still owned Gum Spring Plantation and where her first husband was buried in the Episcopal Church cemetery. The newspaper account of the wedding does not list Tappan Adney as either a member of the wedding party or a guest, although his sister Mary Ruth is listed. Following the wedding, Adney's mother quit her boarding-house business and took up residence with her new husband near his church at Avenue C and Sixth Street in the East Village of Lower Manhattan.

Ruth Adney likely wrote to her son to tell him of her engagement and her plans to establish a new household with her new husband. Adney wrote years later that he did not attend college "because of changed family circumstances." He had enjoyed a strong bond with his father, whom he greatly admired. It is possible, as a young adult, he did not look favourably on the prospect of continuing his education while living in another man's home.

Although Adney was a prolific writer throughout his life and wrote about his father, as far as has been discovered, he never mentioned his mother in his correspondence or biographical recollections. Years later, his mother left a sizable inheritance to Mary Ruth but a token amount to her son. Perhaps she still resented his rejection of a college education after she had worked hard to provide him the opportunity. Or perhaps Mary Ruth needed the money more than he did.

Whatever transpired between mother and son, it is clear that Adney's life took a dramatic turn during his first trip to New Brunswick. He left New York on a summer holiday, firmly set on the path of higher education and probably, like his father, an academic career. When he finally returned to New York on February 28, 1889, he had been away for nearly two years, and his life had been transformed. He was equipped with the experience of immersion in the cultural world of wilderness living and confident in his ability to translate this authentic, first-hand knowledge into illustrated journalism, using his art and writing skills. He began giving lectures on natural history and the Canadian wilderness, for which there was a growing audience. He began the development of a professional career without the need for additional academic education.

His lifelong vocation was anchored in that first trip to New Brunswick; it eventually centred on the preservation of the material and linguistic culture of the Wəlastəkwey and the battle for their Indigenous rights. New Brunswick played to his strengths: a quick, intuitive mind; an independent spirit; an insatiable curiosity; and a fierce loyalty to people and causes he cared about. Dramatically changed, he returned to New York to begin a new life and career.

Adney in his Flushing, New York studio, summer, 1896 (CCHS)

Adney sketching while on a hunting expedition, 1896 (CCHS)

Chapter Four

Tobique Expeditions and Natural History Journalism

Tobique!...one goes back from year to year as to a friend that is always new and never grows old. The spell it exerts...is not to be resisted. —Tappan Adney

Between 1887 and 1896, the wilderness of New Brunswick served as a natural science "laboratory" for Tappan Adney, a place where his book-based knowledge of botany, zoology, geology, and ornithology came alive in direct experience of the great woodland environment.

He made five trips to New Brunswick during those years, three of them to the forests surrounding the Tobique River, which forms the watershed flowing from Mount Carleton in the north-central region of the province to the Wəlastəkw on its western border with the state of Maine. He explored the area thoroughly with Hum Sharp and others, visiting Trousers Lake and Odell Stream on moose and caribou hunts, spending enough time with trappers that he became an expert on the subject, and prospecting on the Serpentine River in search of gold-bearing quartz rock. He chronicled each trip in handwritten journals and typed them up years later.

Although Adney was based and earned his living in New York, the inspiration for his art, journalism, and lecturing came almost exclusively from his travels to New Brunswick and his time spent living there. These years—between ages nineteen and twenty-eight—were a time of discovery and growth during which he established himself as an illustrator and writer in the city of New York and its environs. His drawings and articles were published in more than a dozen New York periodicals, including *Cosmopolitan, St. Nicholas, Harper's Weekly, Outing, Forest and Stream,* and *Our Animal Friends,* a monthly publication of the American Society for the Prevention of Cruelty to Animals (ASPCA).

He spent almost half his time away from the city gathering material for his articles and illustrations. He expanded his own wilderness experience by absorbing the campfire stories of others who had spent their lives in the woods, hunting, fishing, trapping, and lumbering. Clippings of published

Adney's drawing of a moose feeding on lily roots in shallow water, *Our Animal Friends*, September 1893 (CCHS)

Adney's drawing of a fish eagle (osprey), *Our Animal Friends*, June 1894 (CCHS)

work from this time show he made his living as a commercial artist and writer. There are hundreds of examples of his artwork and articles. He made a comfortable living, needing to provide only for himself. He noted that he was paid $25 for the drawings to illustrate a particular article, the equivalent of approximately $830 in today's currency. His eye and hand performed like a photographic process, able to capture quickly the essence of a subject and transfer it to paper. Much of his early artwork focused on animals and particularly on birds.

A significant proportion of his early articles, perhaps as much as half, were published in *Our Animal Friends*. Many of his colleagues from the American Museum of Natural History, the American Ornithologists' Union, and the Linnaean Society were also ASPCA members and regular contributors to *Our Animal Friends*. It was a natural association for Adney. His father had seen plenty of cruelty to horses during the American Civil War and had schooled Adney to treat animals with compassion and kindness.

His first forays into the woods of New Brunswick were caribou and moose hunts for the purpose of subsistence provisioning. He recognized and appreciated the authentic cultural context of such hunting but personally was a reluctant hunter. For many years he was torn between his admiration and respect for the woodsmen he met and his sympathy for the animals they killed. He accepted the killing of animals for food—sustenance for households and community—but he had a moral dilemma with hunting for sport or cash. No evidence has been found that after 1900 Adney ever again hunted or participated in trapping.

What was it about the Tobique watershed that especially fascinated Adney? In a particularly lyrical passage, he expressed his love for the wilderness environment of the region.

> Tobique! The lusty trout lurking in its shady pools; the gaunt moose that roams the forest in round-wood berry season; the shaggy bruin tearing the viscid bark from the fir tree in early summer... all these may not differ from their kind in other places, for nature is one everywhere. The brooks are no cooler, the smell of the balsam no sweeter, nor the crinkle of cold snow under the moccasined foot, no more pleasant music here on Tobique than in a thousand other spots.
>
> But it has so happened that about the forests of New Brunswick are clustered the recollections of my earliest days in "The Woods" and there I first saw and felt that Nature which is only found in some wilderness. Though two generations of men have come and passed on since these woods were first settled along their borders by white men, it seems to me the woods have not changed, nor lost their spell. The wandering moose lingers now with the cattle. The bears, as often as the spring comes around, levy tribute on the young flocks, but only a little more moss seems to lie on the fallen tree trunks, and one goes back from year to year, as to a friend, that is always new and never grows old. The spell it exerts is one not to be resisted.[1]

In the fall of 1891, Adney was back in Upper Woodstock visiting Hum Sharp, who invited him to spend the Christmas season on a caribou hunt around Odell Stream, a tributary of the Tobique. Adney readily accepted. Later that winter, Adney received word that his friend Edmund Collins had died in New York. Collins was a pioneering promoter of Canadian literature who had been the editor of *Epoch*, a New York literary magazine. Adney had been working with him on a writing project, but with the loss of this collaboration had no reason for a prompt return to the city. He extended his stay to November 1892 and spent much of that time on wilderness adventures in Tobique country.[2]

Sharp had previously sent Adney a letter containing a seventeen-page account of the time he became separated from his Indigenous guide and got lost after a snowstorm covered his tracks back to camp. He wandered for a week without food or shelter. He was chased and treed by an angry bull moose. He became weak and was on the verge of surrendering to a frozen death when he found a logging road that led to a lumber camp, shelter, and food.

Adney was not put off by Sharp's life-threatening experience. Wilderness survival skills were a challenge that appealed to him and added to the adventures that enhanced his work as a New York artist and writer. From November 1891, he remained in New Brunswick, roaming the Tobique and Serpentine River watersheds with Sharp and others for a full year.

The Odell Stream caribou hunt began around Christmas. Sharp and Adney loaded a toboggan with supplies in Woodstock and made the fifty-mile trip up the Wəlastəkw valley to Andover by train. They caught a ride with the Inman mail wagon for the next sixteen miles up the Tobique to Arthurette, where they stopped to invite Manzer Giberson, a local game warden and woodsman, to join them. Adney and Sharp continued on, hauling their toboggan up a lumber road on smooth, hard snow, arriving at McNair's lumber camp in a state of exhaustion. They hunted for a week without success, although they saw caribou nearly every day.[3]

A few days after Giberson joined them, they got their caribou, a big bull with no horns. They cached the meat under a pile of snow and continued in the direction of the Miramichi. Before long they came upon multiple caribou tracks, which they followed. They caught up with the animals at dark when it was too late to continue hunting. They found

an old timber road which seemed to lead in the direction of camp and followed it. It was a poor chance for camping out, low spruce land, no dry wood and six inches of snow on the ground.

We kept on the old road and at length came to an old lumber camp. It had settled gradually down into the mud until the walls were only a few feet high and the roof had all fallen in.[4]

Adney's painting of Ambrose Lockwood calling moose,
St. Nicholas Magazine, March 1896 (CCHS)

They scavenged enough split logs to lay a flat roof over the walls of the hovel. It began to snow heavily and the wind rose. They built a fire on the earth floor and made a meal of the gingerbread Adney had packed. He described the situation: "It snowed and it piled up in little piles in the corners, it sifted down our necks and into our ears, or if it fell on us the heat of the fire turned it to water. I lay in the middle, Manzer and Hum on each side."[5]

In the morning they found eighteen inches of new snow had fallen. Hungry and chilled, they continued on the old road, coming shortly to a new lumber camp in operation. After warming themselves and getting some hot food, they returned to retrieve the cached caribou meat. Although an ordeal, the caribou hunt was a success. They had obtained a large provision of meat, and Adney was thoroughly inducted into wilderness living in winter conditions.

In the summer of 1892, Adney and Humboldt Sharp joined Sol Perley of Upper Woodstock on a gold-prospecting trip on the Serpentine River, which flowed into the Tobique at the Forks above Nictau and Riley Brook, an even more distant wilderness area than the scene of their caribou hunt.

Stories of gold in the area had circulated for decades after Andover lumberman George Giberson came home from the woods carrying a large quartz rock with veins of gold running through it. Before he could return for more, Giberson died of typhoid fever without telling anyone exactly where he had found the gold. His death in 1851 ignited a fierce curiosity and intense search by local residents, but no more gold-studded quartz rocks were found.

Prospectors on the Serpentine did find rocks amalgamated with minute granules of gold. To extract the gold the rocks were crushed to a powder, then mixed with mercury to separate and concentrate the gold. The mercury was then burnt off, leaving only the gold. This process was operating on the Serpentine River with a water-powered three-stamp mill crushing the rocks. Adney, Sharp, and Perley set out for the site.

The preparations for months in the woods — gathering all the needed supplies, tools, and equipment — and making the difficult journey to the Serpentine River foreshadowed Adney's trip as a journalist down the Yukon River five years later to cover the Klondike Gold Rush. Everything he learned about wilderness survival in the woods of New Brunswick prepared him for this later supreme test in the subarctic environment.

Three additional men and a towboat were hired to help the party to their destination. Adney marvelled at how skillfully they guided the boat through the treacherous rocks and boulders: "the men in the bow ready to shove this way or that at a moment's notice, or to jump bodily into the seething water to ease her off."[6]

After several days they arrived at the place where gold prospectors had camped the previous year. The first thing they did was clear a patch of ground and plant Early Rose potatoes. Several months later, while sharing a meal of potatoes, a Wəlastəkwi visitor commented, "I never expected to live to see potatoes raised on Serpentine." To Adney it was an indication of "how far we were from what even they regarded as civilization."[7]

Adney spent most of his time exploring, fishing, and sketching. He had been commissioned by *Our Animal Friends* to create drawings of birds to illustrate articles. He walked twenty-six miles to Riley Brook to mail the sketches to New York.

Perley hired another woodsman, Hezekiah Day, to work at the camp. Adney described him as a "red-whiskered, stout, ruddy-complexioned man of some fifty years or more." He had been in the woods all his life, starting when his father and three brothers "were makers of pine timber." Adney wrote that Hezekiah Day was

a man of singularly reserved demeanor, quiet of speech, he had
many tales to tell though he was not a talker, much less a boaster,
and we used to get up close to listen to all he had to say about the
habits of animals. He showed me many things about trapping,
and explained the dead falls of all kinds, old ones scattered all
along the road for sable, mink, otter, blackcat, and bears.[8]

The drawings Adney made of those traps became the centrepiece
of a series of articles he wrote on trapping, published in *Forest and Stream*
magazine in 1893.

After weeks of prospecting on the Serpentine, Perley had not found
Giberson's gold, but he had packed boxes with a thousand pounds of
quartz rock to take back for assay. Everything was loaded into the towboat
and they headed downriver. But the water was so low and the boat so
heavily loaded it grounded only two hundred yards from camp. Perley
decided to retrieve his rocks when the water was higher. They anchored the
towboat to a tree, covering the contents as best they could. Each took his
own personal gear and walked the twenty-six miles to Riley Brook.

Later, Adney decided to return alone with a rifle and small axe to further
observe and sketch the wildlife of the Serpentine area. He camped out,
living off trout, ducks, and partridge plus the small quantity of provisions
he carried. He commented on the profound sense of loneliness and fear of
encounters with bears and moose. His previous experiences of wilderness
living had all been with veteran woodsmen; now he was on his own — a
serious test of his survival skills.

After ten weeks, Adney built a raft and navigated down the Serpentine.
At Pup Falls, he let the raft down the falls on a wire and continued to Big
Falls, where he tried the same manoeuvre. The raft caught between rocks
and could not be dislodged, so he walked the rest of the way to the Forks
of the Tobique and on to Riley Brook. From there, he took the Inman mail
wagon to Andover and the train to Woodstock. He left soon afterward for
New York with, as he described it, "a great store of sketches of woods and
traps and a great store of hunting and trapping lore."[9]

In the fall of 1893, Adney returned to the Tobique woods with an
expedition from the American Museum of Natural History. The museum
was creating a large diorama of north woods wildlife and mounting an

expedition to get a large bull moose to serve as the centrepiece. The hunt was successful, but the expedition led to a confrontation between Adney and the museum administration.

Earlier in 1893, when Adney was working at the museum on the illustrations for Frank Chapman's *Handbook of Birds of Eastern North America,* John Rowley, the museum's taxidermist, approached him "and asked me if I knew a place where he could go and be pretty sure of getting a moose."[10] Adney told him the wilderness around the Tobique River in New Brunswick was the best place he knew and recommended finding a Maliseet (Wəlastəkwi) guide.

He told Rowley he was planning a trip to the same area of New Brunswick and suggested he accompany the expedition. Rowley agreed, and they began making plans. Moose hunting is timed for the fall mating season. A hunter skilled in imitating the call of another moose can bring a bull into close range. The AMNH expedition arranged to arrive just before the opening of the three-week moose-hunting season in September.

The crew from New York—consisting of Rowley, his younger brother, Crop, and Adney—arrived at Andover, New Brunswick, on Saturday and checked into Allen Perley's hotel. They arranged for transport with John Inman, the Tobique mailman, who made a twice-a-week horse-and-wagon trip upriver and would leave Monday morning at dawn. They spent Sunday buying supplies, after overcoming the scruples of the local storekeeper against doing business on the Sabbath.

With supplies secured, Perley and Adney went to the Wəlastəkwey village looking for guides with canoes who could call moose. They stopped by the home of Joe Alexander, who had a canoe and assured them he could call moose. Joe suggested hiring his uncle, Ambrose Lockwood, who also had a canoe, and Ambrose agreed to join the month-long expedition.

Joe and Ambrose paddled down to the Andover hotel and loaded the canoes with part of the gear and supplies. The rest would be brought along on the Inman mail wagon some sixty miles north up the Tobique River to the Forks where the Little Tobique, the Right Hand Branch, and the Mamozekel converge. When they arrived at Riley Brook, they determined another canoe would be needed to distribute the load as they went farther upstream into the woods and to ensure they had enough room for all the specimens they would bring out.

Adney went looking for another canoe and guide. Rowley gave assurances he would be reimbursed for the cost of the additional canoe since it would be used entirely for museum purposes. All the birchbark canoes in the community and their owners were already at work with other hunting parties. The only canoe left was a twenty-five-foot dugout owned by a man named Jimmie. Having been hewn and carved from a whole log, the dugout canoe was three times heavier than a birchbark canoe but could carry an enormous load and would bounce off rocks without damage. Adney hired Jimmie and his dugout, which he dubbed the "Great Eastern."

They set up camp at the Forks. Joe and Ambrose arrived two day later, having poled their canoes upstream against the current. Adney and Rowley had been planning to take the Little Tobique to Little Tobique Lake, but Ambrose Lockwood advised taking the Right Hand Branch to Trousers Lake and Gulquac Lake. He explained that the Right Hand Branch would be more difficult, but their chances of getting a moose were much better in that direction, where there would be fewer hunting parties.

Adney was confident they were right and was obliged to them for placing the success of the expedition above their own self-interest. He admired them and later wrote, "they never shirked or spared themselves labor.... They were splendid canoemen and skillful campmen...."[11] They clearly understood their role, and Adney knew from previous experience how important it was to listen to their advice carefully and then follow it. Wəlastəkwi guides didn't argue with those who hired them; they would advise on the best course of action once and then do what they were told, even if it meant doing the wrong thing.

The expedition launched into the Right Hand Branch, poling against the strong current for five days to traverse the thirty-five miles to Trousers Lake, where they found an old log shanty that became their headquarters camp after some minor repairs. Ambrose suggested a hunting party continue to Gualquac Lake, some twelve miles farther, including a one-and-a-quarter—mile portage. Gualquac, he said, was the best place to call a moose, as the lake had a hard bottom and plenty of water lilies on which moose feed. Ambrose was a fount of information about the habits of moose and was clearly taking the lead as hunting guide. Adney thought it strange, since Joe was hired as the moose hunter and Ambrose as a camp helper. He later discovered that Ambrose was an experienced moose caller and Joe a beginner. Ambrose hadn't said anything because Joe had been hired as the caller. But when it came time to call a moose, Joe deferred to his uncle. Rowley decided he and the two guides should continue to Gualquac Lake.

At the headquarters camp, Adney and Jimmie set out to augment the food supply with fresh and smoked trout. They discovered large trout gathered under the logs jammed into an old dam at the end of the lake. They kept busy for three days. When the catch at the dam diminished, they went to a small lake nearby and caught twenty-five more good-sized trout in one afternoon.

A few days later, as Adney and Jimmie were sitting by the fire after supper, the sound of a canoe docking on the shore of the lake brought them to their feet. Joe stepped into the firelight and announced they had a moose, a big moose — the biggest moose he had ever seen. He stretched out his arms full width to indicate the size of the antlers. The antlers were later measured and found to be fifty-nine-and-a-half inches from tip to tip. Ambrose, too, said it was the biggest moose he had ever seen and that it was about eleven years old. Joe had been sent back to camp to deliver some of the meat to Adney and Jimmie and to retrieve some plaster so Rowley could make a cast of the moose's nose.

The next morning, they set out in the dugout canoe to transport the moose. Adney took his camera. By the time they reached the camp on Gulquac Lake, Rowley had skinned the moose with the hide still attached to the head. They dined on fresh moose meat that night and breakfasted on it the next morning. Rowley mixed the plaster in a bread pan and soon had a perfect mould of the nose that would later be filled with more plaster at the museum to yield an exact copy of the original. Joe and Ambrose slung the hide and the head with the enormous antlers across a pole and walked it down to the lake to load in the dugout canoe.

In addition to the moose centrepiece of the museum's new diorama, other animal and plant specimens were needed to complete the north woods environment of the installation. Rowley, his Wəlastəkwi guides, and Adney trapped mice, muskrats, squirrels, shrews, moles, mink, sable, otter, beaver, partridge, and other birds. They preserved the skins with heads attached to be transported back to the museum in New York, where Rowley would reconstruct them into lifelike replicas.

Rowley also made wax impressions of leaves and bark from all the trees in the area: birch, maple, ash, cedar, pine, spruce, and fir. He first made a plaster mould of the leaves and bark then poured hot wax into the mould to make a perfect copy of the original. Only one sample was needed for each tree, from which any number of copies could be made. Colour would be added later at the museum's workshop.

Before they left their camp at Gulquac Lake, Adney and the guides spent several nights attempting to call in a moose. Adney describes them as bundled in double layers of clothing and wrapped in blankets; the mid-October nights had turned decidedly colder. By midnight, he wrote, frost had settled on the gunwales of the canoe, and chilly, wet dew coated their blankets and "spread over the lake in a sheet of white."[12] He quoted Ambrose's instructions: "Must keep very still."[13] After an extended period of silence, Ambrose rose to his feet, brought the rolled birchbark horn to his mouth and began to call.

A low quick grunt, then a silence, then another low grunt. It was scarcely audible. It was in case a moose might be within a few rods. In a few minutes again the call was raised, this time louder, a low swelling wail, and as the Indian made the call, the horn, high aloft, described a figure eight.

The Indian stood a moment, listening with strained attention for some far away sound, but there was none and he slowly took his seat and wrapped his blanket about himself. Far away is the hooting of the great horned owl lost in the bubbling of a distant brook.

Thus, we waited; the Pleiades rose above the eastern horizon's bank of trees and great Jupiter followed soon, almost a moon by itself. Never had the sky seemed so clear. It seemed as if the remotest star in the heavens contributed its share of light. And there seemed to be myriads of others that blurred the vision.... as if we look and listen on the border of another world.[14]

Several evenings later, they went to the place on the lake where Ambrose had successfully hunted moose before. After a few hours of patient, seductive calling, they heard the unmistakable sound of a moose returning the call from perhaps a mile away. The moose came closer, and they could hear him walking back and forth in the woods, trying to identify the call coming from the canoe on the edge of the lake: "but no persuading of the wily Ambrose could lure him from the security the black woods gave him."[15] Ambrose asked Adney to remember that it was October 13 when he had successfully called in a moose, nearly two weeks after the season had ended.

Rowley decided it was time to leave the woods. They had achieved nearly all the expedition's goals. They broke camp at Gulquac Lake, loaded the canoes, and paddled to the portage. After the arduous carry, they set off down the length of Trousers Lake just as a rainstorm with heavy winds and high whitecap waves came up. The wind was blowing down the lake, driving the heavily loaded canoes through the rough water with only a few inches of freeboard below the gunwales.

Adney was paddling in the bow of one canoe with Ambrose in the stern, calling out instructions. The waves came from behind them like ocean surf. When Ambrose saw a large swell coming, he shouted to Adney to paddle hard so the wave wouldn't flood the canoe. When such a wave hits, it lifts the rear of the canoe and drives the bow into the trough, putting it in danger of submersion. Hard paddling at that point drives the canoe forward and keeps the bow as high as possible as the swell passes under the canoe. After several hours of the most exhausting paddling Adney ever experienced, they arrived at their headquarters camp near the outlet of Trousers Lake. The shelter of the shanty allowed them to dry off, get a hot meal, and rest from their ordeal.

The next day they set out down the Right Hand Branch to the Forks of the Tobique. When they reached Riley Brook, Adney sent his trunk of personal effects to Andover on Inman's mail wagon so he could better distribute the heavy load of museum boxes and gear between the three canoes for safer travelling down the Tobique. The guides' canoes were heavily loaded with moose meat Rowley had given them, which they had smoked and dried. Rowley was irritated at Adney's initiative because it implied further indebtedness of the museum's budget for the hiring of Jimmie and his dugout canoe for the rest of the downriver trip. Adney made no reply. It should have been obvious to Rowley they could not otherwise bring out the museum's collection and their gear in a single trip.[16]

They reached the mouth of the Tobique at the end of October and stopped at the Indigenous village so Joe and Ambrose could unload the moose meat at their houses. With the guides' canoes now less heavily loaded, Rowley proposed to pay Jimmie off and send him home and told Adney he could continue to Andover by hired wagon. Adney declined, explaining it would have been impossible to bring the museum's collection and expedition gear out of the woods without Jimmie and his large dugout canoe, and it was still needed to complete the trip to Andover. He insisted Jimmie should be paid by the expedition for his services. Rowley answered that when he got back to New York he would do his best to see that Adney was reimbursed for his expenses.

But that's not the way it worked out. When they got back to New York, it was clear that Rowley had not even mentioned to his supervisor, Professor J.A. Allen, that Adney had accompanied the expedition, let alone requested approval for extra expenses. When Adney confronted Rowley, he said he had meant to but it must have slipped his mind.

Adney had kept a meticulous record of what he had spent to ensure the expedition's success. His accounting showed what he was owed. Rowley disagreed but had only rough estimates. Adney was now suspicious he was trying to avoid paying and threatened to take the dispute to Allen. Rowley was reluctant for that to happen, but when he offered no resolution, Adney did just that.

Rowley acknowledged Adney had accompanied the expedition but denied he had depended on him for anything. He completely ignored all that Adney had done to identify the place, provide supplies, and haul everything in and back out. Adney was so incensed he wrote a six-page statement to Allen of all he had done to ensure the success of the expedition.

Allen maintained he had no money in the expedition budget for Adney, but he could offer him credit for his contributions in the official museum report. Disappointed and angry, Adney accepted the credit, which turned out to be one sentence at the beginning of a dry, academic listing, much of it in Latin, of the twenty-one species of animals the expedition had brought back for the museum's collection. The one-sentence credit reads "Mr. E.T. Adney also accompanied the party, rendering material aid and contributing to the success of the expedition."[17]

In the summer of 1896 Adney was approached by a friend in New York who offered to pay all his expenses for a trip to the Serpentine River in New Brunswick to collect and bring back quartz rocks embedded with gold. The friend was intrigued by Adney's account of Giberson's gold and wanted to see for himself if there was enough to warrant a mining operation. Adney wrote to Hum Sharp and Sol Perley to ask if they would be available for another trip like the one in 1892.

For this expedition he was equipped with a five-by-seven Premo Box camera and tripod as well as his sketching supplies. The camera was fitted with a Gundlach star lens and a B&L iris-diaphragm shutter. The editor of *Field and Stream* magazine later told Adney his photographs were the best record of such a trip that he had ever seen.

Adney travelled by train from New York to New Brunswick, arriving in Woodstock on September 15. He learned that Perley and Hum Sharp were planning for the gold-prospecting trip on the Serpentine but were not ready to start out for at least two weeks. After purchasing additional supplies, Adney took the train north up the Wəlastəkw Valley to Andover. He crossed the river to Perth and caught the Tobique Valley Railroad, which had been completed and began service to Plaster Rock in 1894.

Adney stopped at Arthurette to visit his friend Manzer Giberson, who was interested in the trip to the Serpentine but laid up with a cut foot. He told Adney to go to Riley Brook to see Amos Gaunce, an old hand at bear hunting who was preparing to check his bear traps. Amos took a liking to Adney and invited him along.

Adney described the area:

Riley Brook settlement lies in a perfectly smooth, level "intervale," or flat, some two miles long on the west side of the river. It lies like a great amphitheater, the hills several hundred feet high rising more or less abruptly on each side. The whole plain is under good cultivation and a dozen or so houses have a neat, thrifty appearance. The woods commence at the edge of the flat....

Every year Amos catches a bear within a mile of [his] house and moose and caribou roam out into the clearing in their wanderings to and fro and often pass right by the houses.[18]

Everyone was awake early the next morning.

By sunrise the whole family were awake when Amos came into the breakfast table. Well, I thought, there was something distinctive in my old rags that had seen more than one season in the woods.... He had on an old coat, half corduroy, half moleskin, in an advanced stage of disintegration, ragged and fringed at every seam, greasy and gray; pants that matched the coat, and a dark reddish felt hat full of holes and shiny with years of wear. This suit was an heirloom. The whole atmosphere anywhere in its vicinity was redolent with the smell of campfires and other odors that a stranger would not so easily classify. "Don't mind Amos, that's the bear 'scent' Amos takes with him," said his wife, who evidently thought some explanation was needed.

When we were ready to start, Amos put the grub into an old seamless sack that by another coincidence just matched his clothes and slung it on his back with a leather "carrying strap," which passed around in front of each shoulder. He took a small axe besides.

"If we git a bear in the trap, I'll let you shoot him," said Amos to me, who was carrying a 45-70 Repeater [rifle] as well as the camera. "I'll be mighty disappointed if we don't git a bear."[19]

With that, Adney was inducted into bear trapping with Amos Gaunce and his partner, Charley Barker, who, Adney wrote, was

a natural woodsman and one of the best hunters on the Tobique. I never saw his equal in following a trail. He could follow, at a swinging gait, a "path" that I could not even see, and I thought I had been about a little in the woods. And he followed it when it was so dark that I could hardly see the trees.[20]

On September 26, Adney wrote: "Dog tired. Twenty miles of tramping with gun, camera, and tripod. Twenty miles of mountains, rocks, underbrush, burnt land, fallen trees, and swamp following an old bear hunter's trail."[21]

On the first hunt, the first few traps were empty, but then came one in which a yearling bear cub was caught in the steel jaws by a few toes of a hind paw. The cub was squealing in pain and was desperate to escape. Fearful that the young bear's cries would attract its protective mother, Amos wanted to kill it quickly. He motioned to Adney as if offering an initiation into the brotherhood of bear trappers.

"Well, are you going to shoot him?" Amos asked. Adney hesitated and then replied, "No, not for any money. Shoot anything in that fix? No."[22] Adney said they could let the cub go and trap it again in a year or so when it would be larger and have a bigger hide to sell. Amos didn't see it that way. He dispatched the cub, skinned it out, cut up its carcass as bait for the trap, and continued on.

Adney never resolved the conflict between his aversion to killing animals and his admiration for woodsmen. Right through his last trip into the woods in 1896, he participated in trapping bear, beaver, mink, and sable (marten). This passage from his journal sums up his ambivalence:

> I have never been a very successful hunter, considering how
> much time I have been in the woods. Yet I do not think that my
> loss. The grand wilderness itself is recompense for any amount
> of trouble and hardship. Health and vigor are better than any
> game.[23]

Adney was essentially a conservationist, his natural history journalism contributing in the same way and at the same time as John Muir to the appreciation and preservation of the natural world. Muir founded the Sierra Club in 1892 and published his first book, *The Mountains of California*, in 1894. Like Adney, he helped galvanize the conservation movement of the time with articles in popular magazines. Like Muir and others, Adney appreciated the intrinsic importance of wilderness preservation and the experience of venturing into remote and still pristine natural areas. But his interest in heritage preservation also included the cultural and livelihood practices of the Indigenous people and the non-Indigenous settlers who lived in close relationship with wilderness regions.

In this respect he diverged from the conservationists who wanted to set up large wilderness parks from which most human activity was banned except recreational tourism. He was an ethnographer as well as a naturalist, and heritage preservation applied to the ways in which human communities relied on forestland, rivers, and lakes for sustenance and sustainable resources. He was always a participant-observer, whether it was building canoes with Peter Jo or bear hunting with Amos Gaunce.

When Sol Perley and Hum Sharp finally showed up, Sol let Tappan know about an arrangement with Newell Bear. Newell claimed he and his uncle, Ambrose, were trapping on the "Bathurst waters" when they discovered some white rocks flecked with a shiny yellow metal. Newell, who lived at Riley Brook, let it be known he would guide anyone back to the spot "for a certain sum." Perley agreed to pay Newell $20 and meet him on a certain day at a camp site on the Right Hand Branch near Seven Mile Hole.

Newell ran a trapline along the Serpentine and maintained a home camp farther up the river. Perley, Hum, and Adney arrived a day late. Newell had not waited. They figured he had set out to check his trapline, which he'd said he needed to do and could take a week or more. Perley hiked to Newell's home camp and left a note written on birchbark, but their failure to meet him as promised got their dealings with Newell off to a poor start.

After four days of waiting, Sharp and Perley were anxious to get on with their gold prospecting. Adney offered to go to Newell's camp and wait for his return. He was particularly interested to see an Indigenous hunter's wilderness camp, take note how the shelter was constructed, and photograph the whole set-up.

The next day, with camera, tripod, Winchester rifle, and food supplies in his backpack, Adney hiked to Newell's camp. It was evident no one other than Perley had been there for some time. Falling leaves had collected in the firepit beneath the smoke hole in the roof. Perley's birchbark note was still hanging from the ridgepole. Adney took the opportunity to take photographs and carefully examine the construction of the first Indigenous wilderness camp he had seen. A large bearskin was drying on a stretcher, a sign that Newell might be returning soon.

Adney was sitting in the birchbark shelter when Newell returned.

...the door parted...and in came a little old man with a pack and an axe. He threw his pack down on the floor and I moved to make room for him. He was a short, but heavy-set man with dark, much-wrinkled features and he gave me what I thought a decidedly sinister look.... I saw at once he was an Indian of strong, pure type.[24]

Newell was annoyed that Adney had been depleting his firewood supply. Adney was at first deferential, explaining his purpose for the visit was to see his camp and take some photographs. Newell commented that Adney took up a good deal of room but began cooking supper and seemed willing for him to stay. As the evening progressed and it became evident that Adney was an eager conversationalist, Newell became friendly and was eager to talk as well.

We soon became good friends. Newell appeared to be in good humor. His profile, with its strongly curved nose, was good, but

I did not like it when he looked me square in the face, as he did whenever he put leading remarks to me about game clubs and shooting licenses. His...face had a sinister expression.... I pictured to mind as never before, the real old-time Indian, the foe of the white man that was driving him from hunting grounds....

We talked on into the night. Newell is more chatty than most Indians I have met. He was down on "laws that wouldn't let Injun ketch beaver nor otter." He was down on the white man that the "Injun fed when he first came here, but now wouldn't let Injun hunt."

Newell was from a family of old time hunters and no doubt it was getting harder to get a living out of the woods than there used to be....

It grew late and I began to grow sleepy.

"When are you ever going to bed?" I asked him.

"...don't get company all time in woods."[25]

When Adney mentioned Sol Perley and the reason for his expedition, Newell's face "showed no change. After a long silence, he said, 'You go tell that man, Injun there when he say he there. Injun not lie. That man, he not come when he say. I not believe that man again. I got my traps set now, more'n thirty bear traps.... I can't afford leave my trappin' now."[26]

It was true: Perley had not arrived at the agreed time. Adney told Newell he didn't know anything about his deal with Perley, but he thought Perley would be a big fool to pay anyone money to go over toward Bathurst. He said he didn't believe there was any more white rock there than on the Serpentine. Sensing trouble ahead, Adney did his best to convince Newell that they didn't need him and that he was here was to take photographs of his shelter.

The next morning Newell announced he would be at his camp on the Serpentine deadwater the first of the following week. He repeated that he had been lied to about the time and place of meeting, and Perley and Sharp would now have to come to him there if they wanted his help.

Adney went back to their camp near the mouth of the Serpentine and told Perley and Sharp what Newell had said. They set out at once and arrived at the deadwater on Sunday night. They found Newell's camp but not Newell. The next day they followed Newell's trapline in hopes of finding him, without success. They eventually found him at a lumber camp working on a pair of moosehide moccasins. He scolded Perley for lying but was completely unfazed when confronted with the inconsistencies of his schedule.

Newell had a great trip planned, but he made it something of a mystery. He said it would be a very hard trip. They would be gone at least two weeks, come out on the other side of the Inter-Colonial railroad, and come home by way of Fredericton. Adney knew the geography Newell described was out of the question and refused to go. He remained in camp, occupying the time by adding to his photographic record, setting and tending mink traps, and fishing.

He was expecting trouble from Perley and Sharp if Newell couldn't produce the white rocks with the gold in them. Eventually, Perley and Sharp returned, reporting a miserable time in the cold and the rain. Hum said they had travelled through rough country with deep gulches and high precipices, which he had not previously seen except in the Rocky Mountains. They realized that Newell did not know the country well. When asked about where he had seen the white rock, he replied, "Somewhere here about." Perley confronted Newell with his failure to show them the ledge of quartz rock he said he could find. Newell became angry at the accusation but backed down when Perley paid him the agreed sum of $20 and called off the search.

Sol and Hum left immediately after this for Woodstock while Adney remained to close the camp and bring out his personal equipment. When he got to Riley Brook, he had a good rest at Amos Gaunce's house and was regaled with stories of moose and bear hunting he had missed while out on the Serpentine. Two days later he left for Woodstock, from where he shipped a fifty-pound box of quartz rocks to his friend and sponsor in New York. He had collected the samples on his own along the Serpentine.

This 1896 trip to the Tobique and Serpentine was the fifth and last of these immersive wilderness adventures. Between these extended trips and his adoption of rural and wilderness living, Tappan Adney developed an artistic and journalistic career in New York based on his experiences in New Brunswick. And now he added photography to his artistic representation of the natural history and cultural life on which he was reporting. Given his formal education and training as an artist, he was a thoroughly sophisticated New Yorker. Yet, by choice and deep inclination, he was drawn to wilderness living and association with the heritage and contemporary lives of Indigenous people in a way that came to define a large part of his vocation.

His reputation as a writer, illustrator, and reporter of natural history and cultural environments had reached a substantial level of recognition in New York.[27] Seven months after returning to the city from New Brunswick, *Harper's Weekly* recruited him for a major assignment: reporting from the Klondike Gold Rush.

Chapter Five

To the Klondike: A Perilous Journey

The most important item on the list is good advice—plenty of it.
—Tappan Adney

Few of the gold-crazed adventurers who joined the Klondike stampede in 1897 were as well equipped as Tappan Adney for the journey's hardships and dangers. He was twenty-nine years old and an experienced woodsman, having sojourned five times in ten years in New Brunswick and repeatedly participated in wilderness expeditions. On his woodland adventures he had endured fatigue, hunger, extreme cold, and injuries. He had learned the wilderness is an unforgiving place for those who are not well prepared.

Harper's Weekly, one of the most popular American newsmagazines of the time, hired Adney to cover the Klondike Gold Rush and provide articles, photos, and illustrations.[1] He was given a $2,000 advance (the equivalent of $75,000 in 2024) to cover his travel and living expenses, with the balance to come after successful completion of the assignment.[2] *Harper's* also arranged with the *London Chronicle* for the concurrent publication of Adney's dispatches.

Although *Harper's* had not previously published Adney's work, the editors were obviously aware of his writing and artistic skills. He had been producing outdoor adventure articles and illustrations for other New York publications since his first trip to New Brunswick. He had established a reputation as a versatile journalist who was reliable in meeting deadlines. His skill and experience as a woodsman made him a sound choice for the Klondike assignment.

Harper's hired him as a special correspondent, and he set to work listing the supplies he would need. His outfit included many items unusual for a traveller to the Klondike: cameras, tripod, film, developing chemicals, a typewriter, typing paper, artist supplies, and plans for a lumberman's batteau—a rough-water boat he had seen working among the log booms on the Walastəkw in New Brunswick. Unlike virtually everyone else, he didn't need any mining tools. His objective was to discover the story of this gold fever stampede, not the nuggets that caused it. He was thoroughly aware of the importance of good preparation:

> One who has never undertaken to gather all that a man will need for a space of ten or twelve months, so that he shall not have to call on anyone else for material assistance, has any idea of the time required. The most important item on the list is good advice—plenty of it.[3]

Time was critical. He bought his cross-country train ticket and steamship reservation in New York on July 30. His coastal steamer, *Islander*, was scheduled to leave Victoria, British Columbia, on August 15 and arrive at Skagway, Alaska, five days later. He had been told the Yukon River would freeze by mid-October, so he had just ten weeks to make it to Dawson and the Klondike region via this route. Before leaving New York, he telegraphed Minnie Bell in Woodstock to arrange a meeting in Montréal as he passed through on his way to British Columbia. He knew he would not see her again for at least a year, perhaps more. After several days together, Minnie Bell wrote in her diary: "Talked with Tappan. It is good to have an understanding."[4] Two years later, on September 12, 1899, they would marry at St. Luke's Episcopal Church in Woodstock.

In Montréal, Adney used the telegraph to secure space on the *Islander* for six packhorses, which he planned to buy in Victoria. During a coal-and-water stop in Winnipeg, Manitoba, he hustled to the Hudson's Bay Company (HBC) to purchase winter clothing, but the store had already sold out of some items. Undeterred, he bought the regulation winter-clothing outfit of HBC employees: a heavy, black, hooded duffle coat that reached to his knees; a twelve-pound duffle blanket; a gaily coloured waist sash worn by the Métis People; a red and black wool knit toque; and the best ankle-high moose-hide moccasins. He purchased the rest of his gear and supplies in Victoria, where he arrived on August 8.

On the train west Adney met a pair of stampeders from Detroit who were planning to buy horses in Victoria. The two had agreed to help each other over White Pass to Lindeman Lake, the headwaters of the Yukon River. One was a US Cavalry veteran, Jim McCarron, who was experienced with horses; the other, a teenager, Burghardt, was a baker and cook who hoped his skills would earn him a living in Dawson. Adney made a pact with them: McCarron and Burghardt would take charge of the care and feeding of Adney's horses, and they would use their combined eight horses to transport all of their outfits to Lindeman Lake. They agreed that Adney's supplies would be first to be transported. Adney arrived in Victoria a week before the departure of the *Islander*, which gave him adequate time to shop for horses, hay, and oats plus his own provisions and have the planking, ribs, and oars for his batteau custom-cut and ready for loading on the steamer.

Compared with Adney, most who left the ports of Seattle and Victoria in 1897 and 1898 bound for the Klondike were naive tenderfoots. The manifests of the coastal steamers during this time list more than a hundred thousand passengers. A yearning for adventure and escape from the stifling conventions of Victorian-era life drove some of the men heading for the Yukon; others, unemployed for years in the lingering economic depression of the 1890s, decided to seek their fortune in the gold fields. All shared the dream of becoming fabulously wealthy overnight.

When news of gold-laden ships returning to Seattle flashed across the telegraph wires, it spread like wildfire across the United States and around the world. Within months, a small remote settlement in northwestern Canada became the focus of tens of thousands of eager men seeking their fortunes. Those who didn't have the money needed to equip an outfit borrowed the funds. Investors who hoped to get rich financed others. Some sold everything they owned to finance the journey, hoping to strike it rich in the gold fields. It didn't occur to them they might not make it to Dawson, or if they did, that they might not find any gold. They were afflicted by "gold fever," a kind of madness.

After the discovery of gold in the Klondike area in August 1896, and before thousands of would-be miners from across North America arrived, hundreds of seasoned prospectors from Circle City, Forty Mile, and other mining towns in the region had already descended on Dawson to stake their claims. When the ill-equipped greenhorns started arriving, the population increase overwhelmed local food supplies. Famine stalked the miners, along with scurvy, a wasting disease caused by a diet deficient in vitamin C. Canadian officials in the Yukon Territory and the federal government in Ottawa pondered what to do when the spring breakup swept the ice from the Yukon River, clearing passage for a new influx of would-be miners.

To prevent a recurrence of food shortages the following winter, the North West Mounted Police (NWMP) were ordered to set up check points and require everyone bound for Dawson to have sufficient supplies to feed themselves for one year.[5] Only those with adequate provisions would be allowed to set out for Dawson. This government intervention helped but did not eliminate the spectre of famine in the gold fields the next winter.

The typical miners' outfit included flour, bacon, canned meats, hardtack biscuits, dried fruit, beans, split peas, oatmeal, rice, evaporated milk, coffee, tea, sugar, salt, and medical supplies. It also included cooking utensils, axes, knives, guns, ammunition, mining equipment, building tools, cold-weather clothing, blankets, and a sturdy tent. A fully equipped outfit typically weighed around twelve hundred pounds; more elaborate outfits could weigh a ton or more.

The border between the US territory of Alaska and Canada had been established a decade earlier. A long thin strip of land on the ocean side of the coast range, stretching from the main part of Alaska halfway to Victoria, British Columbia, is part of the United States. The international border runs along the highest ridges and peaks of the mountains that sit brooding sombrely on the cloud-draped horizon, miles inland from the Pacific Ocean. The stampeders bound for the Klondike had to land at the Alaskan towns of Skagway or nearby Dyea (pronounced *die-yah*) and make their way over the height of land on the coastal range into Canada. Up to that point, the journey was a five-day pleasure cruise from Seattle or Victoria with beautiful mountain scenery all the way. But when the big steamers dropped anchor at the head of Lynn Canal outside Skagway, the stampeders got their first taste of the hard realities they would face all the way to Dawson.

There were no docks at the Skagway landing. The steamship companies assumed no responsibility for offloading passengers and their cargo. Passengers had to arrange with local boatmen to ferry their goods ashore. Supplies were loaded onto scows, rowed to shore, transferred to horse-drawn wagons, hauled to higher ground, and unloaded in the open. Passengers on Adney's ship, the *Islander,* had formed a committee to organize the offloading and provide onshore security for their goods. Horses, immobilized in tightly packed stalls below deck during the five-day voyage, were led down planks onto the scows, then prodded into the frigid water to swim ashore.

Once on shore, each man had to transport his supplies overland to Lindeman Lake, crossing into Canada at either Chilkoot Pass or White

Pass of the coastal mountain range. Men who brought horses used them to haul their outfits up the trail to the mountain passes. Others paid packers to haul their goods on their backs or on packhorses. But the vast majority with little or no money had to pack their supplies on their own backs, 80 to 120 pounds at a time, making numerous shuttles to move their entire outfits from one stockpiling point to another on the trails. Moving a 1,200-pound outfit to Lindeman Lake, twenty-six miles via the Chilkoot Pass or forty-five miles via the White Pass, meant mind- and muscle-numbing repetitions of the routes—a total of six hundred miles on the Chilkoot Trail or more than a thousand miles on the White Pass Trail. Those with horses or who could hire horses had a distinct advantage. Those who made it to Lindeman Lake had to build or buy boats to navigate the nearly six hundred miles down the Yukon River to Dawson and the nearby goldfields.

The extreme effort required to get over the mountain passes became the first test for the stampeders. The Chilkoot Pass, at 3,200 feet above sea level, was the best-known route. Indigenous people had long used the trail as a trade route, but it had a serious drawback: the last half-mile rose eight hundred feet at a forty-degree angle, so steep that loaded horses could not make the climb. Most were left at the base of the summit, where human packers took over, repeatedly plodding up and down the steep, narrow, rocky trail. Some horses and burros were taken over without loads for use on the other side.

Many would-be miners found the passes to be insurmountable barriers to the realization of their ambitions. Most had never been in the wilderness before or done any climbing or packing with heavy loads. After seeing the passes and hearing ominous reports of the grim hardships ahead, many sold their provisions and bought return tickets to Victoria or Seattle. Those who made it to Lindeman Lake and built boats or rafts then had to face the dangers of capsizing and losing their supplies and perhaps their lives on the voyage down the Yukon River. A high risk of death from accident and illness continued for those who reached Dawson and the gold fields. Conflicts resulted in homicides and failure to strike it rich in suicides.

Others realized that mining was not the only way to get rich in the Klondike. Instead of panning for gold, they mined the miners. In tents pitched in and around Dawson, they set up makeshift hotels, restaurants, saloons, dance halls, gambling houses, brothels, and laundries. They started under canvas then moved into wooden buildings. Sawmills, boat building shops, packing services, and mining supply stores were established.

The NWMP estimated the population of the Dawson City area to be less than five thousand during the winter of 1897–98. Only the hardiest and best prepared made it to Dawson in 1897, perhaps only 15 per cent of those who attempted the journey. Adney was among the elite few. He was extraordinarily tough, mentally and physically.

Virtually everyone on the *Islander* decided on the White Pass Trail. The elevation of the pass was lower than the Chilkoot, but the distance to Lindeman Lake was much greater. Adney was skeptical. While waiting in the staging area to unload his outfit, Adney met Charles Leadbetter, an enterprising packer, who offered his assistance. In exchange for the eight horses and their feed supplies, which Adney and his two companions had available, Leadbetter and his packers would transport all their goods over the Chilkoot Pass to Lindeman Lake, taking only four to five days to complete the transfer. Adney and his partners, however, would have to move their goods by boat from Skagway to Dyea four miles away and then inland to the Chilkoot trailhead. The Adney party would also be expected to assist Leadbetter's packers along the trail. Everyone agreed and signed a contract spelling out the arrangement. Leadbetter then ferried the horses to Dyea to work in his packhorse trains on the Chilkoot Trail.

Adney unloaded his outfit from the *Islander* and hired a man from Texas with a thirty-foot dory who was in the business of ferrying people and their goods the four miles between Skagway and Dyea. With everything delivered to Leadbetter's camp, Adney returned to Skagway to investigate White Pass. He shouldered his five-by-seven camera and tripod and his backpack with blankets and food and headed up the White Pass Trail. He spent two cold, rainy days on the trail, taking shelter in the tents of accommodating stampeders at night. By the time he made it halfway to the summit, he had seen enough for his reporting. He returned to Skagway, then to Dyea.

He described the scene on the White Pass Trail: "Where there are no rocks, there are boggy holes. It is all rocks and mud—rocks and mud."[6] They laboured "ankle-deep in sloppy, slimy, chocolate-colored mud," he wrote. "Horses and men, bags and pack-covers are dyed with this brown stain."[7]

We come to an empty pack-saddle....We need no one to tell us that over the cliff a horse has rolled hundreds of feet, and lies out of sight among the bushes. Again an almost unbearable stench announces an earlier victim.

Every man we meet tells of the trials of the trail. Anxious and weary are they.[8]

And yet people kept coming. At Skagway, he wrote, "A steamer arrives and empties several hundred people and tons of goods into the mouth of the trail, and the trail absorbs them as a sponge drinks up water. They are lost amid the gulches and trees."[9]

On his arrival at Dyea he was dismayed to find the supplies he had left stockpiled had been swept up in an unusually high tide and soaked by a foot of water. Fortunately, the lot had been salvaged by an acquaintance Adney had made on the *Islander*. He lost some flour and dried fruit but no other food. His heart sank, however, when he saw water dripping from film containers he had ordered hermetically sealed. His entire supply of film plates for the camera was ruined, and no replacements could be obtained this side of Seattle. He still had a small hand-held camera with spools of film but not enough for the work ahead.

He sorted through his supplies, drying things in a tent before returning to Skagway on August 28 to post an order for more film on a ship returning south. He knew winter would set in before the film plates could arrive, but he hoped the mail service operated by the NWMP year-round could make the delivery by dog sled from Skagway to Dawson.

On August 29, he inquired about when his goods would be moved, but Leadbetter's packers were sullen and angry. Leadbetter had promised to deliver their goods in exchange for their labour, so they too were waiting. Some were on the verge of mutiny. To make matters worse, many of Leadbetter's horses and burros couldn't work because they needed shoes, but the Dyea blacksmith was often drunk and lacked tools and supplies.

Three days later, Adney's goods and those of his partners had not been moved, although their horses were still being used in Leadbetter's pack trains. He and his partners hired four Indigenous men with a canoe to haul their outfits several miles upstream to where Leadbetter had moved his base camp.

When they arrived, they found McCarron's horse lame and unable to work. McCarron and Burghardt saw it as a harbinger of problems ahead. They decided to pack their own goods and asked Adney to dissolve their agreement. Adney agreed to give them one of his horses in exchange for the work they had done for him. He was then left on his own with five horses, now being worked by Leadbetter somewhere up the trail. On the morning of September 2, the simmering resentment of Leadbetter's packers boiled over. Frustrated and angry, they confiscated all the able horses, loaded their own supplies, and moved up the trail, leaving Adney's goods and those of others behind.

Adney returned to Dyea and the US commissioner's office to seek warrants for the release of his horses. He returned to camp late that afternoon to find his horses munching oats and the packers in a better frame of mind, having moved their own goods closer to the summit. At the campfire that night, they acknowledged Adney's right to his horses and left them behind when they resumed packing the next day.

The next day, September 5, Adney sold three of his horses to a group of packers for $50 each, twice what he paid for them in Victoria. The packers then had ten horses, on which they agreed to haul Adney's goods as well as their own. Heading for the next camp with the pack train, he recognized McCarron and Burghardt and their horses, one of which—a small mare—was down on the trail. Her pack had slipped and suddenly shifted, the weight of it taking her down. The men removed the pack. The mare's back was broken, and she had to be shot. Adney wrote: "Wet blankets, saddles not cinched tight, saddles that do not fit, loads unequally balanced, are doing the sad work. We cannot see until the saddles are off what hundreds of horses are suffering."[10]

At Sheep Camp, four miles from the Chilkoot summit, he found his remaining horse. The value of horses plummeted closer to the pass, so he rode it down the trail to sell it. On the way to Dyea, he saw Leadbetter and one of his teamsters coming the other way. The teamster asked Adney if would sell his horse. When he said his price was $25, the teamster jumped at the offer. Returning to Sheep Camp, he took supper in a hotel built with rough-sawn lumber. When the proprietor saw Adney's camera, he said he had some photo supplies abandoned by another photographer and was at liberty to sell them.

> ...he brought out—of all things!—three spools of 4 x 5 daylight film! I took them quickly enough. That very day I was going down the trail in Sheep Camp...when a young man hailed me with "Say, do you want to buy a camera? I see you are a photographer." A stroke of lightning could not have caused me

more astonishment. "I have a camera here, and I guess I don't want it any longer. It's too much trouble." It proved to be the very make of camera that my spools fitted, and, as fortune is said always to run in streaks, he had nine more unused spools and was willing to part with them for their cost in San Francisco![11]

By September 12 snow was swirling on the Chilkoot Pass summit and at Lindeman Lake, but Indigenous packers predicted the lakes and Yukon River would not freeze for six weeks. Burros and horses were starving for lack of grazing. As the weather worsened, packers quit, and rates rose in response. Discouraged and exhausted, many would-be prospectors tried to sell their outfits, but they had little value. Stampeders who had shouldered their outfits hundreds of times to move up the trail and over the pass were not eager to acquire more weight at any price.

While waiting for his outfit to be taken over the pass, Adney reflected on what he was seeing.

The cruelty to horses is past belief.... Their owners have used and abused them to this point, and are too tenderhearted (?) to put them out of their misery. Their backs are raw from wet and wrinkled blankets, their legs cut and bruised on the rocks, and they are as thin as snakes and starving to death.[12]

He described an encounter with one horse abandoned on the trail when his owner no longer had use for him:

A wretched thin, white cayuse came to my tent. He had been driven from four miles above, where his owner had deserted him. It was raining a cold rain. He put his head and as much more as he could inside the tent, trying to get next the stove. He stayed there all night and was around all next day, and he had nothing to eat. I am certain he never felt the 44-caliber bullet back of his ear that evening. Thereupon a general killing-off began, until carcasses were lying on all sides.[13]

Flush with cash that most didn't have, Adney paid a dozen packers to take his outfit across the pass and two miles farther to Crater Lake, but they refused to transport his boat lumber. He knew he must find a new partner; it was lunacy to attempt such a long and dangerous river journey without assistance. He finally partnered with a young Californian named Al Brown who had worked as a paid packer for Leadbetter. He had become stranded when Leadbetter's packing scheme collapsed. Brown had good cold-weather clothing but no food and no experience in the wilderness. In his rush to join the stampede he neglected to bring provisions, naively believing he could work for whatever he needed along the way. Ordinarily, Adney would not have considered such a novice, but Brown had one important skill to recommend him: "he was an expert oarsman, holding the amateur championship of the Pacific coast."[14]

Brown agreed to join Adney in piloting his boat down the Yukon River to Dawson in exchange for food and the transport of his small bundles of clothes and blankets. Adney finally found a trustworthy packer who promised to promptly bring the boat lumber over the pass for $30. Adney and Brown climbed the Chilkoot Pass together, each bearing light packs filled with Adney's cameras and photo supplies, which he didn't trust to packers. After reaching the summit of the pass, they made their way down to Crater Lake, an irregular mile-long glacial basin where their outfits had been piled. It was the first of a series of interconnecting alpine lakes and streams that flowed into the upper Yukon River. They hired more packers to carry their supplies to the head of Long Lake, about four miles down the trail, where they had agreed to meet the packer with Adney's boat lumber.

A storm marooned them for several days with ferocious wind, snow, and rain. Rays of sun occasionally winked through the scudding clouds. They anchored the tent with rocks and hunkered down inside to wait for the boat lumber. After several days, they turned back up the trail to investigate. Along the way they heard reports that an avalanche of snow, water, and boulders had wiped out Sheep Camp, taking many outfits and lives with it. They feared that both the packer and Adney's boat lumber might be gone. They found Sheep Camp in disarray. Many tents and outfits were buried or had been carried away, but only one life was known to be lost. The disaster was the last straw for many who had been wavering. Whether they lost anything or not, it gave many a good excuse to turn back.

Adney was relieved to find his boat lumber safe but the packer's feet had given out. Adney hired two new packers to take the lumber over, this time climbing the pass with them to ensure delivery. Arriving at Long Lake, they found the storm still raging, with tents blown down or flapping like sails in the wind. Suspecting that high wind was a chronic condition they pushed

Adney and the batteau he built to travel 600 miles down the Yukon River to the Klondike gold fields, *Harper's Weekly*, January 1, 1898 (CCHS)

on, hoping for better conditions farther down the trail. At Lindeman Lake, the drop in elevation put them into "a new and smiling country," as Adney put it.[15]

Lindeman Lake is a long sliver of water with a towering mountain on the western edge. The guidebook Adney bought in Victoria described shipbuilding as the principal industry at Lindeman, and indeed it was. They found a sea of tents spread on a flat plain and a swarm of frenetic builders working on about sixty boats in various stages of completion. The most common was a large flat-bottomed skiff with a wide, square stern, about twenty-four feet long and capable of carrying up to three tons of cargo. The fresh, unseasoned lumber cut nearby shrank and warped before boats could be launched. They leaked like sieves. They had to be heavily caulked, treated with pitch, and continually patched to keep them reasonably watertight.

The design of Adney's batteau came from a boat used in log drives on the rivers of New Brunswick. It is a narrow, flat-bottomed boat with raked ends and flared sides, making it highly manoeuvrable. Lumbermen stand in the boat navigating with long spiked poles to keep it from being crushed by the jumble of swift-moving logs. Adney knew there was no better boat in which to attempt a long, hazardous journey down a river filled with rocks, rapids, shoals, and perhaps ice if the freeze-up began before they reached Dawson.

The seasoned, precut ribs and planking he had obtained in Victoria paid huge dividends at Lake Lindeman and beyond. The assembly of the batteau was faster and easier than the other boats. The dry lumber swelled as it absorbed water, tightening the joints with very little leaking. Snow began falling with disturbing regularity as they worked on the boat—six inches one day, a dusting the next, but enough to require setting up a shelter with a covering tarp. Stampeders arrived daily from both passes. Many planned to overwinter at Lindeman Lake or farther on at Lake Bennett and then launch their boats downriver with the spring thaw.

Adney and Brown were determined to reach Dawson before the freeze-up. On October 5, they carried the batteau to the water with the help of other builders. It was twenty-three feet long and six feet wide and sank eighteen inches into the water when loaded with fifteen hundred pounds of cargo. It had taken Adney forty-seven days since his arrival at Skagway and twenty-two days since he first went over the Chilkoot Pass to arrive at this crucial stage of his journey.

On October 6, they were given a morning send-off of hoorahs and pistol shots that echoed in the cold grey sky. Adney had the forecast of freeze-up by November 1 in mind and knew they had barely enough time to make the three-week, six-hundred-mile voyage to Dawson. Brown was delighted with the way the boat handled. He immediately earned his keep by rowing four miles in dead-calm water to the foot of Lindeman Lake. Here they found a group of boats waiting their turns to go through a mile-long, rock-walled gorge of rough water leading to Lake Bennett. Each party unloaded and packed their supplies to the other end and then walked their empty boat with ropes attached at each end through the gorge.

Adney recognized the leader of one party as someone he knew from New York: John Burnham, a writer from *Forest and Stream* magazine. Burnham and his party had completed the gruelling forty-five-mile journey via White Pass to Lindeman Lake. In camp that night, they traded trail stories.

The next morning, after inspecting the gorge, Adney and Brown decided to save precious time by riding through instead of walking the empty boat with ropes. Burnham later described the scene in a *Forest and Stream* article.

> Adney was an expert at river navigation; and his companion, though inexperienced in this kind of work, was a champion oarsman, cool-headed and gritty. I happened to be on the trail… when I heard some men calling out…that the *Harper's Weekly* man was shooting the rapids. I ran across just in time to see the

boat swept by with the speed of a bolt from a crossbow, leaping
from wave-crest to wave-crest, and drenching its occupants with
sheets of spray. Adney and Brown were standing erect in bow
and stern, each wielding a single oar used as a paddle, and from
their masterly course it was evident that they had their boat well
under control. It was all over in a very small fraction of time.
They had avoided by the narrowest margin jagged boulders it
seemed impossible to pass, and in a lather of foam shot out into
the smooth water below.[16]

Their adrenaline-fuelled plunge through the gorge ended with a soft
landing beside their tent, where they had left some of their supplies the
day before. A few miles farther downstream they arrived at Lake Bennett.
Gale-force winds whipped whitecaps over its twenty-seven-mile length and
stranded Adney and Brown for several days. By October 9, they could wait
no longer. They hoisted a small spritsail, made from a blanket, and were
quickly pulled into the wind stream. Larger boats with huge square sails
scudded by, Adney wrote, "at railroad speed." The frigid air and spray
numbed their hands. They couldn't let go of the sail lines or steering oar for
even a second for fear of losing control. About twelve miles down the lake
a gust snapped their mast, forcing them to make for shore to cut a heavier
and stronger one. The next day the wind calmed, and the superior design
of the batteau began to show as the little sail pulled them past the scows
and rafts that had left days earlier.

Midway through Lake Bennett, they were reminded how quickly death
could become a reality for the inexperienced and unwary. A stampeder on
shore was drying supplies and blankets in the sun. He pleaded with them
to stop and rowed out to meet them. Adney and Brown recognized him
as one of a party of three they had seen on the trail. He said that both his
partners had drowned. They had nailed their sail to the mast with no way
to easily lower it. When the gale began to blow, and they were clearly in
danger of losing control, one of the men tried to unfasten the sail but lost
his balance and was blown overboard. The other jumped in to rescue him,
but they were taken by the wind and icy water.

The lone survivor managed to get to shore and now was left to struggle
on with over three thousand pounds of supplies. He offered to give half to
Brown if he would join him, but Brown refused. Others had also declined.
He was desperate to get to Dawson. Seeing they could not help, Adney and

Brown bid him farewell and continued down the lake. Months later, they heard his hands and feet had been severely frostbitten as he tried to reach Dawson while pulling a sled over the ice.

By noon they reached the foot of Lake Bennett, then glided down a connecting stream into Tagish Lake, where Brown rowed the rest of the day on mirror-calm water, amid magnificent mountains that towered in the pewter sky. A trolling line caught a salmon for dinner. That night, preparing the meal, they found a six-inch whitefish inside the salmon. The next morning, Brown's skill at the oars overtook larger boats being rowed with heavy spruce or pine oars. Adney had the foresight to have his oars cut from ash, well known to woodsmen for its unusual combination of great strength and light weight. They landed at dusk in shallow water at the foot of Tagish Lake, near a group of tents flying a British flag. It was the Canadian customs office, where duties were collected on foreign goods entering Canada from the United States. Adney had been careful to purchase all his goods in Canadian stores and had receipts to prove it, so he owed nothing.

At the evening campfire, conversation focused on the weather and when the lakes and rivers would freeze. An old-timer gave an ominous warning: "You will get through Lake Marsh [now called Marsh Lake], then the White Horse; and if you get through Lake Labarge before it freezes, you will make Thirty-Mile River, and possibly Pelly River; and if you get that far before freeze-up, you may get down with the mush ice."[17]

Another man said that for the past three years where the Klondike River joins the Yukon at Dawson had been frozen tight by the thirteenth of October. It was then the twelfth with nearly five hundred miles to go. The still waters of the lakes freeze first. The Yukon, with its many tributaries, is kept open by fast, continuous currents and is the last to freeze. The great river flows for nearly two thousand miles from its source at the outlet of Marsh Lake, traversing the northwestern region of the Yukon Territory and then Alaska. It crosses the Arctic Circle and flows into the Bering Sea near St. Michael, Alaska.

The upper Yukon, flowing from Marsh Lake to Dawson, begins as a lazy watercourse but gains speed and volume as other rivers and innumerable creeks flow into it. The upper river is easily navigated during the warm months, except for a few dangerous rapids and windy lakes. It makes its way through mountain valleys with rocky outcroppings and bluffs, sandy sloughs, and swampy flats. It's filled with shifting bars of sand and gravel, with innumerable small islands and branching channels that sometimes turn into dead ends. Even experienced river navigators, like Adney, must remain alert to stay in the main channel, or risk time-consuming delays hauling off sandbars or rowing back upstream to get back on course.

Adney and Brown hurried on the next day through a sluggish connecting stream into Marsh Lake, a shallow, narrow, and muddy finger of water nineteen miles long. At nightfall they put into shore and found thin ice about twenty feet out. Fearing they could be ice-bound by morning, they ate a quick supper and resumed rowing in the dark, hoping to clear the lake before resting. A mile on they ran into ice. They turned toward the centre of the lake, hoping for open water, but ran into still more ice. They feared the outlet might be frozen but then suddenly found open water and continued rowing the rest of the night.

As the pre-dawn sky began to lighten, they were exhausted and found a landing to rest in the shelter of some small spruce trees. At full daylight they were off again, still within Marsh Lake but carried along at increasing speed, which told them the entrance to the Yukon River was near. That night they slept easier, knowing they were clear of the alpine lakes and now on the Yukon River. But they were still at least 450 miles from Dawson with only two and a half weeks remaining before the predicted freeze-up of the Yukon.

An hour out the next morning, they came to a group of boats gathered on shore in a large eddy preparing to traverse Miles Canyon. It was a serpentine mile of raging water in which the entire Yukon River funnelled into a basalt channel one hundred feet wide with sheer walls fifty feet high. Most stampeders were packing their loads on the trail above and then lining their boats through with ropes. After inspecting the canyon, Adney and Brown decided to ride through fully loaded. They recalled that at Lake Bennett the empty boats had the worst of it, bobbing like corks in a stormy sea.

Shooting the canyon in the batteau was less dangerous than it appeared. They took on some water and had a few risky moments, but Adney's ability to read the river and Brown's strength and skill as an oarsman brought them safely through. They shot out the end of canyon, past others reloading their boats, and continued several miles downriver to White Horse Rapids, the most dangerous stretch of water on the Yukon, named for the white foam leaping into the air from troughs that resembled a herd of white horses.

The rapids had claimed at least forty lives since the Chilkat trade monopoly had been broken and the river opened to white men in 1890. Adney flagged it on his map as a place to be respected.

Men with experience shooting the rapids were making good money guiding greenhorn stampeders through the treacherous water.[18] Adney and Brown hauled up at the head of the rapids to assess the danger. The gauntlet was only a quarter-mile long but filled with a racing current, seething cascades, submerged rocks, and turbulent troughs big enough to swallow a small boat. They offloaded a third of their cargo to give the batteau more buoyancy, covered the remainder with an oiled tarp, tied everything down, and launched into the cascade. Adney described the experience:

> Following the roughest water, to avoid rocks, we are soon in the dancing waves and pitching far worse than in the Canyon. As we jump from wave to wave, it seems positively as if boat and all would keep right on through to the bottom of the river. The water even now is pouring in, and it is plain that the boat will never live through. One thought alone comforts us: the fearful impetus with which we are moving must surely take us bodily through and out, and then—we can make the shore somehow. I count the seconds that will take us through.

And then they were in the rapids.

> From sides and ends a sheet of water pours over, drenching Brown and filling the boat; the same instant, it seems, a big side-wave takes the little craft, spins her like a top, quick as a wink, throws her into a boiling eddy on the left—and we are through and safe, with a little more work to get ashore.
>
> Men who were watching us from the bank said that we disappeared from sight in the trough. Brown is wet up to his waist. Everything is afloat. We jump out leg-deep into the water near shore, and, when we have bailed out some of the water... we unload, pitch tent, and, while tripping back for our five hundred pounds of goods, watch the other boats come through.... Our goods in the boat are not damaged, because the sacks were tight and they were wet for so short a time.[19]

Tappan Adney, *Running the White Horse Rapids* (*The Klondike Stampede*, 143)

When Adney asked the "imperturbable Brown...if he were scared [Brown] replied, 'Why, no. You said it was all right. I suppose you know — it's your boat and your outfit.' I believe that if a charge of dynamite were to explode under Brown he would not wink an eyelash."[20]

It was now the fourteenth of October. Dawson was 439 miles downriver. They had successfully negotiated the last dangerous rapids, but the rapidly changing season was working against them. They warily watched the snowline creep lower on the surrounding mountains. Rain, fog, and slate-coloured skies greeted them most mornings. Adding to the gloom, a few minutes of daylight were lost each day. In mid-August there had been fifteen hours of daylight; by December 21 there would be only six.

To reach Dawson by November 1 they would have to average twenty-four miles a day, a snap in summer weather but perhaps impossible if they had to battle ice as it closed in. They moved on, adding the strength of rowing to the speed of the current, and with continual mental alertness stayed in the main channel, avoiding sand and gravel bars. The "ash breeze" created by Brown's work with the lightweight oars overtook many larger, less agile scows and rafts. One of the rafts had set up a stove to save time by doing all their cooking on board. Adney and Brown tied up alongside, drifting together long enough to share coffee and flapjacks.

Each night at dusk, they dragged the boat on shore. At one point, Brown's boot stuck in the mud and he fell full length into the icy water. He needed to quickly change into dry clothes and get warm, but snow and ice were on the ground and there was little wood to build a fire. The temperature had been just below freezing all day and was dropping fast. They rigged the oars and poles into a tepee and, throwing the tent around them, made a shelter for the night. Adney managed to build a fire and dry Brown's clothes by morning. The next day, as they approached the confluence with the Big Salmon River, they saw what appeared to be foam on the water ahead. On drawing closer they found it was slushy lumps of ice, the first of the mush ice the old-timer had mentioned. It was a harbinger of larger and more dangerous ice ahead.

Nearing the Little Salmon River, thirty-six miles farther on, Adney and Brown stopped at an Indigenous encampment set up for trading. It had furs, mittens, and moccasins, highly valued items for the coming winter. The stampeders generally had tea, tobacco, candles, guns, and ammunition—items Indigenous people were eager to acquire. After making a few minor trades that satisfied both parties, Adney and Brown shoved off. Several days later, about 225 miles from Dawson, they slipped through the Five Finger Rapids and the Rink Rapids without incident.

Each morning they awoke to find heavy frost and more mush ice in the river. Morning fog and mist dissipated with the rising sun. The swift current now bore them along, Adney wrote, "as fast as the most eager can wish," until they reached Fort Selkirk on October 22, 170 miles from Dawson.[21] Fort Selkirk was located a mile from the confluence with the Pelly River. It had been a Hudson's Bay Company outpost until 1853 when, in the absence of the post manager, a band of Chilkats burned it to the ground. For centuries, the Chilkats maintained a trade monopoly on furs from the interior by controlling access via the Chilkoot Pass. The advent of Hudson's Bay Company posts was a direct threat to their livelihood and caused them to strike back in an effort to reinforce their hold on their home territory.

The HBC post was never rebuilt. When Adney and Brown arrived, the site was occupied by an Alaska Commercial Company (ACC) store, a dozen other log cabins occupied by Indigenous families, and a mission station. The ACC agent had gone "outside" and had left the store in the care of

J.J. Pitts, described by Adney as "a little, grave, sober man, with dark, thin beard." After eagerly accepting an invitation of overnight accommodations in the agent's vacant cabin, they ate supper with Pitts and spent "the evening talking over a bottle of Scotch, a rare luxury here." The conversation proved instructive, with Pitts providing "the first intelligent account of facts and conditions [at Dawson] we had heard." Pitts described unprepared stampeders asking him the price of flour in Dawson.

> I tell them it has no price.... Last winter flour was freighted from
> Forty-Mile and sold in Dawson for $40 to $60 a sack. You will see it
> sell this winter for $100.... People outside talk as if the steamers on
> this river run on a schedule; whereas they are liable to be stuck on
> a bar and not get off at all and be destroyed by the ice in the spring.
> The country is not and never has been well supplied. Mr. Harper
> says that in the twenty-five years that he has been in the Yukon
> there has not been a year when there has not been a shortage of
> something. One year it was candles, and the men had to sit in the
> dark. Another year something else. This year it is flour.[22]

Pitts asked if Adney and Brown were well supplied. Adney told him that Brown had no food but was strong and was willing to take the risk of being able to buy food with money he would earn. "That is a very foolish thing for him to do," Pitts replied. "Many people are short, and more may have to leave before spring. The time was when it would go hard with the man who was responsible for bringing in a person like that."[23] Adney realized he had placed himself, as well as Brown, in a potentially dangerous position. In a camp where food is scarce, deliberately coming without provisions is nearly a crime against every other man in the camp.

The temperature the following morning was -5°F with a thick fog blanketing the river. They stood around the big stove in the store examining skins and furs. Pitts was interested in sending moose hides to Dawson, where they were in great demand for moccasins, mittens, and gold sacks. After picking out some hides he hesitated. "No, I won't send them," he said. "I don't think you'll reach Dawson."[24]

The fog lifted at noon, revealing a stream of ice floes pouring out of the Pelly from the right side and filling half the Yukon. Adney and Brown launched the batteau, staying to the left where the river was still open.

The water freezes to the oars, until they become unmanageable
and again and again we have to stop and pound the ice off with
an axe. Mittens are frozen stiff, mustaches a mass of icicles, and
no matter how hard we work we can't keep warm. The current is
swift. We have gone, we judge, twenty miles when the setting of
the sun and the lowering fog warns us to make camp.[25]

The freezing process in northern rivers begins with ice crystals forming
in eddies and still waters near shore. The crystals cluster together and
form larger masses as they float downstream. The tops, exposed to the air,
freeze hard and form small ice floes. The floes closest to shore rub against
the bank and are rotated by the current to form ice pans as big as wagon
wheels, hard on top with a few feet of loose slush below. After the entire
surface freezes, snowshoe or dogsled travel is possible but treacherous. The
current continues to flow beneath the ice, creating thin places where a man
with a heavy pack or a sled can fall through and be dragged by the current
to certain death.

Preparing to camp for the night, Adney and Brown drew the boat up
close to shore, secured it to a tree, then set up camp on a high flat bank. As
they were about to turn in, a long, dull roar drew them to the edge of the
bank just in time to see an ice floe forty feet long go by, scraping the boat.
They scrambled down the bank, unloaded the boat, and hauled it out, safe
from harm. At ten o'clock Adney recorded the temperature as +1°F. The
ominous sound of the increasing ice pans swept along in the current made
them pessimistic about reaching Dawson. Surely, with such temperatures,
the river would freeze tight within a few days.

The next morning, they repeated the daily ritual of chopping ice from
the boat and hacking a channel through the shore ice to reach the main
current. Surrounded by floes, they were swept along but able to manoeuvre
among the ice cakes and keep in open water. At nightfall, they stopped to
help two men whose boat had been badly damaged by the ice. It was lying
in two sections, one on shore and the other stuck in the ice. By morning the
shore ice had frozen enough that the two men could retrieve the damaged
part and repair their boat. As Adney and Brown were pushing off, the two
men told them about a raft loaded with slaughtered beef that was reported
to be hung up on a bar some miles below. Later, when they came to the
raft, lodged squarely on the head of an island, they found it was loaded
with mutton, not beef. They threw one of the carcasses into their boat and

went on. Soon after they saw two men, each hauling a loaded sled upriver on the shore ice. The men shouted to them, "There is no grub in Dawson. If you haven't an outfit, for God's sake turn right back where you are!"[26]

With night falling, they made camp next to three prospectors who were part of the Christy party that included Leroy Pelletier, the correspondent for the *New York Times*. The rest of the Christy party, including two women, had been camped on an island for the past three days, afraid to move among the floes on the river. They had left Lake Bennett a week before Adney and Brown. Next morning, as Adney and Brown were ready to launch, the Christy boat passed by.

Hours later, they saw two miners dragging a sled upriver on shore. One shouted that the ice had jammed tight at the mouth of the White River, a few miles ahead. If true, it would mean the end of their river journey. They were seventy-six miles from Dawson. They worked desperately to make for shore but were caught in a jumble of ice and borne along by the strong current. A huge ice floe hit them broadside, tilted the downstream gunwale nearly to the water, then sheared off just as they thought the boat and goods were lost. Fighting hard, they caught an opening, swung clear of the shore, and made it to mid-river. When they reached the junction with the White River, the ice jam had cleared.

Ten miles on, at Stewart River, they saw boats hauled out on the shore ice, some tents, and even a few log cabins. This was the destination for many who intended to prospect the creeks around the Stewart in search of new gold strikes. When Adney and Brown set up camp for the night, they heard unsettling stories of famine and thieving at Dawson, with two men having been shot for breaking into supply caches. The next morning, October 27, a warm chinook wind was blowing from the coast. The temperature was twenty above at seven a.m. and forty above by noon. The dramatic change in the weather gave everyone on the river a brief respite and a fresh opportunity to keep moving downriver toward Dawson.

That evening, as they headed for shore, the batteau wedged between two floes. They were driven by the current straight toward a huge slab of ice projected upward at an angle and threatening to slide over the boat and crush it. As they struck the slab, the floe pushing them along collapsed, allowing them to slide by the overhanging ice unharmed, but immediately another danger appeared: several tall spruce trees had fallen into the water, barricading their path. With desperate rowing they narrowly missed the trees and landed on the other side near a huge pile of driftwood, perfect for a campfire. They were setting up the tent when they heard a cry for help and saw the Christy boat drifting backwards toward them. Adney threw them a line, secured it to a tree, and hauled in the floundering boat. It had crashed into the spruce trees and had been swept under them, stern first, badly injuring the leader of the group.

The next day they saw more prospectors dragging loaded sleds upriver, making their way back to Skagway on foot. A sign on shore warned "Keep to the left side of the island," which was the only option since the right channel was jammed with ice. After passing Sixty-Mile River, a man on the bank called out: "Fifty-five miles to Dawson! Keep to the right, and look sharp, or you'll be carried past!"[27] That night they camped on the left bank, just above a sudden bend of the river bearing left. The next morning, seeing more ice than ever, they decided to stop for a day and build a sled in case they would need to haul their supplies the rest of the way to Dawson, which they judged to be about ten miles.

The next morning, October 31, they reloaded, chopped a channel into the open water, and began what they thought would be a half day's work. Rounding the bend in the river, they immediately saw a large collection of boats, tents, and people on the right-hand shore.

"How far to Dawson?" they called out.

"This is Dawson! If you don't look out you will be carried past!"[28]

They dug their paddles into the ice and pulled the batteau to a landing among the other boats.

It had been ninety-two days since Adney departed New York and twenty-five days since he and Brown launched the batteau at Lindeman Lake. The perilous journey was over, the dangers met and overcome. Now the real work for which Adney had been sent to the Klondike could begin.

Chapter Six

On the Ground in the Gold Rush:
From Reporter to Ethnographer

...a scene more suggestive of the infernal regions than any spot on earth.
— Tappan Adney

Dawson City sits at the confluence of the Yukon and Klondike rivers. The Yukon flows on a northwest course past the town, with the Klondike streaming in from the east. In the spring of 1896, it was a small settlement on the floodplain where the rivers merge. When Adney arrived eighteen months later, it had become a ramshackle town of several thousand people. In anticipation of explosive growth triggered by the discovery of gold, the town site had been surveyed in a rectangular grid with streets running parallel to the Yukon for a mile and a half.

When Adney and Brown landed, they were welcomed by the Christy party but took some ribbing about spending a day and two nights camped only a mile upriver from their destination. The Christy party had arrived the day before. Leroy Pelletier invited them to stack their goods next to the Christy party tent for safekeeping until he got settled.

Adney soon discovered they hadn't really landed at Dawson proper but a quarter mile upriver at a former Indigenous fishing village, a settlement that later came to be called Klondike City. After securing his supplies, Adney set to work photographing new arrivals on the ice-choked river. The newcomers were dubbed cheechakos, a derisive term that locally meant a know-nothing greenhorn.

The Klondike River had frozen solid weeks before Adney's arrival on November 1. The next day, he walked across the ice to get his first look at Dawson City. He found the rapidly expanding town buzzing with new construction. It was a motley assortment of approximately three hundred buildings, including stores, saloons, hotels, restaurants, dance halls, and residences. The largest of the commercial buildings were the warehouses of two trading companies that brought in supplies on their steamships from the mouth of the Yukon River. Although the town site covered 160 acres,

Adney's illustration *Christmas in the Klondike, Harper's Weekly*,
December 17, 1898 (CCHS)

the only street in practical use was First Street, which ran parallel to the
Yukon, sixty-five feet back from its high-water mark.

Adney walked the length of First Street, gazing with wonder at the
animated scene. Weeks of isolation on the river made it difficult to adjust to
crowds of people again. Men and dog teams hauling lumber and supplies
from town to the mines had packed the frozen street smooth. Woodfire
smoke curled from the innumerable stovepipes protruding from the roofs
of buildings and tents, filling the air with its pungent odour.

People in the streets went about their business with what Adney
described as an "energetic stride," partly because of the cold temperature
and partly because darkness would soon be returning. The saloons and
stores were filled with men who appeared to have nothing to do except
warm themselves by the stoves. At least half of them were identifiable
as cheechakos by their clothing and their earnest interrogations of
old-timers. Sled dogs lay underfoot in the street, curled and sleeping,
oblivious to the cold thanks to their heavy protective coats. Construction
material — squared logs and lumber — was piled randomly about.
Workmen were busily sawing lumber, erecting timbers, and nailing new
buildings into place, making the most of the brief daylight hours for
construction work.

The North West Mounted Police headquarters was located at the junction of the rivers, facing the Yukon and separated from the town by a slough. The police garrison, commanded by Superintendent Charles Constantine, consisted of ten log buildings that provided space for offices, a courtroom, a jail, a post office, a warehouse, a mess hall, and housing for thirty or more officers. Constantine's reputation for fairness, efficiency, and incorruptibility earned him the sobriquet "First in the Yukon."

At the north end of First Street, two-storey structures stood side by side in a ragged row with signs bearing names such as the Moose-Horn, Palace Saloon and Restaurant, M and M Saloon and Dance Hall, Green Tree Hotel, and Opera House. The spaces between the two-storey buildings were filled with tents or small cabins used as restaurants, mining brokers' offices, supply caches, or living space for saloon workers. On the opposite side of the street, along the edge of the river, an irregular line of tents, rough cabins built of wood salvaged from boats, and tents sitting atop scows pulled from the water served as restaurants, offices, and residences.

Beyond the saloons stood a block of large, well-built, squared-log storage buildings belonging to the Alaska Commercial Company. The North American Transportation and Trading Company occupied the next block with a large store, three corrugated iron warehouses, and a bunkhouse for employees. Beyond the trading companies, a large steam-powered sawmill operated day and night to keep up with the demand for lumber. Beyond the mill, more cabins were being built. Finally, at the far end of First Street, in the shadow of Moosehide Mountain, stood St. Mary's Catholic Church and Hospital. Adney later learned the hospital was run by the Jesuit Father William Judge and the Sisters of Saint Ann, and that Father Judge was known as the Saint of Dawson for the compassionate and universal care he provided without cost to the sick and dying.[1]

Prices of goods were posted on the walls of saloons and on the bulletin board at the Alaska Commercial Company store. Whole outfits—food, clothing, mining supplies—were selling for a dollar a pound and "not waiting long for takers," Adney wrote.[2] Flour, the one item in short supply, was selling for $75 to $120 per fifty-pound sack, even more than J.J. Pitts, the manager at the Fort Selkirk store, had predicted.

When Adney returned from his visit to Dawson, he discovered the mutton he had found on the river was missing from his supplies. Two members of the Christy party, who were supposed to be on guard, told a suspicious story: they said the owner of the mutton raft was making inquiries about boats arriving with mutton on board. Rather than have Adney's mutton discovered, the two guards, with the help of a third man, threw it into the river. Adney didn't believe a word of it but had no way to prove otherwise. One of the guards later confessed he had looked the other way while the third man took the mutton. He was facing starvation after he had lost his supplies in the river and his partners abandoned him. Out of pity, Adney decided not to pursue it, but he regretted the loss of fresh meat when he knew none would be available for months to come. His food supplies were adequate for the winter, but the mutton would have enhanced the otherwise monotonous meals.

On November 7, ice slabs in the Yukon jammed the narrows just below Dawson. The ice dam caused severe flooding in Dawson and for miles upriver. Adney's boat, tent, and supplies were safe atop a twenty-foot embankment overlooking the river. Boats tethered below the bank were mangled by the heaving ice, their wood smashed into kindling. The upper Yukon froze smooth, forming a thoroughfare for those still on the river to haul their goods to Dawson by sled.

Leroy Pelletier, the *New York Times* reporter, invited Adney to partner with him in building and sharing a cabin, an offer quickly accepted. Besides their shared experience as working writers in New York City, Pelletier and Adney had much in common. They were both born in 1868. Pelletier was from Houlton, Maine, located near the US–Canada border, only a few miles from Woodstock, New Brunswick, where Adney first launched into north woods adventures. Both men had lively minds. Pelletier, like Adney, was a resourceful, high-energy person. They were both adept at coping with the Klondike conditions. They scouted the area together for several days looking for a cabin site, finally settling on a location four and a half miles south of Dawson on Bonanza Creek, about nine miles below the Bonanza discovery claim that had started the gold rush stampede. The cabin faced the main trail from town, which gave the correspondents front-row seats on the steady parade of miners and their dog teams hauling supplies to the mining claims.

Camping in Adney's tent, with the help of Brown working for food and shelter, they spent a month building their cabin, at one point working in temperatures that dipped to -39°F. The completed cabin was fourteen by sixteen feet. It had a dirt floor and an unusual windowpane made from

Adney's photograph of a miner on the way to his claim, 1898.
(*The Klondike Stampede*, 205)

Adney's celluloid film, which had been ruined when it got wet at Dyea. The cabin was furnished with two beds, two tables, and two chairs, all constructed from local lumber. Following local practice, the roof was covered with poles then a thick layer of moss and up to six inches of dirt, which froze hard in the winter and became impermeable sod in the summer. The cabin was heated with the sheet-iron stove Adney had packed with his outfit and used in his tent during the journey to Dawson.

As early as September 30, a month before Adney arrived, winter starvation became a major concern in Dawson. Men with few or no food supplies were thrown into a panic by an official notice posted on First Street by NWMP Superintendent Constantine warning about the risk of death from starvation. Constantine's notice urged those with meagre supplies to evacuate immediately to Fort Yukon, three hundred miles downriver in American territory, where he said they would find large stocks of food. The collector of customs and the gold commissioner added their voices to the government chorus urging miners to depart. Captain Hansen of the Alaska Commercial Company, a relative newcomer to the region, went about town in a state of great agitation urging those poorly supplied to flee for their lives.

Captain Healy, the manager of the North American Transportation Company, a veteran of nearly twenty years in the region, took a different view. He had seen food shortages and stampedes before. He said Fort Yukon was no better supplied than Dawson and predicted disaster if hundreds suddenly arrived there looking for food. He said the problem in Dawson was not one of quantity but distribution. Healy suggested the two trading companies pool their warehouse supplies and distribute enough rations to needy miners to get them through to the month of June, when new supply ships would arrive and the miners could repay their winter grub stakes with gold from their spring cleanups. Captain Hansen declined, saying that he had to fill his existing orders. He continued preaching doomsday warnings to groups of miners at his First Street store. Healy commented that Hansen was behaving like a hysterical cheechako.

By October 20, approximately fifty men had departed Dawson in small boats headed downstream toward Fort Yukon. Others, hauling sleds upstream, set out toward Fort Selkirk. Adney and Brown had seen a few of the sled haulers shouting dire warnings. By the end of October the evacuees totalled about 250, including a steamer-load of miners who were given downriver passage plus five days of provisions paid for by the government to induce them to leave Dawson City.

The evacuation debate was still a hot item of conversation in town when Adney arrived on November 1. Many folks sided with the government, saying that charity cases had no place in a town like Dawson; they threatened the survival of everyone else. Captain Healy's no-famine view came in for criticism, with some accusing him of hidden profit motives. Adney recorded that Healy's stubborn insistence there would be no starvation in Dawson was misunderstood and maliciously misrepresented.[3] Adney's conversations with old-timers and the nearly full warehouses of both trading companies convinced him that Healy's view was correct, and he said so publicly. More importantly, his account of the incident, with a positive image of Healy, was published in *Harper's Weekly*. Healy was grateful. The two became friends and years later would become partners, of sorts, in a business venture.

Adney settled into his work, interviewing miners and absorbing the history and techniques of small-scale gold mining, along with the peculiar culture of the Klondike stampede with its always glittering prospect of becoming fabulously wealthy and never having to work again. As he proceeded with his research, he documented the gold-mining method of the Klondike: placer mining. Placer mining is working at or near the surface of creek beds in which particles of gold are found. Named by early Spanish explorers in North America, this source of gold was a "placer" (pleasure) to find so easily. All that is needed to separate the gold from the sand and gravel where it is found is a pick, a shovel, a pan, and running water. It was the extent of the placer gold mining sites and the prospect of literally finding gold in shallow stream beds that created the stampede to the Klondike.

As placer claims were rapidly staked out on creek after creek in the Klondike region, and the opportunities for this surface mining dwindled, a new technique of placer mining was invented. Miners began sinking shafts on the hillsides along the creeks. It was well understood that gold in the stream beds had been deposited by erosion of the bedrock where veins of gold are initially formed by volcanic processes. It stood to reason that if shafts were sunk into the sand and gravel on the hillsides, more "pay dirt"—gold-bearing deposits—would be found. This turned out to be the case and this modified placer mining spread over the hills around the gold-bearing creeks of the region.

Traditional placer mining could only be done during summer when the ground thawed and water flowed. In Alaskan mining camps, work stopped for the winter. But with this new technique, Klondike miners were able to work year-round. In the summer when a shaft was dug, the dirt was piled to one side at the top. When an ancient stream bed was uncovered, the sand and gravel were piled separately in hopes it would pay off with particles of gold when they were washed and the gold separated. Gold is nineteen times heavier than water and sinks to the bottom in the washing process. Even tiny particles, known as gold dust, can be concentrated and collected this way. But the circumstance that gave the Klondike its fantasy-like reputation of "hitting pay dirt" and "striking it rich" was the unusually high percentage of its gold that was found as coarse particles, large fragments, and nuggets.

When winter came, fires were lit each night in the bottom of the pits so the ground would be thawed and ready to dig out the next morning. Miners who adopted this technique could continue working all winter, piling up the excavated sand and gravel for washing and gold extraction in the summer. By the time Adney arrived, smoking holes filled the creek gulches and covered the surrounding hillsides of the mining region. A toxic haze of smoke, sometimes mixed with ice fog, hung over the mining landscape, a scene of complete destruction of the natural environment. The forested hillsides in the mining area had been heavily logged for the construction of cabins and commercial buildings. The terrain was now completely stripped of all trees to feed the pit fires. It was a crater-pocked landscape with random piles of excavated dirt and gravel.

A cranking device—a windlass—was installed over each shaft. A miner would descend to the bottom on a ladder with a bucket attached to a rope and fill it with dirt. His partner would haul it to the top of the shaft and dump it nearby. By spring, some of these dumps were thirty feet high. When bedrock was reached, the miner below would enlarge the bottom of the shaft, searching for gravel and sand from the ancient stream bed.

After visiting a site of this shaft-based placer mining along Eldorado Creek, Adney recorded this memorable impression:

> The sun, like a deep-red ball in a red glow, hung in the notch of Eldorado; the smoke settling down like a fog (for the evening fires were starting); men on the high dumps like spectres in the half-smoke, half-mist; faint outlines of scores of cabins; the creaking of windlasses—altogether a scene more suggestive of the infernal regions than any spot on earth.[4]

In addition to hazardous and sometimes fatal working conditions, diseases claimed hundreds of lives. Scurvy killed many. Ironically, the cure, vitamin C, was all around them in the needles of spruce trees, long used by Indigenous people to make tea. As long ago as 1536, the Iroquois of the St. Lawrence River valley showed French explorer Jacques Cartier how to prepare a tea from the foliage of the eastern white cedar to protect his crew from dying of scurvy. This vital Indigenous knowledge was repeatedly lost and rediscovered by European invaders and settlers over the next three and a half centuries, but somehow it was not circulating among the Klondike stampeders in the late 1890s.

At the end of a day's hard labour that would be suitable as prison punishment outside the Yukon, miners retreated to their cabins for another monotonous meal of flapjacks, bacon, and beans, with canned vegetables or dried fruit if they were fortunate enough to have them. Adney described the scene in many cabins.

After the glow of the setting sun has died away, and the night wood has been stacked beside the stove…and the candle burns low, the intense stillness of the winter forest is broken only by the occasional distant wail of a dog…. Even that ceases, and there is no sound but the crackling of the fire in the stove, or a mouse gnawing in a dark corner of the cabin. There is nothing to do but sleep. Fortunately, it is little trouble to do that. All who speak of it confess that they never slept so long or so soundly in their lives.[5]

In the spring the final phase of the placer mining process began. Miners built sluice boxes, wooden troughs about twelve feet long and slightly wider at one end so they could be fitted together to form miniature aqueducts to divert water from the creek. The bottoms were covered with removable washboard-like riffles that would trap the heavy gold particles while the lighter dirt and gravel washed on with the flow. The tension was palpable on cleanup days, not only because it was the culmination of a whole winter's work, but also because the outcome might well determine the future course of the miners' lives.

As Adney and Pelletier gathered stories for their readers, they realized they were missing a crucial tool: an accurate map to expedite travel in the gold fields. They decided to make one, using the cartography skills Adney had learned at Trinity School in New York City.

Consulting a large geological survey map of the area in the Gold Commission office, they discovered that the gold commissioner himself could not locate half the creeks. A formal government survey of the gold fields was not expected for several years. Miners relied on their own mental maps and information gleaned from reliable old-timers. Adney and Pelletier interviewed miners, studied informal maps, walked the creeks, and surveyed to verify what they had been told.

After spending considerable time and money researching and drawing the map, a copy titled "Klondike Gold Fields" and dated March 20, 1898, was published in the May 9 issue of the *New York Times* and on May 14 in *Harper's Weekly*. An expanded, more detailed map, titled "Klondike and Indian River Gold Fields," drawn with much greater precision and corrected to September 1898 was subsequently prepared and appears in the original edition of Adney's book *The Klondike Stampede*, published in 1900.

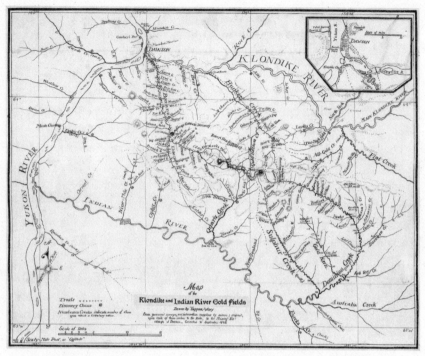

Adney's hand-drawn map of the Klondike gold fields, 1898 (CCHS)

On the outer edge of the map, far from the mining frenzy, Adney named a small watershed tributary Minnie Belle Creek after his bride-to-be. He also prepared a third map in 1898 titled "Overland Routes to Alaska and the Klondike," depicting a much large area of the region along with an insert showing all of Alaska. This map was also drawn with precision and attention to detail.[6]

The maps and dispatches Adney and Pelletier sent to their New York publishers reached Skagway via a dogsled mail service established by the Mounties. A series of NWMP outposts were strategically located between Dawson and the port of Skagway, which remained open to shipping year-round. The first delivery arrived in Dawson on January 4, 1898, but was a shipment of government mail only. The carrier had come in from the Little Salmon River outpost, 285 miles upriver from Dawson, where he had left nine sleds loaded with public mail. He was reluctant to bring the rest until he was sure of the food situation at Dawson for him and his dogs. On February 26, forty dogs pulled into Dawson with the backlog of public mail. From then on dog teams made regular mail runs between Skagway and Dawson.

A letter mailed from Dawson to New York took up to a month to reach Skagway, another week or more to reach Victoria or Seattle, and another week to cross the continent via train to New York. Altogether, total mail time between Dawson and New York was up to six weeks under ideal conditions. Faster, high-priority deliveries were available for a price through private carriers with dog teams that braved the weather and the 527-mile overland trail. Adney shipped a three-pound waterproof tin of manuscripts, sketches, and photographs with a reputable carrier named Patrick Galvin, who had already been hired by others to make the run to the coast. He refused to accept money from Adney for the delivery service.

The trip turned out to be particularly dangerous and difficult, with a narrow escape from starvation when Galvin temporarily went off the trail, away from caches of food. Weeks later, when Adney's package arrived at the Franklin Square offices of *Harper's Weekly*, a note written by Galvin was found inside that read: "I would not do it again for $25,000." Adney later wrote that he had rarely seen such an example of "faithfulness to trust, of pure bull-dog grit."[7]

Working dogs can be found throughout the world, but nowhere have they become so essential to the survival of their human masters than in the northern parts of North America. Indigenous people in the Yukon have used dogs for transportation for centuries. In Dawson, during the winter of 1897–98, Adney estimated there were at least fifteen hundred dogs hauling lumber, firewood, and miners' supplies to the mining claims up to thirty miles out of town.

The best dogs for tolerating extreme cold were malamutes, large animals of seventy to eighty pounds, derived from the grey wolf, native to the Yukon, and bred by Indigenous communities. Their double-layer coat is so dense it insulates their bodies from even extreme cold. They can curl up outside at night in a snowstorm, shake off the snow in the morning, which has helped keep them warm, and be ready to go to work. They can easily pull three to four times their own weight over snow and ice at a walking pace. Pulling a lighter-weight sled, they can maintain a lively trot all day. Adney reported seeing a five-dog team on the trail from Dawson pulling a load of spruce lumber that likely weighed three-quarters of a ton or more.

He wrote that the fights between dogs were inevitable but rarely resulted in any broken skin or blood. Even the most aggressive bites would usually produce nothing more than a mouthful of fur. Although nearly immune to serious damage, the dogs relied mostly on intimidation and bluffing in their fights for dominance. Adney saw one such battle on a Dawson street:

> One fine gray fellow was sitting quietly minding his own business. Suddenly, for no reason that I could see, another of equal size put its countenance close to that of the first, lifted its lips from a double row of hideous ivory fangs, braced forward on its fore-feet, and drew its breath in with a *sh* between its teeth. I never saw a more malignant expression. He stood thus for a whole minute, at each breath throwing more and more intensity into the threat, for such it evidently was, until it was perfectly evident that no limit was set to his rage short of chewing the other dog into small particles. The other dog? Why, he never so much as turned a hair, but sat there with the look that only a Malamute can assume. When the other had lashed himself into a fury, he turned his head the other way, saying as plainly as words could say it, "Oh, you bore me very much!"[8]

Early in January 1898, Adney heard that the Tr'ondëk Hwëch'in band was about to go on a moose hunt. He asked Chief Isaac if he could join the hunt, explaining he had experience hunting moose and caribou in the winter in New Brunswick. Chief Isaac was a skilled negotiator. Adney offered a fifty-pound bag of sugar in exchange for sharing the protection and fireside warmth of the Chief's shelter. Chief Isaac agreed to the offer and the arrangement.

For Adney, it was more of an anthropological experience than a hunting expedition.[9] It was clear the Tr'ondëk Hwëch'in band was still closely attached to their traditional way of life and to accompany them on a winter hunting trip was a unique opportunity. There were Elders in the band who remembered hunting moose and caribou with spears and bows and arrows. They dressed entirely in the skins of animals the women of the band had processed into fine leather and sewn into clothing. Only Chief Isaac and a few others spoke any English. Adney was drawn to learning about the Tr'ondëk Hwëch'in culture with the same interest that had prompted his association with the Wəlastəkwey in New Brunswick. He recorded the details of Tr'ondëk Hwëch'in life in his journal and made sketches of their activities, the first they had seen anyone create. They called them hand

Chief Isaac, Tr'ondëk Hwëch'in band, undated (Anglican Church Diocese of the Yukon Archive)

pictures and called Adney "Picture Man." He sketched and documented everything, from their remarkably effective caribou skin shelters, which kept them warm and dry in the coldest temperatures, to the distinctive pointed toes the women incorporated into their moccasins.

On January 13, the whole village packed and left the place where they had been camped, two miles downriver from Dawson. The entire tribe of sixty-plus people, and nearly as many dogs, loaded their portable caribou-hide shelters and all their possessions onto toboggans and passed through Dawson in a quarter-mile-long line, continuing four miles up the Klondike until the rapidly diminishing daylight required stopping to make camp on the shore of the river. With well-practised skills, all band members took up the task. First, the women with long-handled wooden shovels cleared snow from a space about eighteen by twelve feet for each shelter. Next, the men set up domed frameworks of bent poles lashed together into sturdy, oval-shaped frames ten feet high, ten feet wide, and sixteen feet long and covered them with caribou hides. The hides, sewn together with caribou sinew, were in two sections, and each half was drawn over the bent poles. A two-foot-wide opening was left at one end and covered with a blanket. A large opening was left at the top of each shelter for smoke to escape. Women and children then covered the exposed gravel with fragrant spruce boughs except where the fire would be built.

The completed encampment consisted of seven oval-shaped shelters, each housing several families with children and dogs. The toboggans, loaded with supplies, were lifted onto scaffolds at the side of each shelter to put them out of reach of the dogs, which were constantly hungry and ready to devour anything resembling food, including the rawhide lashings on the toboggans. No one stopped to rest until all tasks were completed and enough firewood was stacked inside the door of each shelter to last until morning. A fire was built in an oblong shape to distribute heat. The smoke flowed out through the opening in the top of the shelter.

Adney stayed in the shelter designated for Chief Isaac and his family plus another family, each group occupying one side of the shelter. There were five adults, three adolescent children, one nursing infant and eleven dogs in the shelter. Six of the dogs were puppies, being raised to replace adult dogs that had been sold to miners. Supper consisted of bread cooked in a frying pan, a few pieces of bacon, and a cup of tea.

The next morning, before daybreak, Chief Isaac went outside and announced in a loud voice that it was time to move. The encampment was dismantled and loaded onto the toboggans as quickly and efficiently as it had been set up. The band travelled ten miles upriver before making camp again, exactly as they had the day before. The next morning, again before dawn, Chief Isaac went outside, but this time he gave instructions for the day's hunt. He informed Adney the hunt would be conducted on the left side of the river. He buckled on his cartridge belt, picked up his rifle, and left. Sometime later, while it was still dark, Adney took his rifle and snowshoes from atop one of the toboggans and fell into line behind two shadowy figures, barely discernible in the predawn darkness, one carrying a rifle and the other a single-barrel shotgun.

As the sky lightened, he saw the one carrying the rifle was a boy of about twelve and the one with the shotgun was the old shaman, the medicine man of the village. After following the river, the snowshoe trail made an abrupt turn to the left into the forest. The old shaman continued along the river while Adney and the boy turned left and climbed the riverbank. The boy quickly disappeared into the dense forest. Adney continued at a slower pace.

At midday, he heard a rifle shot, then another in quick succession. He turned in the direction of the shots and picked up a snowshoe trail, which followed until he saw smoke rising above the trees. When he arrived at the fire, Chief Isaac and four others were skinning a large cow moose.

Adney's illustration *Moose Hunting with the Trochutin* (Tr'ondëk Hwëch'in), *Harper's New Monthly Magazine*, March 1900 (CCHS)

Gathering around the fire, they roasted pieces of the meat on sticks and eagerly scooped up the fat that dripped on the snow. The moose was then quickly butchered. Each hunter wrapped a ten- to fifteen-pound bundle of meat in a spruce-bough package that was slung over his shoulder and carried like a backpack. The rest of the meat was covered with snow and the location marked. The party headed back to camp, arriving after dark, having covered about eighteen miles round trip.

On the return to camp, they saw another member of their hunting party skinning another moose. Later that night, two others returned carrying packs of meat, making a bounty of four moose on the first day of hunting. Everyone was happy and a feast ensued. The following day, the camp moved seven miles upriver. They retrieved the meat and hides cached the previous day. The meat was put on scaffolding, out of reach of the dogs, and the hides brought into the shelters for processing.

The next day, the women shaved off the hair and removed bits of fat, meat, and sinew, a tedious job that took a full day for each hide. The tanning of the hides would take place in the spring, when they would be soaked in a solution of moose brains and livers before being smoked. The pliable skins would eventually be made into moccasins, gloves, clothing, and bags to hold the miners' gold. The prepared hides were hoisted on poles into the trees, out of reach of wolverines, to be picked up on the return journey at the end of the hunt. Toboggans were periodically loaded with meat for transport to Dawson, where miners eagerly paid $1.25 to $1.50 per pound.

Adney accompanied the hunting expedition for a total of six weeks, toward the end of which he became ill. He tried to follow the hunters when they moved up the north fork of the Klondike River but was unable to keep up. He took shelter in an empty miner's cabin. The hunters found him and sent word to Dawson: "Picture man too much sick. Mebbe two days he all right, mebbe two days he dead."[10] Leroy Pelletier came after him with a basket-sleigh and four dogs, but by then Adney had recovered and was on his way to Dawson. They met at a bend of the river and returned to Dawson and then to their cabin.

Adney had been away from the gold fields from mid-January to late February. The Tr'ondëk Hwëch'in band continued hunting for another six weeks, until mid-April. In total they took eighty moose and sixty-five caribou. They kept the food supply their village needed and sold the rest to the miners in and around Dawson. They invested their income in new rifles, ammunition, blankets, and other supplies.

Back in his cabin with Pelletier, Adney resumed his work as a reporter-cum-ethnographer of the Klondike Gold Rush. His training in the natural sciences taught him to collect evidence carefully and to verify facts so that anyone researching the same subject would be able to duplicate his findings. But a gold rush is a constantly changing situation. A seemingly endless stream of people arrived and departed. Events would pop up and then disappear so quickly it was impossible to collect and verify information as he would have preferred. He settled for providing his readers with vivid descriptions of characteristic people and events.

He approached the gold rush as a freakish natural phenomenon, like an earthquake or a volcanic eruption. He was part reporter and part natural scientist, investigating everything related to the odd event and reporting it as thoroughly and accurately as he could. Sometimes the natural-scientist part of his mind got the upper hand, and he would report at length on the birds, animals, insects, trees, rocks, weather, and seasonal variations of the

Klondike region, oblivious to the fact that most of his readers cared more about human-interest stories.

Dawson City was overflowing with stories. Nearly every miner could weave a fascinating tale about his experiences in the Klondike gold fields or of what he saw someone do in the saloons and dance halls. But unlike other reporters, Adney did not spend much time in Dawson. He was not a barfly or gambler like Jack London, who almost died from malnutrition (scurvy) and later parlayed his Dawson experience into stories and books that made him the most popular writer in America.[11] Adney was not a poet like Robert Service, who mined rich veins of Klondike lore, even though he didn't set foot in Dawson until ten years after the gold rush was over. He was not a reporter of politics and economics like Flora Shaw, who was sent by the London *Times* to report on whether Klondike gold would be a good investment for the Empire. Beyond reporting, he worked as an anthropologist, as an ethnographer of the gold rush.

For Adney, individual stories were interesting not simply as human-interest tales but, more importantly, as background to the history of the gold rush. He mostly interviewed old-timers, people who knew the Klondike region from long personal experience. The stories he gleaned from these interviews were woven to good effect into his book *The Klondike Stampede.*

Spring came quickly to the Klondike. The sun lingered a bit longer each day, and the forest came alive with the songs of birds. By mid-April the sun "was shining for as many hours as in the middle United States on the longest day of the year," Adney wrote.[12] The same cosmic forces that had taken away seven minutes of light each day the previous fall were now returning it at the same rate. Snow on the southern hillsides vanished. Trickles of water streamed more each day down the trails and refroze again each night, permitting dog teams to make midnight deliveries of supplies to the mining camps.

By the first of May, muddy water in Bonanza Creek showed that sluicing was underway upstream. Within a few days the final thaw came so quickly it caught Adney off guard. He had been planning to relocate back to Dawson when warmer weather arrived and had already sent a sledload of his supplies into town. On May 3 the spring freshet began overflowing the banks of the Bonanza, submerging the trail, filling the woods, and covering the floor of Adney's cabin with three inches of water. After a few days of swatting mosquitoes and sleeping in rubber boots, Adney took his tent and headed for higher and drier ground on a bluff overlooking Dawson.

From this lofty vantage point, he could see all of Dawson and the convergence of the Klondike and Yukon Rivers. He watched as the ice suddenly broke in the Klondike, sending a wall of frozen debris twenty feet high toward Dawson City. It destroyed two wooden walkway bridges connecting Klondike City and Dawson as though they were made of matchsticks. The flooding covered the centre of Dawson with five feet of water, returning the townsite to what Adney described as the "reeking bog" it had been before the gold rush.[13] Enterprising boatmen were making good money ferrying residents out of the flood zone. The Yukon breakup came on May 10, after which the flooding at Dawson quickly receded; ice floes as big as cabins floated by for days. When the breakup was complete on the Yukon, the first cheechakos from upriver were only a few days behind.

During the flooding, Adney took the opportunity to conduct an informal census. Since virtually everyone in town had been driven to hillside tents, he counted the tents—2,800—occupied by three to five persons per tent, for a total population of between 8,400 and 14,000. The Mounties estimated four to five thousand more were working the mines within a fifty-mile radius of Dawson. Despite the thousands of men idling away the time on the streets of Dawson, more hopeful cheechakos arrived daily. The trading companies, steamship builders, and outfitting stores in Seattle and Victoria continued to build inventory and to expand their operations.

On June 18, 1898, following the breakup of the ice on Lake Tagish, the Mounties reported 7,200 boats had passed through customs with an average of five persons in each boat for a total of thirty-six thousand cheechakos headed for Dawson City. The reality, of course, was that all the gold-bearing ground had been staked more than a year earlier. Both the Bonanza and the Eldorado streams were completely staked out, end to end, by February 1897. There were between nine and ten thousand claims filed in the Klondike district by July 1898. Yet would-be miners continued to arrive, eager and determined, just as thousands of others had the year before. The madness of "gold fever" persisted, but they were all too late.

At mid summer, the sky was still dusky at midnight. The sun would briefly set after twenty hours of continuous shining. If someone said it was ten o'clock, it could be difficult to tell if it was morning or evening by looking at the sky. The "energetic stride" Adney had noticed the year before was now replaced with crowds of listless, dazed men, dragging with slow steps along First Street in Dawson City, where outfits of all sorts were for sale. Adney wrote that "the water-front looked like a row of booths at a fair."[14] The would-be gold miners were trying to raise money to buy a steamship ticket home. The fare between Dawson and St. Michael, Alaska, on the Bering Sea coast was $100, and another $200 from St. Michael on the ocean steamers bound for Seattle. For those who didn't have cash to buy a ticket home, plenty of shovel work was available on prosperous claims to earn the money needed.

Adney left the Klondike on September 16, 1898, on the steamer *John Cudahy*, loaded with passengers and $1.5 million in gold, ending a sixteen-month odyssey that, he wrote, "none of us can hope to see repeated in a lifetime."[15] In mid summer the following year, gold deposits were discovered in the beach sand at Nome, Alaska. When the news reached Dawson, eight thousand miners left within a week for the new site. By then Adney had returned to Woodstock, New Brunswick, to organize his notes and complete *The Klondike Stampede* manuscript. Within a year he would go back to the far north to cover the gold rush at Nome, this time as a correspondent for *Collier's Weekly*.

Chapter Seven

Minnie Bell Sharp and the Last Years in New York

I have had great success in my profession of teaching. I have turned out a greater number of musicians than all the rest of the music schools in Canada put together. —Minnie Bell Sharp

If I am elected, as I shall be, I shall accomplish the greatest work of all. I shall work first for justice and the people…for the good of all, the public weal and humanity. —Minnie Bell Sharp

When Adney returned from the Klondike in the fall of 1898, he first went to Woodstock, New Brunswick, to see his fiancée, Minnie Bell Sharp. He then returned to New York, where he found he had become a celebrity. Readers of *Harper's Weekly*, America's most popular newsmagazine, knew his name from the dispatches and illustrations he had sent from the Klondike gold fields. He brought the gritty and dangerous world of the miners and the strange madness of "gold fever" to the fireside armchairs of eager readers. His reports caught their attention; his drawings and photographs transported their imaginations. *Harper's* tried to recruit him to head its graphics department, but he turned it down in order to remain an independent artist and scholar.

With the waning of the Western frontier in the United States, the romantic fascination with wilderness that had always been a strong element in American culture turned to the North, to the great forests, the mighty rivers, the magnificent mountains, the hidden valleys, and the still pristine wildlife regions of the continent—to Canada and Alaska. Adney's natural history journalism from New Brunswick, published in New York over the previous decade, served and fuelled this interest. The artwork he created to illustrate his stories heightened his profile. He went on to be a founding member of The Explorers Club, serving as its first treasurer. His large paintings portraying scenes of Indigenous life hang to this day in the New York headquarters of The Explorers Club.

He immediately went to work to capitalize on his fame. He assembled his notes, photos, sketches, and dispatches into *The Klondike Stampede*, published by Harper in April 1900. Although many letters, memoirs, diaries, and stories by miners were eventually published, Adney's book is the only fully detailed and illustrated first-person account of the Klondike Gold Rush by a skilled observer and professional writer. The book was a best-seller when first published and has become a primary resource for all subsequent accounts. Pierre Berton, author of *Klondike Fever*, the most complete history of this event, regarded Adney's book as the quintessential resource on the subject. If Adney had written nothing more for the rest of his life, this book alone would secure his place as an anthropological journalist and pioneer of the participant-observer research method.

The Klondike Stampede's instant success put Adney back on the lecture circuit. This time his presentations included a stereopticon slide show featuring glass-plate photographs he hand-coloured to create the illusion of colour photography. In addition to the usual urban venues, he made presentations in Athens, Ohio; Washington, Pennsylvania; and Pittsboro, North Carolina — all places important in Adney's earlier life and the lives of his parents.

His talks included a concern for cruelty to animals, which he had seen on both the White Pass and Chilkoot Pass trails. He had previously done work for the American Society for the Prevention of Cruelty to Animals, and this connection gave him an additional audience. This led to employment with the ASPCA giving lectures on preventing cruelty to animals as well as creating a speakers' bureau for the organization. During this period, he took up residence at the ASPCA's New York headquarters in hotel-like rooms it maintained there. Later, he moved to the Waldorf-Astoria Hotel, renting rooms on a floor reserved for members of the Ohio Society, a social organization for people born in Ohio.

Minnie Bell had not been idly waiting for Tappan's return. She was an enterprising person with artistic talent, organizing skills, and entrepreneurial and political ambitions. Both she and Tappan were strongly defined and highly determined characters. Long before marriage, each had charted career paths to which they remained committed. They made an unusual and in some ways divergent couple, although on one enterprise their choices came together in a significant way.

The first surviving child in her family after the deaths of three previous infants, she was much loved and immensely precocious. New Brunswick historian David Bell writes that at age five "she would be placed amid the admiring circle of her father's workers to read to them."[1] When her talent for music became evident, her father ordered a Steinway piano. At the age of fourteen she spent a year at Compton Ladies' College in Compton, Quebec. She was subsequently a student at St. Margaret's Hall in Halifax, Nova Scotia, as well. In the early 1880s, she went to New York for professional training in voice and piano. She trained with William Mason, who had been taught by the renowned Hungarian composer Franz Liszt. Her studies and training prepared her for performance and teaching. When she returned to Woodstock, she opened a studio for teaching voice and piano with what she described as "the best modern methods."[2] She became a concert recitalist, a music teacher, and the proprietor of a music school.

Minnie Bell was three years older than Tappan. They first met when she took up residence at his mother's boarding house in New York City. At the time she invited his sister, Mary Ruth, and Tappan to her home in New Brunswick for a summer holiday, she was twenty-two and he would shortly turn nineteen. At this stage of life, a three-year difference is considerable. It seems likely to have been Minnie Bell's friendship with Mary Ruth that prompted the invitation. It is not hard to imagine, however, that as both Tappan and Minnie Bell were well educated, talented, and high-spirited they might have been intrigued by each other.

Minnie Bell went to New York in the fall of 1887 to continue her music studies. When she returned in the spring of 1888, Tappan was still living with her family and would remain in New Brunswick until February 1889. There would have been ample opportunity for the two young adults to become well acquainted. Minnie Bell likely saw that Tappan was an unusually accomplished person for his age. Perhaps, the fact he was an artist was especially interesting since this put them both in a similar professional category. Her interest in him may well have been reciprocated for the same reason.

Adney returned to New Brunswick for extended visits four more times before 1896, so it is reasonable to assume he and Minnie Bell continued their association and remained in touch. What we know from her diary entry quoted in chapter 5 is that they had an "understanding" before he left for the Klondike in 1897 and were married on September 12, 1899, at St. Luke's Episcopal Church in Woodstock. Tappan hand-painted a pattern

Minnie Bell Sharp in her wedding gown,
September 12, 1899 (CCHS)

of maple leaves on his bride's wedding dress for the occasion. He was thirty-one and she thirty-four. The wedding was a large, formal affair; the church was packed with family members and townspeople who had known Minnie Bell all her life. Many residents had also come to know Adney over the years of his visits to the area. He was now a celebrated writer and artist, published in New York magazines, and the author of a bestselling book.

But before the marriage, Minnie Bell had moved to Victoria, British Columbia, where she purchased the already established Conservatory of Music, which she operated from 1893 to 1899.[3] During this time, she returned to Woodstock on several occasions to attend to the management of the family orchards. Her brother, Franklin, had taken over the business from their father but died in 1892. Her sister, Lizzie, attempted to carry it on, but the business declined. On her visit in 1897, Minnie Bell was confronted with a situation that augmented her notoriety. The trustees of the school district presented her with a delinquent school-tax bill on the Sharp orchards. She refused to pay the full amount because, as she argued, the orchards were no longer productive and the land was much less valuable than the assessment recorded. She was arrested and put in jail. The trustees said they were making an example of her because she rode a bicycle, wore expensive clothes, and took expensive trips.

While in jail she obtained a copy of the provincial legislation that related to her situation and discovered that since she was not, at the time, a resident of Carleton County, she was not liable for the tax bill. She confronted the trustees' lawyer, who admitted he was not aware of this detail. She was released after seventeen days of imprisonment.

If this release from jail meant the trustees had given up on Minnie Bell Sharp, she was not done with them. She sued them for false arrest and imprisonment. The case went to trial and she won, although the jury awarded her only a token dollar in damages instead of the $2,500 she claimed. The trustees appealed the verdict. A second trial was held. Minnie Bell won again and this time was awarded $75 in damages.[4] The legal wrangling and litigation began when Tappan was away on his Klondike assignment for *Harper's Weekly*. But Minnie Bell was a good researcher and capable of dealing with legal matters on her own.

In 1900, Minnie Bell opened the Woodstock School of Music, which she continued to operate for two decades, with studios in several outlying villages. An advertisement in 1913 described it as "the most successful Music School in Canada" and gave the extensive musical background of the proprietor. Her promotional material explained that "the aim of the school is not to grind out graduates with diplomas" but to equip students with practical musical skills. This stance provides an important insight into Sharp's philosophy of education. Apparently, she had a firm grasp of the principles of progressive education associated with the American philosopher John Dewey. Like Dewey, she focused on the intrinsic value of experiential learning.

Tappan Adney was also drawn to this same kind of learning. Instead of entering the ivy-covered halls of academia and getting officially credentialed, he entered the tree-covered landscape of New Brunswick and became highly skilled in cultural preservation through first-hand experience. No wonder these two independent and resourceful artists became a couple.

Their married life was also unconventional. In April 1900, Adney left on another reporting assignment for the new gold rush in Nome, Alaska. In the fall, he returned to New York for more lecturing and illustrating work but went to Woodstock periodically. In the fall of 1901 Minnie Bell and Tappan hosted a concert and reception that featured a display of his paintings and drawings. Their son, Francis Glenn (he was always known as Glenn), was born in 1902.

The family spent various periods of time together in New York City over the next several years. In 1906, Adney took up residence with his

Minnie Bell and Tappan with their son,
Glenn, 1902 (Adney family collection)

wife and son in Woodstock, and for the next ten years they attempted to revive and run the Sharp orchard business. Minnie Bell continued her music school and organized two choral groups, one for children and one for adults. One concert program lists Mr. Tappan Adney as conductor. The program indicates he also composed piano music for Minnie Bell.

This period ended in 1916 with Tappan's enlistment in the Canadian Army during the First World War. Minnie Bell remained in Woodstock but later joined her husband as he developed his artistic and ethnographic vocations in Montréal. Although they lived apart as much as together, the intensity with which each engaged their vocations and the intelligence they undoubtedly recognized in each other seems to have created an enduring affinity. Both had parents and childhood environments that rewarded creativity and fostered the development of self-esteem, independence, and self-confidence. They were both business-minded about the value of their artistic work, yet neither of them seems to have been particularly adept at handling finances. Their livelihoods were sometimes marginal and later in life shadowed by debt.

Minnie Bell Sharp was a pioneering feminist. She rode a bicycle, which at this time was promoted as an act of social liberation for women. In addition to her accomplishments in music and music education and her astute legal mind, Minnie Bell was interested in politics, and not only as

Minnie Bell Sharp Adney's portrait
that accompanied her autobiography
when she ran for election in 1919
(Adney family collection)

an observer: she wanted to be part of the governing machinery.[5] Her entry into politics was a deliberate confrontation with patriarchy.

She ran for office at a time when it was unusual for a woman to do such a thing. Women were granted the right to vote in federal elections in 1918, but not the right to run for office or sit in Parliament. Minnie Bell put her name forward for election to the Canadian Parliament in 1919. The *Carleton Sentinel* endorsed her candidacy and asked her for a personal "sketch," which it published under the bold headline, "Minnie Bell Adney: An Autobiography." Aside from her diaries, this autobiographical essay is the best account we have of the work ethic, musical talent, unrelenting drive for high achievement, humanitarian concern, and broadly prescient outlook on political affairs and public policy that she inherited from her family and advanced in her own dramatic way.

> When four years old, I had my life planned out what I would do and
> be. And then, as always, I had unlimited faith in my power for "great
> achievements."... At six years I was working, sitting in the big frames
> of the hothouse beds, counting out "Sharp's Famous Drumhead
> Cabbage" plants.... At eight years of age, I was a competent cook,
> making pies, cakes and biscuits. I had my own supplies...my own
> utensils as well as my own sweet, determined will.

...my father kept a...music room. In one end was a Steinway piano...and fine choral organ. My father adored the "harmony of sweet sounds." I was encouraged in every way to cultivate my musical gift.

At the age of twelve I could harness, drive and manage a horse and was the general "factotum" carrying letters to mail and doing all the light trucking.

Our place was a mecca for the infirm and the poor. No one was turned away. Everyone could come and sleep and eat and rest. More than once we had two or three families living on the premises. My father did not believe in "jailing for debt" and so not being able to alter the law he simply paid the debt and freed the debtor.... Father and mother one fall brought the "poor children" from the "poor farm" in family lots and kept them all winter feeding and clothing them, and we always kept a sort of private "orphanage."

I went to New York to study music. I lived like a millionaire's daughter, my father lavishly spending money on me. I had the finest masters both for piano and voice....

I studied the first three years with Nunes, a royal graduate of that greatest of all schools, the Paris Conservatory.... The last two years in New York I taught music and paid my own expenses.

In 1893 I went to British Columbia where at Victoria I conducted a conservatory of music for six years. It was considered the best on the coast.... I have had great success in my profession of teaching. I have turned out a greater number of musicians than all the rest of the music schools in Canada put together....

The "star" job of my life so far was when after I volunteered by wire to help with the flu epidemic at St. John's Engineering Depot. I was accepted and placed in charge of an important department of the hospital just opened for sick nurses. I worked at cooking and assisted with the nursing. There were seventeen of them. I went on duty... at 7 a.m., and off at 8 p.m. I had two kitchens, two stores and two orderlies help me. "I delivered the goods" all right. All the nurses got well. It was said to be the only military depot where none died. I got no money for this, not even travelling expenses.

THE Conservative Candidate
"BY THEIR FRUITS YE SHALL KNOW THEM"

MINNIE BELL ADNEY

Greatest Piano Virtuoso, Music Teacher and Horticulturist of her time and generation. First British born woman candidate for Federal government.

ELECTION CARD

To the Electors of the Federal Constituency of Victoria-Carleton :

I hereby desire to serve notice on the Electors of the above Constituency that it is my intention to offer myself as a candidate in the Election to be held on October 29th, 1925.

I feel I am eminently fitted to be a candidate both for service to my country in war and in peace. My father's family, his son, his sons-in-law and his grand-children have a combined record of a quarter of a century or twenty-five years of service in the Great War and two of my direc' ancestors fought on the fields of Abraham.

Three Foremost Issues :

1. OUR SOLDIERS—JUSTICE, NOT MORE, NOT LESS, FOR EACH AND EVERY SOLDIER, OUR SACRED DUTY. THE SAVIOURS OF THE WORLD ARE CANADA'S PREFERRED CREDITORS. COMPLETE RE-ESTABLISHMENT, NOT CHARITY.

2. GOVERNMENTS—FEDERAL, PROVINCIAL AND MUNICIPAL—MUST ADVANCE PUBLIC WORKS FOR EMPLOYMENT, PROVIDING FOOD AND CLOTHES FOR THE NEEDY, NOW.
   AT THE SAME TIME LAYING THE FOUNDATION OF PERMANENT RE-CONSTRUCTION, AND A GREATER CANADIAN NATION.

3. MOTHERS' PENSIONS—TO PROPERLY FEED AND CLOTHE THE CHILDREN OF CANADA—OUR FUTURE CITIZENS—TO MAKE THEM ASSETS INSTEAD OF LIABILITIES. THE TIME IS NOW.

Governments are for making and enforcing laws to protect the life, the liberty and the property of the people. That is its chief business, and not to operate railroads or banks or church affairs.

Our governments, both Provincial and Federal, must get rid at once before the country is destroyed and deserted, of the government owned railroads. Sell them or give them away. The country would be millions of dollars better off if rid of these devouring octopuses.

Sessional Indemnities—Five hundred dollars to be the limit for a Sessional Indemnity or pay. Men who have good incomes should serve free.

Any member of any government who took increase of indemnity in 1918 after the Armistice was signed and before the soldiers are paid and satisfied is a thief, the goods are on them. A pickpocket is a king beside such.

Our government is a big unwarlike machine like the Juggernaut of old, grinding and ploughing over the country crushing the life and the salvation out of the people.

A solution for the problem and perhaps a cure for this terrible state of things would be to put the country under military rule, court martial the government members, all of them, and give them what they deserve, a term in the penitentiary with hard labour. While they are

"doing time" establish a government from the ex-service men and women who could make some workable laws, get rid of these octopuses, the government owned railways, scrap the junk in the senate, pay the soldiers' debt and reduce the taxes and cost of living (so the children will get enough to eat) There would be plenty of money to do it, taken away from the criminals when they go into prison and then still lots left over to open up our country's great natural resources and bring back into Canada from the United States the ex-service men and all that vast multitude forced out of Canada by these convicts at work for the first time at honest employment (doing time) for their country.

Minnie Bell Adney,
Candidate By the Grace of God.

Minnie Bell Adney's campaign card for election to the
Canadian Parliament, 1925 (CCHS)

And then comes her political platform:

> In conclusion, if I am elected, as I shall be, I shall accomplish the
> greatest work of all. I shall work first for justice and the people: for
> adequate recompense for our wonderful soldier boys who gave for
> us the prime vigor of their lives, and wrote the word "Canada"
> large across the history of our lives; for the children of our land,
> the men and women of tomorrow, that they may have ample
> opportunity to blossom forth as ideal citizens of our land, true to
> themselves, their country and their King; for our common cause,
> without destruction of classes or creeds or the drawing of stringent
> political lines; for the good of all, the public weal and humanity.[6]

The election officials were not allowed to put her name on the ballot.

She ran for election three more times, and in 1925 her name was allowed to appear on the ballot. She pledged to work for an economy in which all children could be reared in security. She got eighty-four votes.

Again, we can see her insightful, logical mind at work. Linking the welfare of children to a political economy that provides security was a progressive idea of good government only just emerging at that time. She was bold in her aspiration to have a voice in government and prescient in her advocacy of progressive public policies for the common good. Considering the style and fluency of her writing, she must have been equally skilled at public speaking. Minnie Bell was a pattern-breaker, endowed with intelligence and drive, undeterred by the conventional expectations of a woman's role. Being married to Minnie Bell must have been a continual challenge. Being married to Tappan was likely no less.

Eight months after their wedding, Adney was again headed north to cover the gold rush at Nome, Alaska, as a correspondent for *Collier's Weekly* magazine. He booked passage on the steamer *Valencia*, which departed Seattle on May 30. In a coincidence, the famous photographer Edward Curtis was on the dock at the same time as Adney. Both men were taking photographs of the pandemonium as passengers boarded the ship and a crowd of well-wishers waved them off. One of Curtis's photographs taken at this time shows Adney standing atop a large packing crate on the dock with his tripod-mounted four-by-four camera.

During this assignment, Adney wrote six articles, illustrated with a total of thirty-two photographs. Two are devoted exclusively to the voyage from Seattle and the dangerous process of getting through the pack ice, which was still thick and sometimes impassible as late as early June. He stayed on site four and a half months, leaving Nome on October 16, 1900, just before the freeze-up.

Comparisons between the Klondike and Nome gold rushes appeared in his dispatches.[7] Features of the environments were the same in both places, such as the explosive population growth. First came the saloons, gambling joints, restaurants, brothels, and bunkhouses, all set up in tents at first but quickly converted to wooden structures. Then came offices for doctors, dentists, and lawyers, as well as larger structures for warehouses, banks, hospitals, and churches.

Both camps had their share of get-rich-quick dreamers who expected to find gold in plain sight waiting to be picked up. Many of the men who showed up had no understanding of the patience and hard work it would take to succeed. The Nome Gold Rush, however, had a high percentage of prospectors and miners from the Klondike and other gold camps in the region who came with realistic expectations. Both the Klondike and Nome gold fields were almost completely staked with claims early on by the discoverers and first arrivals, forcing latecomers to prospect for new discoveries or return home.

In the Klondike, wood was plentiful and sawmills worked round the clock to meet the insatiable demand for construction lumber. At Nome, where there was no forest, only beach and tundra, dozens of ocean steamers brought in millions of board feet of lumber from Seattle as well as coal for heating. The banging of hammers and rasping of handsaws could be heard night and day under the nearly constant sunlight of summer. In the Klondike, something was always in short supply. In Nome, food was plentiful and cheap, supplied by competing steamship companies and stored by the ton in warehouses behind the beaches.

Only a small percentage of those who started for the Klondike gold fields made it there. Virtually all who boarded ships in Seattle or Victoria for Nome arrived at their destination. In the Klondike the gold was coarse and flaky and found either in stream beds or in shafts that led to old stream beds as much as twenty-five to thirty feet below the surface. In Nome the gold was extremely fine, like particles of flour, and was found in the beach sand or just a few feet below the surface.

Coal-fired steam engines and heavy dredging equipment had been brought from Seattle and set up on the beach. Adney counted hundreds of such machines working in Nome as he cruised the length of the beach in a rented boat. Putting steam engines to work became even more feasible when deposits of coal were found near Nome. No such engines existed in the Klondike until years after the initial rush. Both the Klondike and Nome mining areas produced millions of dollars of gold, literally tons of it in their first few years of operation. Both regions continued to produce for many years afterward, and both are still mined today on a small scale.

On his return trip, Adney spent time exploring the Canadian Rockies. He took the Canadian Pacific Railway from Vancouver through the mountains to the Grand Hotel at Lake Louise. He made advance arrangements for a guide to provide supplies and transportation for a week-long snowshoe trek to the headwaters of the North Saskatchewan River on the east side of the Rocky Mountain range. He returned to Lake Louise to resume his train journey to Montréal and then to New York, arriving November 20.

When Adney returned to New York, he began corresponding with John J. Healy, the larger-than-life character he had met in Dawson in 1897. Healy was co-owner of the North American Transportation and Trading Company (NATT), which operated a small fleet of steamships transporting miners and supplies from Seattle to Nome. The NATT also maintained a warehouse at Dawson, filled with tons of food and supplies. This is where Adney saw Healy face down a mob of frightened and desperate men. The dire forecasts of impending food shortages and starvation in the Dawson area over the coming winter had driven them to action. They had come, armed, to raid his warehouse. Healy met them at the door, unarmed, and calmly assured them adequate food supplies were on hand and he would make sure it was equitably available. He was eloquent and persuasive. The mob was completely defused. Adney publicly supported Healy in his effort to counter the panic.

Healy wrote to him with fond remembrance three years later in 1900. As their correspondence grew, Adney learned about Healy's colourful life before Dawson and resolved to write his biography. Healy had served in the US Army, escorting wagon trains on their journeys through the western plains and mountains before the Indigenous nations had been defeated and confined to reservations. He operated a trading business with the Indigenous communities in the Montana territory. He had been the sheriff in a county the size of New England. He performed this lawman's job on the frontier for five years without carrying a visible gun. Healy's letters were filled with tales of courage and near-death experiences on the Montana plains at a time when it was still a lawless and dangerous territory. In his unpublished biography of Healy, Adney recounts tales of heroics and daring on the Montana frontier involving Healy. Adney was able to corroborate Healy's stories via Richard Amory, Healy's deputy sheriff, who later became a colonel on the staff of the governor of New York state and a friend of Adney.

Healy, like Adney, had an extraordinary mind. After reinventing himself as a prospector, storekeeper, county sheriff, steamboat captain, and miner's supply capitalist, he decided to make himself over one more time as a railroad baron. He proposed to build a railroad tunnel under the Bering Strait to connect Asia with North America.[8] He called the tunnel the Panama Canal of the North. (The Panama Canal was under construction at the time.) Healy saw Adney as an adventurous thinker and solicited his support for the project.

The tunnel would be an engineering challenge but not impossible given the technology and tools of the time. It would be forty-four miles long, the longest in the world, but conveniently interrupted by the Diomede Islands, where air-ventilation shafts could be built. The maximum water depth of the Bering Strait is only 180 feet. Below that, the entire seabed is solid granite. Although such a project would face technical and physical challenges, the actual tunnelling through solid bedrock would be less structurally complex and, in some ways, easier than the construction of the New York City subway system, where the walls and ceilings had to be shored up every few feet to keep the tunnels from collapsing.

The proposed tunnel was the key to a much larger plan to build some four thousand miles of railroad tracks in both Alaska and Siberia. Such a gigantic scheme would need equally gigantic financing and require the cooperation of the American and Russian governments. For all the technical and physical challenges the project posed, it first had to clear formidable political hurdles and develop a credible financing plan. Raising as much as $200 million was the first step.

The first American transcontinental railroad was financed based on a thirty-mile-wide US government land grant for the length of the route. To finance his project, Healy needed similar land concessions from the US and

Russian governments. Without the land deals, investors would keep their chequebooks closed. Unlike the US transcontinental railroad deal where the need for fast, reliable transportation between the east and west coasts of the country was self-evident, the Trans-Alaska Siberian Railroad, located in remote corners of both countries, would be a tough sell.

Healy and his business partner, Baron Loicq de Lobel, formally created the Trans-Alaska Siberian Railroad Company. De Lobel was a French nobleman trained as a civil engineer whom Healy met in London at a mining conference. With $6 million in seed money raised with the help of Wall Street capital brokers Abbott and Helm, Healy travelled extensively, chatting up the press, lobbying congressmen, senators, and administration officials. He arranged a meeting with President Theodore Roosevelt to seek support for the project. He saw Roosevelt as a kindred spirit, a big thinker and a visionary who could see the enormous potential of Alaska and a railroad link with Asia. Meanwhile, de Lobel was working the Russian side of the project and had obtained a favourable response from Tsar Nicholas II. Healy reasoned that if the Russian government agreed to support the project, US government approval would follow, and eager investors would be quick to respond.

Healy visited New York in 1903 seeking investors for the railway project and renewed his friendship with Adney. Healy always had more than one iron in the fire. Whenever he found minerals or land that could serve as a town site, he would create a company to hold the asset while he searched for financing to develop it. Often, these companies would in theory support and overlap each other. When Healy visited New York he held a controlling interest in a handful of companies, at least on paper. They were all capitalized enough to meet legal requirements for incorporation, and all had real boards of directors. But without bigger money backing them, they existed only on paper, and their stock was essentially worthless.

Healy was feeling discouraged when he arrived in New York, having been recently betrayed by old friends and colleagues who had conspired to oust him from the leadership of one of his companies, the Central Alaska Exploration Company. He reached out to Adney for both friendship and active support in promoting his business ventures. He made a gift to Adney of one hundred shares of stock in the Alaska Northern Railway Company as a gesture of goodwill and an incentive to help make the company a success. Each share was valued at $100, making the total value $10,000.

It was quite an incentive, but both Healy and Adney knew the stock was worthless unless the company was up and running.

Adney saw it as a long-shot opportunity to make enough money for his family to live in comfort for the rest of their lives. He shelved his artwork and magazine articles and began working full-time for Healy, drafting affidavits to congressional committees, letters to influential members of Congress, legal documents for Healy's various companies, and press releases to reporters in New York and Washington. Up to that time, Adney had been paying his bills with royalty money from book sales. He likely saw that working for Healy and promoting the tunnel and railway project could improve the chances of its success, and they would know in a year or so which way it would go. World events, however, conspired to drag things out.

Just as it seemed de Lobel was making headway with the tsar and his council of ministers to consider the tunnel scheme, war broke out between Russia and Japan. Tensions had been simmering for years. Russian censorship was clamped onto all outgoing and incoming mail. De Lobel fell silent, leaving Healy stewing and anxious. The war started early in February 1904 and raged on for eighteen months, ending in September 1905. Nothing further could be accomplished during this time. Early in 1906, word came from de Lobel that the railroad tunnel project was back on the table. The tsar had signed an edict approving the idea. He appointed a commission to study the proposal and gave advance approval to whatever decision it would make. An eighteen-month deadline was set to complete the study.

The thread of hope from Russia came too late. Healy had lost most of his holdings in the companies he had set up. All his interlocking and codependent companies had come crashing down. With this blow, Healy realized the Alaska Northern Railway Company would probably never come to be, or if it did, he would not live to see it. Healy divided his shares in the company and gave half to Adney and half to his old friend from their Montana days, Richard Amory. Adney wrote to Minnie Bell on May 3, 1906:

Dear Minnie: Yesterday I became the sole owner of $475,000 in stock and of $725,000 in bonds of the Alaska Northern Railroad Company. Will it be worth anything, or will we paper the walls of our house someday with the handsome yellow certificates?[9]

Glenn Adney and his dog outside the family home in Upper Woodstock, 1912
(Adney family collection)

Toward the end of that same letter, Adney mentioned he was in debt for room and board and that every day he remained in New York meant more debt. The same was true for Healy, who retreated to San Francisco to live with a daughter while awaiting the decision from the tsar's commission. In April 1907 the message came that the tsar's ministers had rejected the proposal to build a railroad tunnel under the Bering Strait.

Adney hesitated no longer. With the collapse of Healy's imaginary business empire, there was nothing to keep him in New York. He settled his bills, likely by selling artwork, and returned to Upper Woodstock, Minnie Bell, and their son, Glenn. He never again lived in New York, the city where he had earned a living through his art, journalism, and research for almost twenty years. At age thirty-eight, he was without a reserve of financial resources and discouraged. But in returning to Upper Woodstock, to his five-year-old son, and to his wife, Tappan Adney had a new opportunity, one to which he and Minnie Bell devoted most of the next decade.

Chapter Eight

The Orchard Business in New Brunswick

I intend…to try to apply in practical form, in new orchards, these results of his [Francis Peabody Sharp's] *latest and mature experience, as far as I am able.* —Tappan Adney

Adney's marriage to Minnie Bell came with the legacy of the Sharp family orchard and nursery business. It had once been a flourishing enterprise on the frontline of innovative techniques for developing commercial orchards in northern climates. But it was now bankrupt, having gone from the largest commercial orchard in Canada to a remnant of neglected and unproductive trees. On the death of her father, Minnie Bell inherited most of the land, much of which was mortgaged.

Resurrecting the Sharp family orchard business may seem an unlikely solution for Tappan and Minnie Bell's financial situation, but it was an opportunity open to them: they had access to land that once produced abundant apple crops, and the challenge clearly engaged Adney's interest. He quickly discovered, however, that success would require rescuing not only the Sharp orchards but also the apple business in Carleton County and the legacy of Francis Peabody Sharp. To appreciate the scope of the undertaking Adney faced, Sharp's revolutionary contributions to horticulture must be taken into account.

In the late 1880s, Carleton County was the largest apple-growing region not only in New Brunswick but in all of Canada. It owed this distinction to the work of one man. The wide-ranging and innovative horticultural research of Francis Peabody Sharp during the previous sixty years led to revolutionary discoveries in hybridization and cultivation methods. Sharp was doing his research more than thirty years before the provincial government established a department of agriculture and more than sixty years before the first professional horticulturist was hired in New Brunswick to advise farmers on planting and managing orchards.

Minnie Bell Sharp with employees in Francis Peabody Sharp's orchard, 1895
(F.P. Sharp fonds, NBM)

Some of Sharp's cultivation methods would become standard practice in the orchard business. He frequently wrote articles on horticulture for local newspapers and was sought after as a speaker at agricultural meetings. He was, in effect, New Brunswick's first professional horticulturist. He owned and operated the province's only horticultural research station for more than fifty years.

He planted trees from his nurseries on his own property and leased large tracts of land to expand his orchards. He took on mortgages to finance the orchards and experimental nurseries. Lewis P. Fisher, a wealthy lawyer and the first mayor of Woodstock, held most of these mortgages. He appreciated and respected Sharp's pioneering work.

Although Sharp cultivated a wide variety of fruits and vegetables, apple production was the focus of his business. He also hired out himself and his employees to help maintain other growers' orchards. During the spring, summer, and fall seasons he often employed more than one hundred men. He produced cider and vinegar, as well as honey from his beehives, which in turn ensured good pollination of the orchards. He also operated a windmill for grinding bone meal to enrich his soil. In the spring he operated a commercial maple sugary. A local barrel-making business and a canning factory relied on his orchard business.

In addition to apple trees, Sharp's nurseries produced plum, cherry, and peach trees as well as grape vines, raspberries, and gooseberry bushes. He employed as many as fifteen workers in his nurseries, which, at their largest, occupied twelve acres of ground and contained nearly a million plants. He also raised horses, cattle, sheep, pigs, and chickens.

Sharp conducted microscopic studies of the flow of sap in the tissues of fruit trees and examined soils with the same thoroughness. He conducted numerous experimental trials to test his theories, and he applied and tested various cultivation and tree-training methods based on his findings. One of these trials involved pruning small plum, peach, and apple trees in a fan shape, bending them to the ground in the fall so they would be protected with snow cover, and raising them again in the spring. The trial was successful and allowed Sharp to establish commercial orchards for the first time in an area of Canada previously considered too harsh for some varieties of fruit trees to survive.

One of Sharp's most significant discoveries was what he termed "the Law of Antagonism between Stalk and Root." From his observations of sap and mineral flow in stalks, he discovered that when roots must compete for essential nutrients, trees switch to survival mode, putting most of their energy into flowering and fruiting. Equipped with this knowledge, he planted apple trees six to twelve feet apart instead of the usual twenty-four to thirty feet. He prepared the ground in a unique fashion to support this close planting. After planting, he would apply special cultivation methods and a special surgical notching to force the trees into early fruiting. In one dwarfing experiment, he created several rows of apple trees only three feet high heavily loaded with apples that could easily be harvested from the ground.

Following up on sharing Sharp's discoveries, Adney wrote to Dr. W.T. Macoun, dominion horticulturist at the Dominion Agriculture Farm in Ottawa, with the following information:

> I am sure Mr. Sharp has gone further than anyone else in
> approaching the question of HOW TO CONTROL stalk-and-
> fruit forces of the tree. I am sure no PRIORITY of discovery
> can go to the United States.... I happened to have opportunity

for a lengthy conversation with Dr. N.K. Brittain, of New York,
the well know[n] Botanist…and in speaking of Mr. Sharp's…
discovery of the "Law of Antagonism," he stated to me
quite plainly, that to his knowledge the LAW WAS NEW TO
BOTANICAL SCIENCE.[1]

Sharp plowed his profits from the nurseries and orchards into research
and experimentation. He was heavily mortgaged based on expected results
from his improved and more productive cultivation methods, which,
he anticipated, would put his orchard business ahead of the rest of the
industry. All this had been fully developed when Adney first travelled to
New Brunswick in 1887 as a guest of the Sharp family. As the letter quoted
above indicates, Adney's scientific and ever-curious mind observed and
understood the significance of Sharp's experimental research.

In 1887 Francis Sharp turned sixty-five and turned over the management
of his orchard and nursery business to his sons, Humboldt and Franklin.
He had trained Franklin, in particular, in the orchard business and
especially in his revolutionary cultivation and tree-training methods. Sharp
convinced his son to plant what became known as the Big Orchard. Initially
it consisted of twenty thousand apple trees on seventy acres in Upper
Woodstock. This orchard was expanded from time to time and eventually
grew to cover one hundred acres.

In reflecting on this massive project in later years, Adney observed that it
was the first instance in the history of horticulture when such a large number
of a new variety of apple were planted at one time. Of the young, grafted trees
planted, approximately twelve thousand were the Crimson Beauty variety
developed by Sharp, another six thousand were the Wealthy variety, and the
remaining sixteen hundred were experimental hybrids, the second major
hybridization trial the elder Sharp had conducted. These experimental crosses
held good promise for producing new, high quality, commercial varieties.

The trees in the Big Orchard were planted close together so that Sharp's
unique methods could be applied to turn the orchard into a showcase for his
discoveries. Little did Adney know when he first observed this revolutionary
orcharding that, nearly two decades later, he and Minnie Bell would be
struggling as husband and wife to save this model orchard from being cut
down by strangers.

By the turn of the century, Sharp's business enterprises were in decline due to a series of calamities and neglect. In 1881, fire destroyed the Sharp home, barns, storehouses, and tree-storage cellars. They had no insurance. Although a new house and some other facilities were rebuilt, the loss was irreplaceable. The following winter, Francis Sharp was stricken with serious illness, which Minnie Bell referred to as "pneumonia and brain fever." In the spring of 1882, he sold his entire nursery stock of sixty thousand plums trees to Chase Brothers of Rochester, New York, and used the money to build a new family home, storehouses, and tree cellars. In July he signed a $1,000 mortgage with L.P. Fisher at a rate of 8 per cent per annum. Many years later, after his death in 1903, this mortgage, along with others, would come to haunt Minnie Bell and Tappan.

Francis Sharp had barely recovered from the fire loss and rebuilding when the US government imposed the McKinley tariff of 1890 on imported agricultural crops. The tariff was designed to protect US farmers from crops grown by foreign competitors. It imposed such a high duty on fruits and other crops imported into the United States that it priced them out of the American market. The tariff dealt a devastating blow to Sharp's apple and plum business. "The fact is there are more apples produced than we have a market for. Before the McKinley tariff we used to send to the States, but we have been knocked out of that," Sharp said in a newspaper interview.[2]

In 1892, Sharp's son and business partner, Franklin, died of tuberculosis. The loss left a critical void in Sharp's business succession plan as well as in his heart. He had trained Franklin in his revolutionary methods of fruit growing and other areas of horticulture. At about the same time as Franklin's death, the entire plum orchard of seven thousand trees on the home property was wiped out during a severe winter with no snow cover. The financial impact and Sharp's failing health put his businesses into decline. No more fruit trees were produced and sold from the nursery business after Franklin's death. With the accumulated debt incurred by Sharp's research and experimentation, the stage was set for business failure.

In 1901, daughter Lizzie took out a $3,000 mortgage on one of the Sharp properties, presumably to keep the family afloat financially. She was living with her parents and attempting to keep them comfortable. At the time of Francis Sharp's death in 1903, at the age of eighty, the nursery business was no longer in operation and the orchard business was in decline. There were many outstanding mortgages and very little income.

The following year, Maria Sharp and her daughter Lizzie also died, both from pneumonia. There was a mortgage sale of certain Sharp properties that same year, all held by L.P. Fisher. In 1906 Humboldt gave up the part of the orchard business he was still operating and went west to Red Deer, Alberta. Jennie Rankin, the youngest of Sharp's daughters, now married, had no interest in the orchard business. Minnie Bell and Tappan were the only ones left to manage what remained of Sharp's once vast orchards.

At the time of Sharp's death, Adney prepared a three-and-a-half-page obituary that reveals his great admiration for his father-in-law and his accomplishments in the world of horticulture. This obituary is the first indication that Adney was thinking about picking up the legacy of Francis Peabody Sharp. He wrote:

> It is beyond my poor power to do justice to the service which
> Mr. Sharp has rendered his native County, Province and Country.
> More than sixty years were devoted to experiments, of which
> (I say with no disparagement of any) he alone knew the full
> meaning and grasped the possibilities beyond, and it is the regret
> of many, I am sure, that he did not publish.... It would have been
> of priceless value and it was the one thing needed to establish
> firmly his reputation and make it universal. I tried to persuade
> him to put his knowledge in lasting form, but like many another
> of high attainment he was not prepared to regard his work as
> finished.[3]

Perhaps it was when researching Sharp's letters to Minnie Bell and organizing his thoughts for the obituary that Adney became aware of the potential of the Big Orchard for resolving his own financial situation. The Big Orchard could perhaps become the Big Hope for the Adney family, supplying them with the income they needed.

After Franklin's death, Francis Sharp had looked to Minnie Bell to carry out his plans for the Big Orchard, as she was the only remaining family member he was confident could carry on the legacy. However, she was then in Victoria operating her music conservatory. Sharp began a four-year letter writing effort to persuade his daughter to come home and take over the business. He wrote lengthy letters, revealing his revolutionary discoveries and detailing his unique cultivation methods for her to use in the Big Orchard. Adney described this situation in his letter to Dr. W.T. Macoun:

After the 1892 death of his [Sharp's] son, the great orchard
of trees, PURPOSELY PLANTED…VERY CLOSE was yet
unproducing, and…Mr. Sharp… desired my wife to return…
and take over the orchard title and entire control.

In the endeavor to persuade her to give up a good business
there [in Victoria], Mr. Sharp set forth in detail, the results of
a lifetime of experiment with fruits and their culture, and the
manner of their application to an orchard which… would soon
go to the dogs. In these letters he again and again points out
the reason why he has not complied with requests to put his
experiences into [a] book before he died.… While stating his firm
belief in his DUTY TO THE [HUMAN] RACE to make all
public, still, before him was the "great orchard," and he desired
his FAMILY to make some use of his discovery FIRST, in a way
that this great orchard alone would enable them to do, an object
lesson to the world.

So in going through his many and long letters of that period
I [found] what I, as well as many others, supposed had DIED
WITH HIM. And he expressly states the extreme difficulty of
composition, in his advancing age, saying "I will probably not
write these things in any other form."

Adney concluded the letter with "I intend, if I remain here, to try to
apply in practical form, in new orchards, these results of his latest and
mature experience, as far as I am able."[4]

Sharp had been cautious when speaking about his discoveries at
conventions or in interviews with newspapers, deliberately withholding
and protecting his valuable information for his family's benefit. In a letter
to Minnie Bell about a paper he had delivered in 1896 to a meeting of
the Dairymen and Fruit Growers Association of New Brunswick, he
commented that she "will see that it is remarkable for what is left out."

In an earlier letter to Minnie Bell, her father told her he was working
on an important paper for presentation at a fruit growers' convention in
Ottawa, where he would reveal his revolutionary findings. But then he
threw in a curious comment clearly aimed at enticing her to get involved
with the family business in which he gives her the opportunity to ask him
not to reveal his secrets to the horticultural world.

> All I can gain now by giving away any of my discoveries, which
> have cost so much in study, experiment, and time, is a recognition
> of priority in discovery.... Were there any prospects I could USE
> these discoveries...or that they would be used by my family,
> I would refrain from giving them away.[5]

Apparently, Minnie Bell did not show the kind of interest in the Big Orchard her father hoped for, because he proceeded to complete the paper. Sharp was too ill to travel to Ottawa for the convention, but he sent his paper to be read. It arrived too late and was never presented. Adney was not able to locate the paper in Ottawa, but he did find draft portions of it among Sharp's records. With these and Sharp's letters to Minnie Bell, Adney was able to assemble a record of the knowledge provided by Sharp's scientific experimentation.

Once again, as throughout his life, Tappan Adney's interest in the arc of human knowledge as it comes from the past, is preserved and applied in the present, and is passed on to the future served him well in his new position, along with Minnie Bell as the custodian of her father's legacy. Whatever aspect of natural history and human culture engaged his interest, his instinct for research and assembling information was at the centre of his vocational orientation. This was the stance of serious commitment with which Adney now approached the heritage of Sharp's orchard business and the potential for its commercial revival.

Apparently, Francis Sharp had Tappan in mind for the orchard business long before he had shown any interest in this prospect. In letters, Sharp would often instruct his daughter to "tell this to Tappan." In May of 1893 he wrote about his discovery of artificial forcing of fruit:

> Tell this to Tappan, for I assure him that...this discovery,
> if published, would be worth many thousands of dollars,
> for it will change the whole method of growing fruit.
> Trees will be planted close together, and kept of such size
> that all fruit may be picked from the ground — saving
> more than half the expense of harvesting...for it is a great
> fact that when the whole force of the tree is devoted to the
> fruit, not only is the quantity immensely increased, but
> also THE QUALITY.[6]

At the time of these letters, Adney's interests were otherwise engaged, or perhaps Minnie Bell did not share them with him. It wasn't until almost fifteen years later, when the family's situation demanded a new livelihood, that Sharp's letters would offer Adney the potential path of horticultural enterprise.

The potential for the Big Orchard was never realized. In 1904, the year following Sharp's death, the orchard was sold when the mortgage on the land, held by L.P. Fisher, was foreclosed. The property was sold to S.C. Parker, a fruit grower from Berwick, Nova Scotia, who immediately cut down the trial plot of hybridized apple trees Sharp had planted. They had not yet started bearing fruit, so if there were any valuable new varieties to be discovered among them—like the celebrated New Brunswicker and Crimson Beauty Sharp had previously developed—they were forever lost.

When Adney later wrote about the circumstances of this loss, he expressed great disappointment in Fisher for calling the mortgage, selling the property, and depriving the Sharp family of the opportunity to realize the financial support the Big Orchard could have provided.

> In all of these transactions [with the elder Sharp] Mr. Fisher made money, and lost none. Yet it was the hand of the same Fisher, half a century later, that signed...a foreclosure sale of a piece of property, on which he held a mortgage of no greater amount than the value of one crop, which represented the latest, and the highest, attainment in orchard cultivation in the Maritime Provinces, and removed it thereby from the Sharp family. It may be said in extenuation, that his lifelong friend was now dead. It was only the legacy of this great fruit grower's work to his family that was thus taken.
>
> There went with this property thousands of trial apple hybrids, originated by Mr. Sharp, the result of many years work, an irreparable loss to...Canada...and to the whole world—for these precious hybrids were immediately cut down by the new owner.[7]

Adney immersed himself in Sharp's research, learning everything he could about plant life in general, not only apples. He read through all of Sharp's old letters and documents. He researched the beginnings of horticultural societies and pioneer horticultural publications, identifying names and dates to confirm the uniqueness of Sharp's discoveries. He didn't want to embark on a mission to apply Sharp's profitable cultivation methods and risk his reputation and even greater debts without the assurance that Sharp truly was a pioneer in the scientific advance of horticulture.[8]

He found numerous notes on the cultivation methods. They detailed how Sharp had laid down the fruit trees for winter survival, his methods for inducing dwarfing and early fruiting, and his nutritional programs, including many records on more than just apples and fruit trees. Adney noted:

> Mr. Sharp was more…a Horticulturist, than a Pomologist, that is, not so much merely an "Apple" man as a "gardener." All phases of gardening interested him, indeed he comprehended the full meaning of Horticulture—the most perfect method of tilling the earth so as to produce the best result in the form of fruits, foods, and objects of beauty from the vegetable kingdom.[9]

Humboldt, Minnie Bell's younger brother, maintained and harvested apples from the original New Brunswicker orchard on Sharp's Mountain across the Wəlastəkw from Upper Woodstock until the spring of 1906. He then packed up all the remaining trees in the nursery—ten thousand—and headed west by train to Red Deer, Alberta, which proved too cold for a nursery business. He eventually settled in Armstrong, British Columbia, where he established a nursery business in 1910. He wrote to Adney, asking him to send apple seeds and scions from certain varieties of Sharp's apple trees. Adney wrote to Humboldt for details of grafting and pruning and other "secret" techniques that Humboldt had learned from his father.

Adney became increasingly annoyed with the new owner of one of the Sharp orchards. He expressed his concern in a letter to the Department of Agriculture in Ottawa that a "Nova Scotia packer" who had bought one of Sharp's New Brunswicker orchards was selling the apples under the name Duchess of Oldenburg, an imported Russian variety. Sharp had gone to great lengths to grow and show the differences between the two varieties. But there were now people who tried to take the hybridizing credit from Sharp by claiming that his New Brunswicker was in fact the Duchess of Oldenburg. Adney saw it as a blatant attempt to defame Sharp and rob him of his legacy. When Adney's ire was aroused and he took on a case, he did a thorough job; his typewritten letter to Ottawa is fifteen pages long, in which he notes the remnant orchard he and Minnie Bell have in their possession. "We ourselves have only a few trees, at the outside not hardly more than a dozen barrels to market.... The orchards which Mr. Sharp himself planted are, and have been, for a long time owned by other people."[10]

Tappan and Minnie Bell set out to work with the orchard that remained on property they controlled, and at the same time, Tappan began organizing his defence of Sharp's legacy. He also became aware of the larger community in which Sharp had worked. Over the years, he had planted many orchards for other people and had received annual payments for maintenance on these properties. Adney decided to enlist the apple growers of Carleton County, who knew and honoured Sharp, to help present his horticultural achievements to the world.

Adney took up this new research and documentation project with characteristic persistence. As a student of natural history and as a social scientist, he was particularly attracted to the broad field of heritage preservation, which was a prominent feature of the opportunity now before him. His decision to resurrect the Sharp orchard business was about both preserving Sharp's legacy and advancing the economy and culture of apple growing in Carleton County.

He began working on a general history of the apple industry in the Upper River Valley region of the province, along with an explanation of the cultivation practices and descriptions of varieties of apples grown by his late father-in-law. The book project, titled *Commercial Orcharding in Carleton County*, was aimed at present and prospective growers in the county. It was an ambitious project he did not complete. Apparently, he reconsidered the utility of such an exhaustive account and turned his attention instead to the creation of an abbreviated and more practical guide. *Fruit Growing in Carleton County* was published in February 1911.

In the same year he submitted a lengthy document to the provincial government for inclusion in its annual report to the legislature on horticulture. The twenty-page article, "Francis Peabody Sharp, His Work in Horticulture," was published by order of the Legislature in 1912. It extols the virtues of Sharp's revolutionary cultivation methods and experiments without, of course, revealing exact details.

Meanwhile, the lower Wəlastəkw Valley had been identified as a suitable region for apple growing, and the New Brunswick government began promoting the area for planting orchards. In 1909, a young man from Ontario, A.G. Turney, was hired as the first government horticulturist. A few years later Adney maintained that a decline in Carleton County's orchard production was only partly due to the aging of the orchard trees. He said they were also suffering from not having Sharp's experience and expert advice, which was further compounded by "improper advice from outside influences." He was referring, of course, to Turney. Sharp had always been adamant that cultivation methods and varieties of fruit in one region could not simply be applied to another region of different geography and climate.

A year later Turney invited Adney to join the New Brunswick Fruit Growers Association. He quotes a resolution by the association at its last meeting in February 1910 to start moving its place of annual meeting and exhibition around the province, thereby catering "to the fruit growers of all New Brunswick." Turney then added:

> ...we would strongly urge upon you the advisability of becoming a member and participating in the great work of developing the fruit industry of the Province. We need your help and hope to receive it. We think you need our help. We have been struggling along individually for years — let us now grasp the spirit of the age and "work together."

Then, Turney sweetened the deal, or perhaps offered a challenge Adney couldn't refuse:

> A careful perusal of the prize list embodied in the accompanying pamphlet will convince you that this exhibition, to be held November next in St. John, presents opportunities for obtaining renown and prize money never before offered in the Province. We know that the exhibition will eclipse anything of the sort ever held in New Brunswick and by working together we are confident of rivaling any similar exhibition held in the Maritime Provinces.[11]

He closed with a line, shown here in italics, that Adney had written in previous correspondence about Carleton County growers: "Trusting to receive your support in the development of *the great natural fruit sections of New Brunswick*, I am, Yours very truly, A.G. Turney." The carefully worded invitation worked, and Adney joined the New Brunswick Fruit Growers Association. The New Brunswick Museum holds membership cards for the years 1910 through 1913 in its Adney collection.

Not long after, however, a statement Turney published in the *Maritime Farmer* of January 24, 1911, angered Adney and other Carleton County apple growers:

> New Brunswick's premier apple lands are to be found in the lower
> St. John Valley, between Saint John and Fredericton, and are
> only 20 to 80 miles from Saint John, the national winter port. To
> the man who desires to grow apples I do not know in all Canada
> of a country where the prospects and markets are better, or the
> environment more ideal.[12]

An article submitted anonymously to the *Carleton Sentinel*, but obviously written by Adney, responded at length and offered this challenge:

> What right has Mr. Turney, the horticulturist whose salary is
> paid for by the people in the northern half of New Brunswick,
> to deliberately ignore the section which raised the first barrel of
> apples ever sold in the market, and has been raising a large and
> profitable surplus of 5,000 to 18,000 barrels a year for the past
> 30 years? If there is any "premier" apple section it is ours....
>
> The section that first produced the Dudley Winter, the New
> Brunswicker and other hardy varieties native to Northern New
> Brunswick and Eastern Maine, may have its credit and fame
> taken from it by Ontario and Ontario-educated men, but...
> not by...men we have helped to bring here to serve us in an
> official capacity.[13]

Adney was now forty-three. When he undertook a determined defence of Sharp's legacy, it was with an air of authority anchored in his research. The fact that the provincial horticulturist was deliberately ignoring the heritage of apple growing in Carleton County seemed to him wrong-headed.

Adney had approached Turney with a plan for testing Sharp's experiments in Carleton County, but Turney was not impressed. Adney was annoyed and insulted by his lack of interest. He wrote to his member of Parliament, F.B. Carvell, slamming Turney for using Ontario cultivation methods and blasting the grower from Nova Scotia.

> I do not have expectation of taking up any of these subjects very far with our new Horticulturist, for when I outlined a plan for him to take up certain matters by further experiment and study of his own, to either prove or disprove, with credit to himself, he has (although very courteously) referred to them as "assertions." I commonly take pains in discussing any subject temperately with a person whose intelligence is equal or superior to my own, not to make "assertions" in the sense that I understand the term....
>
> They have outlined a "Plan of Work" to make New Brunswick "a great commercial orchard country," and I perceive that our local horticulturist already has his hands full. I suppose it is more important to plant new orchards, and to "renovate" the old ones, than to attempt to go very far into abstract matters!
>
> THERE WAS A TIME when Horticulturists from Nova Scotia to Iowa, and Quebec, found it worthwhile to study methods of orchard cultivation from Mr. Sharp...one who has accomplished almost the miraculous in this hard country in way of forcing production of fruit on vast quantities per acre.
>
> "Nova Scotia methods" have killed the big Sharp orchard mostly and methods highly successful in Ontario have been so far unsuccessful here.... It was a saying formerly of Mr. Sharp's that "New Brunswick would have been a great orchard country long ago if it had not been for 'Ontario methods' — if fruit growers had studied more our own local peculiar conditions."[14]

Carvell replied with encouraging news:

> I quite agree with you that the late Mr. Sharp is practically the only man who has ever made a success of the orchard business in New Brunswick. I may tell you that for the last two years I have had under discussion with the Minister of Agriculture the establishment of an experimental farm in Carleton County.... I may tell you that things are looking fairly prosperous at the present time and of course, should the farm be established, without any question the orchard part of it would be an important feature.[15]

To Adney's disappointment, the experimental farm and research station established in 1912 was not located in Carleton County. In yet another move favouring the southern part of the province, it was located in York County near Fredericton.

Another incident that frustrated Adney occurred at the apple exhibition in Saint John in 1911. At the opening of the show, Premier Hazen read from a printed document titled "Can New Brunswick Grow Apples?," in which there were answers from three prominent people: G.H. Vroom, dominion fruit inspector; A. McNeil, chief of the Dominion Fruit Division; and Francis Peabody Sharp. The premier read the first two responses, which were full of vague generalities, but omitted Sharp's, which read:

> The conditions of Russia, as to fruit production, should of itself
> be strong prima facie evidence that ours may be great fruit
> growing country, for no part of New Brunswick can compare
> for cold with sections of Russia in which are found the largest
> commercial orchards in the world.[16]

Adney typed the following comment onto a copy of the sheet from which the premier had read: "Why did he omit this, which was the most valuable of the whole lot? Having got their apples together for a picture, and to write about, were they then done with F.P. Sharp and with Carleton County?"[17]

Frustrated, Adney began his campaign to rescue and promote Sharp's reputation by organizing the Carleton County Fruit Growers Association. The initial meeting of interested growers took place on February 3, 1911, at the Woodstock School of Music. A local newspaper reported the meeting under the headline "Carleton County Fruit Growers Meet and Organize—Neglect of the Hazen Government Causes the Present Action."

> The immediate cause for organizing is the seeming neglect
> of Carleton County and northern New Brunswick in the late
> activities of the horticultural department...and to demand
> recognition as the only commercial apple section of the province.

The participants elected officers for their new organization. Adney was elected secretary. The article continued:

The full text of the opening address of the organizer, Mr.
Adney, will be given in our next issue. In the meantime it is
desired to be made known that…the general horticultural
policy of the government is supported, but the facts…seemed
to show that…our county as a fruit producing section is being
discriminated against and our due share can best be secured
through an organization strong enough to demand recognition
as the only, as yet, commercial apple producing section of New
Brunswick.[18]

At this first meeting five "objects" were set for the new organization
that closely matched Adney's agenda, the first of which he was already
working to achieve. Adney made a final attack against the new provincial
horticulturist regarding the long-standing dispute about the authenticity of
Sharp's New Brunswicker apple:

A vigorous protest was unanimously made at the attempts
of outside foreign influences, supported by the Provincial
Horticulturist, to change the name of our native apple,
the New Brunswicker, to that of a foreign and much inferior
variety, the Duchess of Oldenburg.[19]

But Adney was fighting a losing battle. The government had already
established twenty-three demonstration orchards in the fifteen counties of
the province, promoting them as horticultural showplaces for various fruit
varieties and cultivation methods. Modern forty-gallon orchard sprayers
applied toxic chemicals that reduced insect and fungus damage. Growers
were encouraged to adopt this practice. The government supplied trees and
supervision for planting as well as free courses on orchard management. In
1911 the New Brunswick Fruit Growers Association provided its members
with fifteen thousand trees at a cost of twenty-three cents per tree, less than
half the retail cost.

St. John River Valley Fruit Farm and Land Company was also
established in 1911. It acquired nine hundred acres near Burton and
planted two thousand apple trees. The next year five thousand more trees
were planted. In 1912, the Springhill Fruit and Land Company planted
two thousand trees on extensive holdings near Fredericton. Orchards of
commercial size were being planted throughout the province, most notably

in the lower Wəlastəkw Valley and Moncton areas. By 1913 there were twenty-five commercial size orchards, all, to Adney's great frustration, using Turney's Ontario horticultural methods. Although the government attempted to educate growers in the methods Turney promoted, and the number of large-scale orchards increased, total production for the province did not rise to the level Sharp's orchards had achieved in the mid-1800s.[20]

Adney was disappointed not only with the government but also with some growers in Carleton County who were intrigued by the new demonstration orchards elsewhere in the province as well as apple-growing practices in Nova Scotia. He published an article in a local newspaper in which he incautiously berated growers in his own association.

He blamed declining production in Carleton County on local growers failing to replace their old orchards. He noted that apple production in the county went from eighteen thousand barrels in 1890 to five thousand barrels in 1910. He faulted New Brunswick growers for being led astray by the planting of thousands of untested new trees. He also referred to S.C. Parker, a prominent Nova Scotia grower and secretary of the Nova Scotia Fruit Growers Association, without naming him, who was now the owner of the Franklin Sharp orchard. He suggested that this grower recognized the quality of the New Brunswicker apple and Carleton County's proven capacity for commercial apple production.

In another newspaper article he again criticized the farmers in Carleton County for neglecting future opportunities for their children by switching to cultivation methods and apple varieties being brought into the province by the government. Although frustrated, outmanoeuvred, and sidelined by government spending, Adney didn't give up his campaign for the recognition of Sharp's methods and his apple varieties. On April 14, 1913, he published a lengthy article in the *Maritime Farmer and Co-operative Dairyman* profiling six prominent and successful fruit growers in Carleton County who were using these cultivation methods and apple varieties.

A.G. Turney, for his part, seemed to realize that Adney's knowledge of Sharp's legacy was a valuable part of horticultural history. In 1912, he wrote to Adney asking him to submit an article on Sharp for a revision of the *Cyclopedia of American Horticulture*. The request had been made at the urging of the renowned horticulturist Dr. Liberty Hyde Bailey, who was the editor of the *Cyclopedia* project and wanted Sharp to be recognized for his achievements. Adney complied without hesitation. His article was included in the *Cyclopedia*.

In February 1914, Adney posted an advertisement in the *Carleton Sentinel* offering for sale native-grown apple trees three to five years old, which would suggest he had started a nursery business in addition to managing the orchard on the property Minnie Bell still owned. In the same advertisement he represented himself as an agent for Grasseth Arsenate of Lead and Grasseth Bordeaux Mixtures, a pesticide and fungicide used on apple orchards at that time. Being a distributor for farm chemicals would have augmented Adney's income. Minnie Bell's music school added to the family income as well, which, all together, was likely meagre. There is no indication the orchard business or other sources of income provided the Adney family with adequate and secure finances.

During this time, Adney began writing a column in the *Woodstock Press* titled "Doings in Hardscrabble," another minor source of income. Writing in the tradition of the humorous parts of Benjamin Franklin's *Poor Richard's Almanack* and the satirical vein of Mark Twain, Adney adopted the voice of a slightly cynical country bumpkin who is nevertheless a keen observer of human machinations and foibles.

In 1912, Adney designed a house for his family on the knoll above the former Sharp home and nursery buildings. His plans show a living room, kitchen, two bedrooms, a pantry, an attached woodshed, and another large shed. Only the first section of this plan was completed, the living room and two bedrooms. Adney referred to the house as a bungalow.

The lack of additional records beyond a certain time suggests Tappan and Minnie Bell gave up on their plan for reviving Francis Sharp's orchards. The Big Orchard had passed into other hands, and they never had access to sufficient property to develop anything more than a small orchard and nursery business. Their financial situation continued to be meagre and uncertain.

But Adney did not abandon his campaign for the public recognition of Sharp's horticultural legacy. Minnie Bell, too, was persistent in keeping her father's name before the public. Her father figured prominently in her autobiography, published in 1919 when she became one of the first women to run for political office in New Brunswick. She placed great emphasis on how important it was for her to grow up working with her father in his orchard business and his great achievements in the field of horticulture.

My father had a most beautiful garden and orchard, which under his hand blossomed and bore most abundantly.... He raised to perfection apples, plums, red and golden raspberries, blackberries, pears and grapes.... By the time I was ten I was learning the nursery and orchard business — indeed in the late winter the whole family and house became a factory for making trees. A busy hive of from twenty to fifty workers.... I learned the whole business of making trees, planting and raising, packing and shipping fruit, gardening, taking care of horses, cows, sheep, bees and pigs — in fact I was a regular farmer.... My father planted what was then the largest and finest orchard in Canada. It contained twenty thousand trees under the highest state of cultivation.... My father, Francis Peabody Sharp, was easily the greatest man of his time, doing more for his country than any other man within its bounds.[21]

In 1921, fourteen years after he began his campaign on behalf of Francis Sharp, and long after he was no longer living in Woodstock, Adney demonstrated his continuing obsession with the controversy over the origins of the New Brunswicker apple.

Essentially, the controversy over whether the New Brunswicker apple and the Duchess of Oldenburg apple were different varieties challenged the authenticity of Francis Sharp's work, suggesting he was a fraud. Adney studied the physical differences of the two varieties and corresponded with pomologists in Canada and the United States on the matter. He gathered crucial facts to create an unassailable case for Sharp's creation of the New Brunswicker apple as a distinct variety. He also provided the evidence of a direct witness, Darius Shaw, who was employed in Sharp's nursery and had seen the first New Brunswicker go from seedling to an apple-bearing tree.[22] He eventually published a lengthy article in the *Woodstock Press* on August 2, 1921, in which he showed that a mix-up had occurred in the distribution of these two varieties by Stark nurseries. in the United States.

Adney and Minnie Bell spent nine years working to revive both the Sharp orchards and Sharp's reputation as a horticultural pioneer. They were unable to make an adequate living and eventually gave up the effort. But Adney's vigorous written defence of Francis Sharp's pioneering contributions to apple growing in cold climates remain tangible evidence that a horticultural pioneer once lived in Upper Woodstock, New Brunswick. His discoveries and innovations significantly benefitted his region, his country, and the practice of apple production worldwide.

Adney as an officers' training instructor, Canadian Army, Royal Military College, Kingston, Ontario, 1916 (Adney family collection)

Chapter Nine

An Interlude of Military Service

The…immediate past dropped entirely out as to many memories as well as habits. Circumstances however enabled the stringing of them together in that I saw the need for better visual instruction, such as could be had in scale models of Engineer field works. —Tappan Adney

The First World War had been underway for two years when Tappan Adney decided to volunteer for the Canadian Army. He was accepted and "taken on strength" as a lieutenant at Valcartier, a suburb of Québec, on October 3, 1916. He subtracted four years from his age on his officer's declaration paper, giving his year of birth as 1872, making him forty-four, because the army's cut off age for enlistment was forty-five. Wartime enlistment stories frequently tell of young men eager to serve who advanced their age to qualify. It was rare for a middle-aged man to do the reverse, but Adney was an adventurous person, and this move was yet another adventurous step. As it turned out, its consequences and the creative use to which Adney put the opportunities that followed became the context in which he developed significant contributions to military infrastructure, the artistic heritage of Canada, and the preservation of Indigenous culture.

He listed his son, Francis Glenn Adney of Woodstock, New Brunswick, then age fourteen, as next-of-kin on his declaration paper rather than his wife, Minnie Bell. This has been seen as indicating a break with his wife. Considering his continuing care for Minnie Bell in her later difficult years, a more plausible explanation may be that Adney had confidence Glenn would be a solid support for his mother whatever the future might hold. Such confidence was not misplaced, as became evident in Glenn's later support for both his parents.

Adney's medical record on entering military service indicates he was six feet one and three-quarters inches tall and weighed 175 pounds. The examining doctor noted varicose veins and a stiff big toe on his right foot.

This latter impairment, as we know from his journal, was the result of a mishap with an axe when he was working with a lumber crew on his first trip to New Brunswick.

The certificate of medical examination signed by the doctor lists Adney as fit for service in Canada. He was first attached to the Canadian Expeditionary Force and assigned to the Engineer Training Depot at Saint-Jean, Quebec. As required by the army, he also applied for Canadian citizenship, which was granted by the County Court in Woodstock on May 2, 1917.

Adney's time in the Canadian Army was relatively brief and the documentation is sparse, but it's not difficult to imagine a larger picture of the situation as he was taken into service. It seems likely he would have been a peer in age and life experience with the officers in charge. In some cases, they may have even been younger. It must have been an unusual situation to have a mature man who identified professionally as an artist and writer appear among the ranks of enlistees.

In the interviews that would have taken place after he was accepted, someone in the chain of command decided where to place this highly intelligent, multiply skilled, well-spoken, and supremely self-confident man. They realized an artist and craftsman with advanced communication skills could be an asset in the officers' training program of the engineering division, and assigned Adney to the Royal Military College at Kingston, Ontario. It's easy to imagine a commanding officer interviewing Adney in order to determine how to utilize his skills. We have a good indication of what happened at this point from a letter he wrote in 1941 to Diamond Jenness, an anthropologist colleague.

> The...immediate past dropped entirely out as to many memories as well as habits. Circumstances however enabled the stringing of them together in that I saw the need for better visual instruction, such as could be had in scale models of Engineer field works. Chief of Staff Gwatkin saw the point and thereafter was on that work. From what I had observed early at the American Museum, I introduced realistic effects by use of paper-pulp modeling over wire network or lathing.[1]

Three aspects of Adney's situation are clearly indicated in this description. First, he proposed to the chief of staff that the construction of scale models would improve the training of officers in the engineering of battlefield infrastructure — "I saw the need for better visual instruction."

Second, Chief of Staff Gwatkin immediately understood what Adney was talking about and provided full support for model-building as means of improving the training program. Adney was fully versed in the efficacy of experiential learning. From his childhood education outdoors with his father to working with Peter Jo on the construction of birchbark canoes to his participation in the Klondike Gold Rush to the task of orchard renewal and management, Adney was an expert in the methods and techniques of experiential learning. He now saw how to apply them in the context of battlefield engineering and officer training and was given the opportunity to do so. Adney's proposal created a teaching position, to which he was assigned.

Third, Adney reveals something important when he writes about the effect of signing up for military service: "The…immediate past dropped entirely out as to many memories as well as habits." Without requiring analysis, his description of this experience reveals a characteristic of his response to opportunities and challenges. When a new area of research, artistic engagement, or livelihood opportunity compelled his interest, he could shift focus with an extraordinary concentration of attention to follow up what now seemed more important. This can be seen in the way he mastered the design features and construction techniques of building birchbark canoes. It can be seen in his voyage down the Yukon River with winter closing in. It can be seen in the focus of attention it took to rapidly prepare a five-hundred-page book on the Klondike Gold Rush for publication. It can be seen in the way he took on the defence of Francis Peabody Sharp's horticultural legacy. This is the way Adney characteristically worked.

When Tappan Adney signed up for military service, he had half of his salary sent directly to Minnie Bell. After almost a decade of struggling to generate an adequate livelihood from the orchard business and Minnie Bell's income from her music-teaching business, the security of a regular salary must have been a relief. For the time being, at least, the stress of putting together a sufficient income no longer required constant attention. The chief of staff's recognition of his potential for upgrading the officers' training program and Adney's position at the Engineering

Adney training officers in bridge construction, 1917. Adney is the tallest figure on the far right leaning forward at the railing. (CCHS)

Training Depot and the Royal Military College opened the door for this shift in attention.

The innovation Adney proposed was to create scale models of battlefield structures to improve their design and shift the knowledge of how to build them from abstract to hands-on learning. From the photographic evidence of the work Adney undertook and supervised, the training program included building large tabletop models and full-scale structures of the kind that were needed on the frontlines of the war in Europe. It is not hard to imagine the focus of attention, the sense of design and engineering, and the application of craftsmanship Adney brought to this work or the satisfaction he likely enjoyed from employing this combination of talent and skill.

Adney brought a design feature to battlefield infrastructure that reduced the hazards of trench warfare. By employing a zigzag design when constructing trenches, the blast effect of exploding munitions that landed in the trench was mitigated. Instead of the explosion's lethal force extending some distance both ways along a linear trench, the zigzag walls stopped the blast zone from spreading. The existing photographs of Adney's models and constructions provide a clear and detailed representation of the work he did for the Engineering Training Depot and the Royal Military College.

On August 28, 1918, Tappan Adney was recommended for promotion to captain, but the war ended before the advance in rank took effect. His service had been continuous for two years and three months. He was discharged on December 31, 1918. His demobilization papers show he was immediately employed as the vocational supervisor of the Ste. Anne de Bellevue Military Hospital. The vocational program of a military hospital was concerned with the rehabilitation of injured veterans allowing them to resume a working life. It is likely that Adney's reputation as an effective administrator of training programs in the Canadian Army put him in good position for this continuing employment as a civilian.

Adney's demobilization papers show his son, Glenn, as next of kin, but they also show his separation allowance of three dollars a day went to Minnie Bell. She continued to receive this war-service gratuity for all of 1919. Glenn, now seventeen, graduated from Woodstock High School second in his class in June 1919 and was regularly playing the piano for various events in and around Woodstock. He entered McGill University in the fall as a scholarship student and immediately began playing piano in an orchestra. Glenn also performed with a jazz band he organized while still a student. He was a talented and enterprising young man.

It is uncertain how long Tappan Adney continued working at Ste. Anne de Bellevue Military Hospital. In January 1920 he received a letter from Leroy Pelletier addressed to him at the Royal Military College in Kingston. Pelletier, Adney's cabinmate from the Klondike days, was responding to a Christmas greeting. It may have been the last address he had or Adney may have been working for the college on contract at this time.

In November 1920, Adney received a letter from Harlan I. Smith addressed to him at 153 Sydenham Street, Kingston. Adney had known Smith from the early days of the Explorers Club in New York in 1904, when Smith was an archaeologist associated with the American Museum of Natural History. He was now with the Geological Survey Division of the Department of Mines of the Government of Canada. Adney had written to him about potential employment at the Victoria Memorial Museum in Ottawa. On March 29, 1921, Smith sent him a letter of reference to use in trying to get a position at the museum. At this time, Adney was also corresponding with Edward Sapir, a leading anthropologist and linguistic ethnographer who had become a prominent figure at the Victoria Memorial Museum. Sapir went on to become a professor at Yale.

From all this we learn that Adney had relocated to Kingston and was seeking a position within an institutional setting where his ethnographic research, cultural preservation, and artistic skills could be employed. He later took up residence in Montréal, where the cultural environment provided the opportunities he needed to establish professional contacts and employ his vocational skills.

Chapter Ten

Art and Ethnography: The Montréal Years

In the case of Missinaibie, I did the work I was sent to do, and I think I did it fairly well, too. If McGill, as Mr. Judah assured me, had no money to pay for it, they couldn't deprive me of the satisfaction of doing a first class job, which I have all my life aimed to do, regardless of monetary compensation.
—Tappan Adney

When Tappan Adney was discharged from the Canadian Army at the end of 1918, he apparently had contacts and relationships that enabled him to anticipate working as a self-employed artist. On leaving the army he was immediately employed as vocational supervisor at the Ste. Anne de Bellevue Military Hospital. By 1920 he was corresponding with members of the extended Adney family from a Kingston, Ontario, address. He was doing extensive genealogical research into the history of his family in the same way he previously researched the Sharp family in New Brunswick. Simultaneously with this research into Scottish and British history, he became interested in heraldry and heraldic art. As with anything he researched, he became deeply knowledgeable on the subject and, in this case, highly adept at producing heraldic art.

In the early 1920s the Royal Military College at Kingston added Currie Hall to the Currie Building. This new addition was an assembly hall that memorialized the service of the Canadian Expeditionary Force in World

Adney's business card advertising his heraldic design work (CCHS)

153

War I. Currie Hall was designed for ceremonial occasions and was highly decorated. When Currie Hall officially opened in May 1922, the interior decorations included heraldic shields of all the provinces plus the Yukon Territory that Adney had carved and painted. This work was done in association with Percy Erskine Nobbs, the most prominent heraldic art authority in Canada, who supervised the interior design of the hall.

Adney's letter of November 29, 1922, to Mrs. W.J. Hornaday of Lebanon, Ohio, on genealogical work provides further information about his situation at that time.

> I have been so frightfully busy getting a new start in my profession. I am doing some work not equaled in Canada. Two designs, including a carved panel of arms, are now on exhibition at the Canadian Royal Academy. Have just finished and taken to engraver an armorial bookplate (panel design) and I expect to have much private work to do, but it is slow getting a start. I design wholly in the manner of the best work of the later Plantagenet and early Tudor manner, as about everything in the last 300 years is the stereotyped, ugly, undecorative, unbeautiful "art" of the coach painter and undertaker, but with the revival of Gothic architecture has come a revival of the beautiful heraldic art with which it was so closely associated, which is a revelation to those who have not given it study and who take their idea of heraldry from the steel and copper plate stuff of the past couple of centuries.[1]

Although this report of doing work for which he was paid sounds promising, the comment about "slow getting a start" likely indicates his financial situation was not yet prosperous. In another letter to Mrs. Hornaday on December 21, 1922, he gives his address as "Care of Glenn Adney, 206 Milton St., Montréal." An eleven-page typewritten letter, dated December 30, 1923, from Adney to Mrs. Hornaday, again on family genealogy, is headed with the address "Shagpat Studio, 364 Dorchester St. West, Montréal, Canada."

In his 1941 letter to Diamond Jenness, he writes:

> I learned some other things.... I introduced into practical decorative Heraldry and lived off that doing new and distinctive

Adney's model of an Indigenous canoe-making site, commissioned
for a Canadian Pacific Railroad display, undated (CCHS)

work in Montréal. Then when I went back [to the canoe] it was
indirectly. The return was...due to the encouragement given by
you and Marius [Barbeau] touching the Canoe construction.
I picked up a thread out of the remote past, scale models I
had made (of which one has now a place in the Malecite coll.
American Museum) and I could say I was not ashamed of that
early work. I made realistic group models of canoe building for
the CPR [Canadian Pacific Railroad], turned carved pulpboard
into relief maps, and managed to make a living.... Nothing one
has ever learned to know or do well is lost yet one cannot ever
foresee in what direction it will be employed; opportunity may in
part be created but it mostly depends upon someone observing
you [to] be a living creature and not "dead from the neck up"
and find in you just the man though there might be better ones
to be had.[2]

On June 29, 1925, Adney received an order for "6 panels of arms in
relief with gold & silver leaf: New Zealand, Canada, Australia, England,
Scotland, Ireland." At the top of the order Adney wrote: "C.P.R.—New
Zealand Exp. For Nov. 1, 1925." Later information indicates the display
took place in Wembley, England, but perhaps the Canadian Pacific Railroad
arranged to have the carved national shields displayed in exhibitions at
various places throughout the Commonwealth.

At the same time Adney wrote to Edward Sapir:

In only a few days I expect to start on our job [for] New Zealand exhibition for C.P.R., and there is other C.P.R. exhibition work (at Toronto), and with the T. Eaton work—all coming in rushes, with scarcely warning, makes impossible the setting aside of any time...to getting out to a few of these "last places" of the bark canoes.[3]

Again, Adney mentions the canoe project. It's clear in his letter to Sapir that he has been "getting out" to do research on canoe designs and canoe building, and he needs to find time to continue this work. From the middle of the twenties to the early thirties he returns to the canoe project and works with determination on constructing the models that become the foundation of his legacy. Again, we see here a shift in focus; in this case, a return to the ethnographic research and preservation of Indigenous material culture that captured his attention when he first landed in New Brunswick in 1887 and apprenticed to canoe builder Peter Jo.

In later years, Adney identified the way this shift happened. Diamond Jenness urged him to again take up the model canoe building project. This encouragement by a leading ethnographer of the time confirmed Adney's assessment of the quality and cultural importance of this preservation work. This shift brought him back to the canoe project and motivated him to turn his attention to developing the grand sweep of its ethnographic and geographic reach to the whole of North America. He knew the precision of the work he had previously done was museum quality. He envisioned expanding the canoe project into an ethnographic documentation of all the regions of the continent that would constitute a contribution to the field of ethnography and the preservation of Indigenous material culture without precedent.

He probably realized, as well, that he was one of the few ethnographic scholars with the skills to accomplish this kind of documentation. He also knew that to serve its full potential, the project required a written account, complete with detailed drawings. Building the models and assembling the book was an opportunity to make a unique contribution to the developing field of North American ethnographic scholarship. It was no small matter that he was encouraged by Jenness and other leading figures in the discipline to continue and complete the canoe project.

Although Adney was now motivated to devote more time to the canoe project, he had to continue with work that provided an income. In 1925

Adney's carved oak panel in the
Champlain Dining Room of the
Château Frontenac, Québec
(photo: Luc Antoine Coutuier)

the Montréal Arts Club held an exhibition of his work titled "Sketches and Notes of Canadian Outdoors by E.T. Adney." During this time he designed and carved a group of medieval baronial shields for the Windsor Hotel in Montréal. In 1926, he designed and carved forty heraldic shields commemorating historical figures and families from the province of Quebec for the Champlain Dining Room of the Château Frontenac in Québec. He also carved the marble and oak hearth decor for the fireplace in this same room.

His artwork appears on the cover of a 1926 publication promoting the Nipigon River Bungalow Camp. This commission may have come from having done work for the Canadian Pacific Railroad. The CPR line that ran north of Lake Superior made a stop at this site, and Canadian Pacific promoted it as a destination for vacationers and fishermen. He also entered a contest to design a new Canadian flag sponsored by a Quebec newspaper. From over eighteen hundred entries Adney's design was declared the winner, but the Canadian government did not adopt it.

In 1929 Adney designed the seal of the Royal College of Physicians and Surgeons of Canada. In response to Glenn Adney's 1960 inquiry seeking information about this project, he was told that his father had also designed the stained glass installations in the University of British Columbia Library and carved the provincial crests in the library of the Royal Military College in Kingston, Ontario.

An example of Adney's heraldic art,
Sir William Osler's coat of arms,
undated (CCHS)

The Adney Collection at the Carleton County Historical Society (CCHS) in Woodstock, New Brunswick, contains several large folios of heraldic art, which includes the following description:

> A valuable classified collection of original drawings and photographs from original Heraldic material of the Medieval period [in] England, when Heraldry was a beautiful decorative Art, and before its decadence and utter corruption into a thing of "unmitigated ugliness" through the advent of the little books, "All about Heraldry" for use of designers, coach painters and undertakers, and those of the "new" men who were taught to regard the right to armorials as a mark and evidence of Gentility. I intended for illustrations of a Book on Decorative Heraldry, the project did not go through. —E.T. Adney[4]

The full extent of Adney's heraldic art may yet be identified. In 2011 David and Marlene Henley, publishers of the *Woodstock Bugle*, were having dinner at the Château de Frontenac. In the course of the evening they noticed a plaque identifying Tappan Adney as the artist who had carved the forty baronial shields encircling the Champlain Dining Room. David and Marlene reported their find when they returned to Woodstock. Their discovery created a small sensation among Adney researchers, who had been unaware of this major collection of his work. Additional examples of his heraldic art may await discovery.

By 1927, Adney was so well known as an expert on Indigenous material culture he was contracted to act as a consultant for a major artistic project. The Hudson's Bay Company commissioned two large murals depicting historical themes for installation in the lobby of its corporate headquarters in Winnipeg, Manitoba. Canadian artist Adam Sherriff Scott had been engaged to produce the murals with Tappan Adney to oversee the accuracy with which the appearance of Indigenous people, their canoes, and other artifacts were presented.

The Montréal newspaper *La Presse* published a photograph of one of the murals on August 20, 1927, with a caption in French translated as follows:

> Photograph of a mural painting, being executed, destined for
> the headquarters of the Hudson's Bay Company at Winnipeg.
> This painting, on a single special canvas, the largest that has been
> executed to date in Canada, measures 54 feet long by 10 high. It
> is the work of the Canadian artist-painter Adam Sherriff Scott,
> of Montréal, in collaboration with E.T. Adney, for the types of
> people, the costumes, the canoes, and other accessories. The
> scene is the area around Fort Garry (today Winnipeg), at the
> confluence of the Red and Assiniboine Rivers, in 1859. Indians,
> Metis, woodsmen, canoers, traders, wigwams and costumes, all
> are of the time. The decoration of the canoe, in the foreground,
> is that of the time of the French (1752). Shown are a herd of
> cattle, a steamboat and a sailing ship; in the center, a missionary
> and Governor Ellice.[5]

In 1999, the archivist of the Hudson's Bay Company reported that the murals still existed, but due to building renovations only one remained on display at that time. In 2014, the Hudson's Bay Company donated both murals to the Manitoba Museum.

Although Adney was using his research and artistic skills to provide an income, his central interest during his Montréal years came back to ethnography and the preservation of Indigenous culture. In addition to his personal project of canoe preservation, he was eager to connect

Hudson's Bay murals on display in the elevator lobby of the
Company's Winnipeg headquarters, 1987 (CCHS)

with others working in the field of ethnography and was looking for employment opportunities with institutional settings. Adney carried on regular correspondence with prominent research scholars in the field, but his prime opportunity for finding professional employment lay with Lionel Judah, the curator of the Ethnological Museum at McGill University.

Judah had begun his career in museum work years earlier as a technician cleaning biological specimens in the Medical Museum at McGill. He worked under the supervision of Maude Abbott, a biology professor at McGill and founder of the Medical Museum. Judah's record of published papers is composed of one on the cleaning of biological specimens and two on the size and care of glass jars used to store biological specimens. By 1925, however, he had been promoted within the museum's administration to curator of the ethnographic division.

According to information provided by the Redpath Museum (the Redpath Museum eventually took in the collections of the Ethnological Museum), the relationship between Adney and McGill began when Lionel Judah learned about the model-canoe collection from Adney's landlord, who was about to seize it for non-payment of rent. Judah offered to store the canoes in the Ethnological Museum for safekeeping. Adney paid off his back rent, and as of June 1928, the canoes remained on loan to the Ethnological Museum.

Adney built most of his model canoes between 1925 and the early 1930s. Records from 1930 show ninety models on loan to McGill. Considering the research he was also conducting on canoe design and construction from all regions of the continent, this rate of sustained production was a major achievement. Consider, too, that at the same time he was doing other work to earn an income. Unfortunately, Adney was never able to secure paid employment at the Ethnological Museum. He was recognized and valued as an honorary consultant — essentially a volunteer. The barrier to being a paid consultant, according to Judah, was always the museum's lack of an adequate budget.

As the Great Depression took hold in 1930, the museum's funds were increasingly constricted. However, Lionel Judah apparently found money for a potential research project that had recently come to his notice, and he tapped Adney as the man for the job. Indigenous rock paintings at Lake Missinaibi in northern Ontario had recently been reported. Judah asked Adney to photographically document the site. He offered no compensation for professional services or consideration of time spent on the job, only expenses. Adney agreed, which indicates his commitment to ethnography and his interest in this project. It's also likely he still entertained the hope that, by volunteering his professional services to the museum, paid employment might come his way. Unfortunately, this did not happen, and in fact, this project "for expenses" led to conflict with Judah over reimbursement.

Indigenous rock art has long been of interest to anthropologists, but it wasn't until the 1960s, with the publication of *Indian Rock Paintings of the Great Lakes* by Selwyn Dewdney and Kenneth E. Kidd, that the extent of its occurrence in this region was well-documented. The documentation began thirty years earlier with Adney's work. His pioneering report of this research, illustrated with photographs and drawings, is in the holdings of McGill's Rare Book and Special Collections. The folio is titled *McGill University Expedition to Lake Missinabi* [sic] — *Indian Rock Painting 1930 by Tappan Adney.*

The word *expedition* suggests a convoy of explorers and supplies, but in this case, Adney and two canoemen were the entire team. His sixteen-page report includes a set of drawings of various rock paintings, headed by the note that "These are original notes of Pictographs, from which, with assistance of photographs, drawings were made suitable for reproduction if desired." A series of seventeen drawings follow, and a map of the area is included. The report also presents information on the history and geography of the region. Adney names the two Indigenous men who assisted him: Cephas Medicine-Rattle, a Cree, and Walter Soulier, an Ojibway. He later wrote to his friend and colleague George Frederick Clarke — a dentist, amateur archaeologist, and author — in Woodstock, New Brunswick:

> Two wonderful canoemen, an Ojibway and an even better man, a Cree, from Moose Factory. Never saw such paddling, straight away work mostly, deep water man trained with the big fur trade canoes now extinct. The Ojibway was not much of a paddler except very strong, a great man on the portages.

Adney used a six-by-eight plate camera with an eight-by-ten Goertz "dagor" lens, which he described as

> of great efficiency, seeing how all but one of the groups photographed had to be taken from the water from a moving canoe.... Thus with the camera we obtained a good record of the rocks and situation of the writings, the hand drawings gave a record that might be read. And that was the main object of the expedition[6]

He made the following statement in his report:

> I did the work I was sent to do, and I think I did it fairly well, too. If McGill, as Mr. Judah assured me, had no money to pay for it, they couldn't deprive me of the satisfaction of doing a first-class job which I have all my life aimed to do, regardless of monetary compensation.
>
> No charge made for personal services in the 11–12 days of the trip. Nor for considerable time and work and study in preparation of the report; coloring of photographs; interpretations of inscriptions. The service was gladly and freely rendered as a part of assistance I was giving in various ways to McGill, through Mr. Judah, so as to advance the project of a modern public museum. Service I could render, but money outlay of any magnitude I was hardly in a position to make. —E.T. Adney[7]

Adney expected to be reimbursed for his out-of-pocket expenses. He submitted a summary of his costs in July 1930 but received no response. Nearly eighteen months after the expedition, he sent a four-page letter to Judah detailing the reasons why the expenses of the expedition exceeded the original estimates. Finally, on January 12, 1933, two and a half years after the expedition, McGill University paid Adney the $91.60 he was due. He noted at the bottom of the transmittal letter that this settled the arrangements for the Missinaibi expedition.

A more serious issue arose between Adney and Judah in 1932 with respect to models of a "Malecite hunter's camp" and an otter deadfall trap that Adney constructed at Judah's request. Judah was preparing the museum for an evaluation by Dr. Cyril Fox of the British Museum and wanted these models to enhance the Ethnological Museum's representation of Indigenous culture. In an arrangement that Adney understood as helping defray the costs of building the models, he received a total of $25 in five weekly installments from McGill. Apparently, Judah regarded this payment as having purchased the models, and the dispute erupted. Adney appealed his position in a letter to Sir Arthur Currie, principal of McGill University. On November 10, 1932, Judah wrote to Currie indicating he did not understand how the university was under any further financial obligation to Adney.

In a memo of December 5, 1932, Adney amplified his position:

> All other models of canoes entered [on the books of the museum] after January 1932 are free of any lien, and all other models and other items entered [under] Loan, [are the] property of undersigned. [The model canoes on loan to McGill prior to 1932 were being held as collateral for a loan of $1000 made to Adney by the University.] This includes two items done in 1931, Malecite Hunters Camp, and Otter Deadfall, Malecite, prepared in anticipation of survey by Dr. Cyril Fox, falsely entered in museum books as an accession by gift, respectively of Mrs. Walter Molson and Mrs. C.B. Keenan, parties unknown to the undersigned, who did receive from the Bursar, McGill funds of $25, paid in 5 weekly installments, merely as help, to that extent, in preparing at suggestion of Lionel H. Judah, curator of the ethnological museum, so as to show to Dr. Fox what other lines of Canadian ethnology would be able to be developed, besides the canoes. It was not a sale outright nor a sale in any sense. Undersigned has protested to the Principal, Sir Arthur Currie verbally and in writing asserting undersigned's ownership of said items. Value, not less than $250 to $350. —E.T. Adney[8]

This controversy was referred to Dr. J.C. Simpson, secretary of the Faculty of Medicine, who interviewed both Adney and Judah. He summed up the situation as best he could in a letter of December 28, 1932, to A.P.S. Glassco, secretary of McGill University:

> In view of the contradictory character of the evidence, I find it very difficult to offer any definite opinion as to the responsibility of the University—legal or moral. It seems undoubtedly the fact that the models are worth many times the amount that Adney received. The point at issue seems to be that Adney claims that he would not under any circumstances have been willing to do work of this character at the rate of $5.00 a week, while Mr. Judah claims that, in view of his financial condition at the time, he was glad to do the work for even this small sum. As to which of these

views is the correct one, I feel that you are probably in a better
position to judge than I.[9]

When Adney left Montréal for Upper Woodstock in 1933, the ownership
of the camp and trap models was unresolved. On February 16, 1933, in
an apparent effort to separate Adney from McGill University, Secretary
Glassco wrote a letter asking him to tender his resignation as honorary
consultant to the Ethnological Museum. Adney noted at the bottom of the
letter that this was Lionel Judah's way of trying to counter his ownership
of the hunter's camp group and his demand for reimbursement of ninety
dollars from the Missinaibi expedition.

Ten years later, in February 1943, Adney reopened this issue, sending
a cheque for $25 to the secretary of McGill University, stating that it is to
"clear a certain lien that was placed on a certain model of an Indian camp
that among other things I have been leaving at McGill." The McGill files
indicate the cheque was returned to Adney, who had it certified and sent
back to the McGill bursar, Mr. Bentley, along with a forcefully argued letter.

Somehow, this situation was resolved in Adney's favour despite the
recommendation of T.H. Clark, curator of the Redpath Museum, that
the camp and trap models be considered McGill's property. Adney sent a
letter dated March 27, 1943, listing the items to be returned. He directed
them sent to the New Brunswick Museum, to which he was donating them
in care of his friend and colleague, Dr. J.C. Webster, a request with which
McGill University complied in resolution of the ownership issue.

Dr. Cyril Fox's report, *A Survey of McGill University Museums*, included this
significant assessment and recommendation:

6. The Ethnological Museum
   ...On this floor there is collected the important ethnological
   material removed from the Peter Redpath Museum, together
   with ethnological material from other sources, mainly Canadian
   Indian. There is a very important loan collection of models
   of canoes of the aborigines of North America made by Mr.
   Adney....
   ...The university should take steps to acquire the unique
   collection of canoe models, which shows how the study of
   technique in a particular industry can extend and correct the
   literary evidence bearing on the location, relationships, and

migrations of tribes, and which also shows how the modern
Canadian canoe was evolved under European influence. The
models are all to scale and beautifully wrought. The possession
of this collection would encourage the study of those aspects of
ethnology which McGill University ought to, and in time will,
make its own. Its loss would to the same degree be a set-back to
the development of this research.[10]

Adney must have been particularly pleased with Dr. Fox's report and
recommendation. It confirmed the significance of his ethnographic work for
the future of the Ethnological Museum and his stature as a professional in
the field. Unfortunately, McGill failed to act on Dr. Fox's recommendation.
Despite the warning in his report, which should have carried great weight
with the administration, the university lost the model canoe collection in
1939, the full account of which is detailed in the next chapter. Adney was
undoubtedly pleased as well to have prevailed against Redpath's curator
and to have the hunter's camp and trap models, long in dispute, eventually
brought to the New Brunswick Museum.

The last direct communication with Lionel Judah, while still in Montréal,
may be a short note from Adney on May 14, 1933, in which he wrote:

Dear Mr. Judah:

Mr. Cleveland Morgan gave me to understand that it was his
wish that we two should work harmoniously together for the good
of the Museum movement and the University. I will do my best
in that respect, but when you spoke of something to that effect in
the museum Saturday I did not want to discuss it in presence of a
third party who was with me.

He [Morgan] did not put it in just those words. I told him I
would. He told the Principal that my services to the University
could be such that the University could hardly afford to lose
them. Of course I appreciate that expression of his feeling,
but my ardor for the whole museum movement at McGill has
considerably cooled.

Yours truly,

E. T. Adney[11]

Minnie Bell's activities during the years Adney was in Montréal pursuing his artistic and ethnographic work are not well-documented but can be outlined from references in correspondence, Woodstock newspaper articles, and accounts in her diary.

When Tappan elected to remain in Kingston and the Montréal area after the war, Minnie Bell continued her music school in New Brunswick. These were also the years when she dramatically challenged the political conventions of the time, mounting election campaigns to become a member of Parliament representing the Carleton–Victoria riding of New Brunswick. There are also references in correspondence indicating Minnie Bell was living with Tappan in Montréal at the beginning of this period. At one point she applied for the position of inspector of fruit for Canada and, at another, was making plans to open a music school in Montréal.

Adney made a trip to New Brunswick for canoe research during the summer of 1926 and later wrote a letter to George Frederick Clarke describing his discoveries at Tobique. In a postscript, he wrote: "By the way, everything I did at Woodstock is happily perfectly approved of, and a general realignment and readjustment seems in sight after a 'nightmare' of some years. I appreciated your meeting me at the train and making my start easier."[12]

It seems evident from this reference that Minnie Bell did not meet her husband on his arrival in Woodstock. Does this indicate some degree of estrangement? It appears that Tappan and Minnie Bell may have lived apart for most of ten years, each pursuing their ambitions. However their relationship played out over these years, by the early 1930s Minnie Bell was living in Montréal and being cared for by Adney. Her health was deteriorating, her emotional balance was precarious, and she was losing her vision to Fuchs corneal dystrophy, an inherited eye condition.

Their son Glenn, meanwhile, was sailing through his university studies at McGill, a mathematics major on scholarship and a performing musician. Glenn's training on piano by Minnie Bell had given him the skills of a professional, and he found gigs playing in Montréal hotels. He completed a bachelor of science degree in mathematics in 1923 and returned for graduate studies in music. Glenn was clearly a multi-talented and brilliant student. Given his parentage, this is not surprising.

He differed from his parents, however, in a significant respect. Perhaps it was his talent for mathematics and his experience of his parents' chronic struggle to generate an adequate income as artists that led him to a different vocational decision. He eventually took up a career of solid employment as an actuary with the Metropolitan Life Insurance Company in New York. But he also enjoyed being a performing musician for the rest of his life.

In addition to advancing blindness, Minnie Bell's level of mental and emotional distress was increasing. A general paranoia distorted her relationships. Her distress and disorientation became such that Glenn urged his father to find a place for her in an institutional setting where her care could be professionally managed.

This advice was not without warrant. In the early thirties Tappan and Minnie Bell were living in very meagre circumstances. Tappan still had artistic work, and the canoe project was in full swing, but his wife was now entirely dependent on him and their housekeeper, Mrs. Atherton. Employing a housekeeper who could also act as a personal attendant for Minnie Bell would have added to their living expenses but was likely essential at this time. Still, Adney declined Glenn's advice.

On March 16, 1931, Minnie Bell wrote a letter—dictated to Mrs. Atherton—to a former piano student, Susan True, in which she mentioned meeting Glenn's fiancée: "I'm glad you had such a lovely time down at the Grill and met my future daughter, whom I love very much. Glenn & she are making a love match."[13]

Francis Glenn Adney and Margaret Isabel Robertshaw were married on April 30, 1931, at the American Presbyterian Church in Montréal. Although this must have been a happy occasion for Tappan and Minnie Bell, eight days later Glenn wrote a forceful letter to his father, in which he addressed the difficulty of their relationship:

Sunday
Dear Dad:
　　…Now as to my Mother. You were to take over management of her affairs but hardly a day has passed without you running to me with some decision that has to be made. As long as I can contribute I will but it must be understood once and for all that I am not to be worried about details. I only know too well the task you have with her but as I told you if you wanted to keep her out of an institution you would have to do it. I have absolutely reached the limit of personal worry about her. For the past year I have begged you to give me a rest from the worry attached to her with very little response. Now this is final. I don't want to hear of any of

the details of the establishment. Why should you tell me she needs a small table. Surely you can see that she gets it. If this appeal fails believe me it may be necessary for you to take the court action you suggested to Mrs. McLean to obtain money from me. I am not in your happy position that I can take a vacation but I am going to get some relief or know the reason why. Now remember, I will give money but I don't want you harassing me at the hotel.

Your son, Glenn[14]

From Glenn's description, Tappan appears to be stressed as well, perhaps to the point of having difficulty with routine decisions around the care of his wife. This is a vulnerability we have not previously seen in his conduct. Adney was now sixty-four, well into the stage of life in which the deficits of aging begin to show up in various ways. He had been working under great pressure for over a decade to secure an adequate livelihood and the hoped-for results of financial stability had not been achieved. The stress with which he had been dealing was not just around the care of Minnie Bell but for his own future as well.

Another letter from Glenn two weeks later is somewhat softer in tone.

Dear Dad:

I am enclosing cheques covering the next two weeks' money for my Mother. I will know to-morrow whether I am to stay at the Windsor. If I stay I will give you $20.00 every Tuesday starting June 2nd. That will average the same as paying the rent and $15.00 per week in addition. It will help a great deal if I am not bothered with the details of household operation. If it should turn out that I do not stay at the Windsor it would mean that in all probability my income would be cut in half and in that case we would have to get together on a conference to discuss ways and means.

Love,
Glenn[15]

It must have been difficult for Glenn to provide this support for his mother when he had just married and was in danger of losing his orchestra job at the Windsor Hotel. Adney, while continuing his research on canoes and steadily enhancing the value of the project, was at the same time working hard to find a buyer who understood the ethnographic importance of the model canoes and appreciated the collection's value. Should such a buyer be found, the financial status of the Adney family would take a dramatic, positive turn.

Caring for Minnie Bell was becoming increasingly difficult. Adney recorded verbatim some of their conversations.

Sept. 26, 1931
"A concerted plan to do me up, to get rid of me" (claiming that she was "begrudged" enough food to live on)....Angry because she can't eat everything, can't swallow certain kinds of food— the throat "raw." A conspiracy between Glenn, Mrs. Atherton, and ETA to get rid of her by not rubbing plenty Absorbine— pepsins—witch hazel, brandy...

November 20, 1931
As days pass, here, grows irritable toward all and everything around her. Started morning today. Irritable, phoned Hickey, [Doctor] Hickey coming out in PM. Irritable. Brain races. Thinks of helplessness, blindness handicap to action, everything. Her condition. Growing helplessness. Impairment of faculties, memory of her music, rheumatism, in fingers, touch of bronchitis....

Has been this way, always. Ambition for career, fame, very great. But this blocked by assuming family responsibilities, father, mother, sisters. Intense struggle with herself, what she wanted to do, what has kept her from doing it, although her own volition. Voices this. Very trying for those around.[16]

In February 1932, Peggy, Glenn's wife, wrote to her father-in-law:

Dear Dad,
I read your notes more thoroughly when I arrived home. Now while I don't want to quarrel with you I can't let you say Glenn has abandoned his Mother. You know perfectly well that is not the case. Since he first started working he has supported her and

done everything he could for her and after he lost his job last June
you know that he gave you every cent he earned, which came
from the Union position he held, to keep things going, while we
lived on a few dollars I made and a few Glenn made by getting
"club" jobs.... So I can't see where the "abandonment" comes in
at all....

I hope you will be able to get Mom down to N.B. as you plan.
She will be so much better off and much happier after she gets
down there with the people she knows and is able to do a few
things around the bungalow. However, I'll see you in a couple
of days.

Peggy[17]

A new voice, sympathetic but firm, had joined the Adney family.

By the early 1930s, Tappan Adney had substantially completed the
preservation of Indigenous canoe construction. He had built well over one
hundred models. His research papers comprised the raw material for a
landmark book on the cultural history and construction of bark canoes.
During his last few years in Montréal, he tried various avenues to find
an institutional buyer for his canoe collection at a fair valuation. From
the standpoint of museum quality work and the function of his models
in accurately portraying Indigenous material culture, Adney knew his
collection should be worth a great deal to museum professionals who
understood what they were being offered.

Unfortunately, the administrators of McGill's Ethnological Museum
failed to realize the significance of what they held in storage as collateral
against a $1,000 loan made some years earlier to Adney. In a grievous
failure of professional imagination, they did not properly value
Adney's accomplishment and deprived Canada of what could have
been a centrepiece of its ethnographic heritage. Adney's research and
contribution to Indigenous studies was well recognized and appreciated by
anthropologists of the time — in particular, Edward Sapir and Diamond
Jenness, both leading professionals who corresponded with Adney as a peer.

Adney contacted other institutions he thought might respond positively.
In 1930 he offered the canoe collection to the Henry Ford Museum for

$25,000, but the museum did not respond. The economic collapse of 1929 was still looming large over their fiscal management and investment decisions.

Adney then turned to the Smithsonian Institution in Washington and the Field Museum of Natural History in Chicago. The Smithsonian appreciated the importance of the collection but had no funds available for its acquisition. A narrow-minded administrator at the Field Museum told Adney they were not interested in canoes of any kind. As late as 1936 he contacted the Heye Foundation at the Museum of the American Indian in New York City, but they turned him down as well. He sought financial assistance for the completion of his canoe book but was met with similar responses. In 1933, with no clear means of financial support available, Adney made plans to return to New Brunswick, where he and Minnie Bell at least had the small house he had built years earlier on the Sharp property in Upper Woodstock.

Before making this move, Adney made an unusual approach to the Montréal Association for the Blind, with which he had become familiar due to Minnie Bell's visual impairment. He proposed that if one of the association's patrons, a Mr. Hugh Paton, purchased his model canoe collection for $25,000, Adney would donate $5,000 to the association. He received a letter from the association's president, Philip E. Layton, saying that any approach to Paton would have to be directly from Adney. It would not be appropriate for the board of the association to approach him with this proposal. There is no record of a follow-up.

An additional perspective on Adney's situation and thinking in early 1933 can be gained from a letter he wrote to Cleveland Morgan, a member of the museum committee who was sympathetic to Adney:

> A casual remark of yours...makes me reluctantly realize that
> for some years past and especially during the past year, there
> was a plan laid with almost diabolical skill to assure to me a
> position in the growing scheme [*scheme* means the museum's
> development plan], but equally to have it understood, by
> suggestion, that I was not fitted for occupying a post of much or
> any responsibility. The idea was, and was frequently broached
> to me, so that I know the plan perfectly, was to have me and
> keep me in a subordinate technical position, a model-maker, an
> instructor in preparation of museum specimens (supplementing

the other man's field).… But I did find it necessary in my note to
Mr. Glassco to indicate that such a job, nor even a curatorship
was not what I had been expecting from the museum scheme as
it might develop, if the routine duties involved were to militate
against my completing the large work of mine on the canoe, an
immense work in a new field that is entirely my own.[18]

Two observations emerge from a close reading of this letter. First, it
is fair to say that Adney's analysis of his relationship with the museum
administrators strikes a note of paranoia. However, this does not mean
his assessment is incorrect. Given the objective history of the relationship,
particularly the way his work for the museum was repeatedly exploited, he
is likely correct about the administrators' intention toward him.

Second, the position Adney saw for himself in the development
planning ("scheme") of the museum was not to be offered a curatorship
but to have his whole canoe project — research, construction, and
documentation — taken on board as a central feature of the Indigenous
ethnographic division, which would make Adney a senior researcher in this
field. A position such as this would have given him a salaried role in the
development of the museum and given the museum a creative centre of
development such as Dr. Cyril Fox had foreseen would result if they acted
on his recommendation.

The failure of the McGill museum administrators to realize they were
being offered a body of innovative research casts a shadow across the
whole field of heritage preservation in Canada at this time. The failure to
give Adney a secure position from which he could continue and expand
his ethnographic research foreclosed a significant opportunity. But the
concomitant loss of Adney's canoe collection to Canada is a misfortune
boarding on the tragic. In his letter to Cleveland Morgan, Adney identified
a significant part of the problem. He wrote that in Canada there is a
"manifest tendency to build a wall around every little or big institution."

In addition, it seems fair to observe that at this time museum administrators
and, indeed, Canadian society in general had not yet opened their eyes to the
fact that Canada's living heritage rests on not two but three cultural traditions:
francophone, anglophone, and Indigenous. Indigenous cultures were still
regarded as primarily historical, as a curiosity that was fading away as
assimilation into colonialism eliminated its specific and unique characteristics,
values, and worldview. All this has now changed. Indigenous cultures have

reemerged as nations in their own right within the territory called Canada, which, of course, was their home before the European invasion.

This resurgence of the Indigenous factor across the cultural landscape of Canada is a seismic shift that is only beginning to make its influence fully felt. The colonial heritage of transplanted Europeans in North America faces an increasingly sharp assessment of its moral governance and ecological stewardship.

The ethnographic worldview of museum administrators in the 1920s and 1930s was blinkered by the still-prevailing colonial ideology that consigned Indigenous cultures to historical interest. Adney's ethnological orientation, however, had a vital connection to contemporary Indigenous life. Wherever he travelled, he made it a point to meet the Indigenous people of the region, such as the six weeks he took from his Klondike Gold Rush reporting to go hunting with the Tr'ondëk Hwëch'in band in the Yukon.

None of this frontline engagement with contemporary Indigenous life and material culture appears to have been a priority interest to the administrators of the Ethnological Museum at McGill or, as it turned out, the gatekeepers of North American museums generally. Adney was an outlier. His canoe project seems to have been seen as a historical curiosity without relevance to the preservation of a living tradition, his models regarded more like toys than museum-quality recreations. Administrators could not foresee the relevance of Adney's research and documentation to the preservation of Indigenous material culture and its resurgence in the hands of future canoe builders. The consequence of this misjudgment was the loss of Adney's collection to a new privately funded American museum, and his companion canoe book eventually found its way to the premier American publisher of ethnographic and cultural heritage literature.

Adney followed his letter to Morgan with a memo to the General Museums Committee dated February 19, 1933, in which he detailed at length the duties and obligations of an honorary consultant. He also noted that Lionel Judah was no longer the curator at the Ethnological Museum. At this same time, and despite his past disputes with Judah, he received a commission from the museum to catalogue its Molson basket collection. This recognition of his expertise in the field of Indigenous material culture must have given him a degree of satisfaction.

By May 1933, Adney was preparing to leave Montréal for Upper

Woodstock. He gave up his telephone and sent some recently made canoe models to the Château Ramezay for storage. In July, he prepared a list of his personal property at places in Montréal in the event Glenn needed it. The places mentioned are the McCord Museum, the Ethnological Museum, the Château Ramezay, the Canadian Handicrafts Guild (Henry Birks of the Heraldry Department), Adam Sherriff Scott at St. Famille Street, the CPR exhibits warehouse on St. Antoine Street, and the Pathological Laboratory at McGill.

When Tappan and Minnie Bell arrived in Woodstock, New Brunswick, by train, he had to help her with every step; she was now blind and in poor health. They took up residence in their small house in Upper Woodstock. It stood on a wooded knoll adjacent to where the large three-storey Sharp house, along with barns and outbuildings, once stood. The bungalow, as he called it, had suffered years of neglect and was in need of repair. It had neither plumbing nor electricity. The house was located a considerable distance from the road. Keeping a path open in the winter was a constant task. Despite these conditions, Adney was more than pleased to be home.

In September 1933, Lionel Judah wrote to verify Adney's new address and said there were some things he would like to write to him about. Apparently, a collegial friendship was still intact from their years of association, despite their occasional conflicts. In reply, Adney wrote the following about his homecoming:

> It is an indescribable relief which I did not realize until I arrived here from the strain of the past couple of years. It is a wonderful place, a mingling of old orchard trees, a now great timber of spruce and a bungalow which needs an infinite number of repairs.[19]

Adney had returned to the place where Lanes Creek enters the Wəlastəkw, the place where he first met Peter Jo building a birchbark canoe, the place where after a short walk he could again enter the forest with its ever-renewing plant life and its various forms of wildlife carrying on the never-ending story of their species' survival. This is where he had made the transition from New York artist and Central Park ornithologist to a denizen of the deep woods and a pioneering ethnographer of Indigenous culture. No wonder he felt a great relief. He had come back to the place that was the springboard for his primary vocation and where, once again, he would be in direct contact with his friends among the Wəlastəkokewiyik.

Although he had sole responsibility for Minnie Bell's care plus housekeeping duties, he continued to work on the canoe book and construct additional canoe models. He returned to his research and analysis of Wəlastəkwey, the language of his Wəlastəkwi friends. He was nearing the culmination of his canoe building project, and the preservation of his collection was yet to come. His immersion in language study and a renewed association with the Wəlastəkwey foreshadowed the final contribution Adney would make to the preservation of Indigenous culture.

Chapter Eleven

A Legacy of Canoes

When sky shall be no longer blue and fair, and brooks shall cease to sing
the song of summer, and lordly moose no longer tear the lily from its bed of
mud, and lusty trout no longer flirt and jump for very love of living; when
smiling birch and sombre spruce, and all nature, shall break their spell and
cease to beckon, then, but not till then, shall I no longer love the birch canoe.
—Tappan Adney

Lewis Henry Morgan published *The League of the Iroquois* in 1851. Rarely does a new field of scientific research suddenly appear with such scope and depth as North American anthropology did with the publication of Morgan's book. The Iroquois had fascinated him since his school years in upstate New York. His education and career took him into law and business, but his passion was the study of how human societies are organized and function. Tappan Adney was thirteen when Morgan published his last study, *Houses and House-life of the American Aborigines* (1881). Considering the prominence of Morgan's books in intellectual circles, Adney may have been acquainted with them before he encountered the Wəlastəkokewiyik in New Brunswick; if not, when he began to research the literature on Indigenous cultures of North America he would have certainly discovered Morgan's work.

In subsequent decades, the study of human societies distinguished itself from the study of general history. Anthropology, along with ethnography, rapidly advanced into a fully developed academic and research discipline. Adney came of age along with the first generation of anthropologists and ethnographers after Morgan. He corresponded with prominent figures in the field on research questions and themes of mutual interest. His correspondents included Edward Sapir, a leading scholar of linguistics, and Diamond Jenness, a pioneer of both Canadian ethnography and applied anthropology. He also corresponded with Marius Barbeau, Canada's premier folklore anthropologist and ethnomusicologist; Frank

Speck, pioneer scholar of Eastern Woodland Indigenous cultures; and Clark Wissler at the American Museum of Natural History.

Adney was well aware of the growing community of anthropologists doing ethnographic work during this time. Most prominent were Franz Boas at Columbia University, who was making a study of the Kwakiutl People of British Columbia; Paul Radin, whose study of the Winnebago culture was recognized as an extraordinary achievement; and Frank Hamilton Cushing at the Smithsonian, who innovated the participant-observer method with his study of the Zuni way of life.

Like Adney, Cushing was an outlier in the field of ethnography. He had collected Indigenous artifacts since childhood in upstate New York. He published his first scientific paper at age seventeen. Cushing was a student at Cornell University for only a brief time when, at nineteen, he curated an ethnographic exhibition that caught the Smithsonian Institution's attention. He was recruited by the Smithsonian and appointed curator of the ethnological department of the National Museum in Washington. The Smithsonian seems to have been open to recruiting and promoting people on the strength of their experience rather than their academic credentials. They did the same thing with Howard Chapelle, who was appointed to the head the Smithsonian's transportation department and later became central to securing the publication of Adney's canoe book.

Adney's canoe project began in the summer of 1888 when he apprenticed to Peter Jo. He already knew Jo from having joined him, along with Humboldt Sharp, on a caribou hunt the previous winter. Since landing in the Wəlastəkw region of New Brunswick in the summer of 1887, he had been thoroughly inducted into the woodland, river, and lake environments and the adventures of the outdoor life. He would have been familiar with the use of birchbark canoes, but to see one built from materials harvested directly from the forest offered a new level of insight into the Indigenous way of life and its skilled adaptation to the resources of the land.

Adney was a dedicated student of natural history, eager to learn from hands-on experience in whatever environment he encountered. The knowledge, techniques, and skills employed in building a birchbark canoe caught his attention and sparked his imagination. As an artist, the elegant simplicity of the canoe's design and the graceful beauty of the finished product struck a chord with him. In addition, he was intrigued by the way

Adney's drawing *Peter Joe at Work*, an illustration for his article "How an Indian Birch-Bark Canoe is Made," *Harper's Young People*, July 29, 1890 (CCHS)

this unique boat was created from materials gathered from the forest using only minimal tools.

In the summer of 1888, Peter Jo took him into the woods to gather canoe building materials. Working along side his mentor, Adney built a full-size canoe and began building his one-fifth-scale models; this, he later explained, was the scale that allowed him to use traditional materials and precisely demonstrate traditional construction techniques.[1] He also began documenting the canoe building process with drawings and a written account he first published in a supplement to *Harper's Young People: An Illustrated Weekly* in 1890, and again, in an expanded version, in *Outing* in 1900. This was the first-time detailed information on the construction of the birchbark canoe was recorded, illustrated, and published.

When Tappan Adney entered the world of Peter Jo, he likely had a sense of cultural diversity within the context of natural history. New York City, where he had been living, was a crossroad of cultural influences and a centre for the study of natural history. With the encouragement of his father, he had been a student of natural history since childhood. His studies at the Art Students League and exposure to its aesthetic and intellectual milieu would have advanced his cultural awareness. He was intellectually prepared to understand and appreciate the cultural significance of the Indigenous way of life.

> It seemed to me then as it has ever since from contact with the
> Indian in his primitive life untouched by the white man's culture,
> that the Indian had attained that which the Japanese possessed,
> not so much a low standard of living…as a high standard of
> simplicity, which under the same conditions the white man has
> not essentially improved upon.[2]

This unusual comparison signals that Adney was thinking like an anthropologist, a perspective that served him well as he became increasingly involved with Wəlastəkwey language and culture.[3]

We have seen how Adney came to conceive of the canoe project during his years in Montréal and how he worked to advance the collection toward completion. Many distinct canoe designs from different cultural regions were no longer being built; the working knowledge and craftsmanship were on the verge of extinction. He systematically set out to research this heritage of Indigenous canoes and build models that would preserve each variation of design and construction.

> The object has been to build the models in such accurate
> proportions that they shall take the place of large specimens;
> be displayed and compared to far better advantage in the limited
> space of a museum; and so that a large canoe can be accurately
> constructed, or drawn, from the model alone.[4]

Adney began concentrating on his model collection and the compilation of a companion book early in 1925. He had previously made perhaps fewer than a dozen models from intermittent research but with no underlying plan. With the encouragement of professional colleagues, he now planned to produce a collection of model canoes presenting the variations in design from across the continent plus a monograph illustrated with detailed drawings. The encouragement came from Edward Sapir, then chief of anthropology at the National Museum of Canada (now the Canadian Museum of Histroy) in Ottawa; Marius Barbeau, who, with Sapir, was a leading figure in the development of anthropology in Canada; and Diamond Jenness, Sapir's successor after Sapir left the museum in 1925 to accept a teaching position at Yale University.

Adney conceived of the models and the book as complementary. Each would support the other in the preservation of this primary feature of Indigenous material culture. He saw a double opportunity: to establish himself in the rapidly developing field of North American Indigenous ethnology and, by selling his model collection to a museum, free himself from the struggle to obtain adequate income, which was a constant source of stress. He worked on his models in secret, wanting to keep the field of canoe studies to himself. He told only his Woodstock friend George Frederick Clarke what he was doing:

> I am leaving the institutional people severely alone. I don't mean
> to let them have an inkling of what I intend to do...they will
> be lukewarm at best, cold to a certainty and hostile privately.
> I intend to play very foxy...until none of them can muss the
> subject. The fact is, I myself know more than any one specialist
> that I know of.... The technical knowledge I acquired when
> working beside Peter Jo at Upper Woodstock is more than I find
> any [other] writer...possesses, and is the key to the whole subject.[5]

Adney and Clarke maintained a lively correspondence between 1925 and 1933, including instructions from Adney on how, when, and where to obtain the materials for continuing his canoe project. Clarke relied on Noël Polchies and Nicholas Sacobie, his Wəlastəkwi friends, to collect the materials, which he then shipped to Adney in Montréal.

Noël Polchies was the chief of the Wəlastəkwey First Nation at Woodstock. He and Clarke were close friends for many years. He was the grandfather of Peter Paul, who later became an important colleague of Adney in his language studies. Nicholas Sacobie, second chief of the Woodstock First Nation, took over gathering the material for Adney when Polchies died in 1927.

Adney set to work with amazing speed and determination. By 1930, the collection numbered ninety models—an astonishing output.[6] Subtracting the ten or so models built before 1925, he created approximately eighty models in five years, an average of one every three weeks.

Adney's research was comprehensive and exhaustive. He was so meticulous about accuracy and detail he sometimes destroyed unsatisfactory models rather than leave their "inaccuracies of treatment" as misleading specimens. For example, in his research on the distinctive humped-gunwale

Model canoes built by Adney
displayed in the dooryard of his Upper
Woodstock bungalow in the late 1930s
(PANB 1937 P93\CA\2)

canoes of the extinct Beothuk People of Newfoundland, experimental
models proved useful in showing ways they could *not* be built. Bathtub tests
revealed that the sharply V-shaped hulls of Beothuk canoes would have
required rock ballast to remain upright in the water.

During this time Adney also continued his canoe research. He issued a
steady stream of inquiries looking for old canoes and canoe builders. He
made field trips to investigate promising leads. He kept up a voluminous
correspondence with Sapir, Jenness, and Clarke. He continued his unpaid
consultant's job with McGill University's Ethnological Museum. And all the
while he was doing freelance artwork, including heraldic art. Adney later
estimated he spent an equivalent of more than seven years of continuous
work, seven to eight hours daily, on field trips, research, gathering and
preparing materials, and constructing the models. He valued the collection
at $30,000 in 1930, which would be approximately $505,000 today.

Although the majority of Adney's canoes were built during his Montréal
years, he continued to create models when he returned to Upper Woodstock
in 1933. And there was still the matter of organizing his research and
assembling the illustrated book that would provide cultural information
about the canoes and the knowledge of how they were built.

When Adney settled into his bungalow in the woods overlooking the
Wəlastəkw, the legacy of model canoes he had created must have brought
him a sense of satisfaction. The collection, however, was in storage in

Montréal. He had been unable to find a museum that was able or willing to purchase it. His financial situation was marginal, and he had sole care of Minnie Bell. Before he left Montréal, Adney wrote to Lionel Judah indicating his interest in museum work had abated. Perhaps he realized that settling into his last years as an independent scholar was the way of life for which he was best suited.

The Ethnological Museum ceased to exist in the early 1930s. Its global ethnology collections were transferred to McGill's Redpath Museum, and its collections representing Canadian history, including that of Indigenous people, went to the McCord Museum, also at McGill. This is where Adney's model canoes were, in storage, when a husband-and-wife research team from The Mariners' Museum in Newport News, Virginia, discovered them in 1938.

Fred and Nola Hill were on a field trip when they visited the McCord Museum and saw Adney's canoes, covered in dust, carelessly piled on top of each other in a storage room. They had the professional knowledge and imagination to immediately appreciate the historical and cultural value of what they had found. The Hills were impressed with the quality and variety of the models and inquired about the builder. They were told that Tappan Adney, a former consultant to the Ethnological Museum, had made the models, and they were in McGill's possession as collateral for a $1,000 personal loan the museum had made to Adney years earlier.

As field representatives of The Mariners' Museum, the Hills' mission was to find and purchase artifacts of maritime history to expand the holdings of this newly established institution. When they heard how Adney's model canoes came to be stored at McGill, they saw an opportunity. They went in search of the man who had created this singular record of North American Indigenous watercraft. "We went after him with all the tenacity of a ferret seeking food in a hidden retreat. Telephone books gave no clues. Old issues in the library, however, gave his name and address," Nola Hill later recounted. "We felt like Scotland Yard officers must feel when they approach their object of search."

They eventually found Adney in his bungalow in Upper Woodstock surrounded by his research papers, newly built canoe models, and the materials for constructing still more. Adney had been living alone since his wife, Minnie Bell, died in 1937.

...we found Mr. Adney living alone among...handmade
furniture, some of his beautifully constructed canoe models,
and the few small things he was able to save from his Montréal
creditors. But he had many little friends. He lived close to
Nature...dozens of birds and squirrels visited him daily and
ate from his protective hands. One small room was literally
packed with birch bark stock for models, willow and ash cuttings
seasoned for use, and spruce roots for sewing the seams.[7]

Fred Hill reported their find to Homer Ferguson, the president of The
Mariners' Museum, who travelled to Montréal to see the models and
was equally impressed. The Hills began a conversation with Adney, his
son Glenn, and officials at the McCord Museum about acquiring the
collection for The Mariners' Museum. This keen interest was a welcome
contrast to the rejections Adney had received from the administrators of
other museums. Having a permanent institutional home and the care of
professional curators for his canoes was an appealing prospect. He wrote
to Diamond Jenness in January 1939:

It is becoming all but certain that my whole collections of
model canoes will go to an American museum, after I vainly
sought to place them with the Canadian National at almost
any terms.... The museum is the new Mariners' Museum....
Their field representative who came to see me over a year ago, is
coming in the spring to discuss details.[8]

At this point, there must have been a glimmer of recognition at the
McCord Museum that the canoe models were not just a curiosity of
craftsmanship. Administrators tried to block the sale of the collection. The
museum had loaned Adney $1,000 and had taken the canoes as security.
The term of the loan had expired and it had not been repaid, so the
museum claimed ownership of the collection. Legal counsel assured Adney
no court would uphold this claim, and a deal was made with the Hills for
the sale of the canoes at the McCord Museum and the models currently
at his bungalow in Upper Woodstock. The arrangement included paying
off Adney's outstanding loan from McGill with interest, a total of $1,500,

and a personal loan from Glenn of $1,000. McGill backed off its claim and agreed to the deal.

It was an easy decision for Adney. As part of the arrangement, The Mariners' Museum offered Adney a $100 monthly stipend while he finished the canoe book, which it would publish and pay Adney royalties on each copy sold. After protracted correspondence, all agreements and arrangements were settled by February 1940. The Mariners' Museum took possession of the model canoes, transported them to Virginia, and began sending Adney monthly cheques.

The Hills were sensitive to the circumstances in which they acquired Adney's canoes. Nola Hill remarked: "I was not without misgivings that the Museum had paid off the loan of $1000 and took a very fine collection from the country where it rightfully belonged."[9] When Adney wrote to Diamond Jenness, who was at the National Museum of Canada, about the sale and transfer of his canoes, Jenness replied:

> It's a shame your model canoes cannot stay in Canada. I would give a good deal to be allowed to purchase them for our museum here, but we operate on such a shoestring.... Someday, when it is perhaps too late, the Canadian people will wake up and decide they want a real museum in the capital city.[10]

With the monthly stipend from The Mariners' Museum, Adney's financial situation became marginally stable. He lived alone in a frugal manner. He was seventy-two and received a Canadian old-age pension of $20 a month. He may also have had a small pension from his military service.

But Fred and Nola Hill took extra steps to support Adney so he could finish his work on the canoe book. They kept in personal touch and regularly visited him. Nola described their relationship:

> ...we made annual and sometimes semi-annual visits...checking on the progress of his book. We stocked his sometimes depleted larder with canned goods for the long winters, and supplied a [new] typewriter.... Electricity was installed in his humble abode, the roof was repaired, the building tightened and banked around the foundations against the ravages of the freezing winds. We took him to the local stores and supplied him with

heavy underwear, warm jackets and clothing, although from
the hardiness of outdoor life, he seemed as rugged as an old
pine knot. He was an independent person and would not accept
assistance from personal sources, even from his own son. But this
[the arrangement with the museum] was business.[11]

Nola Hill recalled Adney's first visit to the The Mariners' Museum in
November 1940. The Hills met him at Grand Central Station in New York.

A man over six feet tall, erect and military in stature…he stepped
from the train wearing a coonskin cap…complete with a long,
straggly tail dangling about his neck…. The front of his well-
ventilated overcoat…featured the markings of some…varieties of
soups, and was buttoned out of line. Where a button or two were
missing, shiny nails served the purpose. Overshoes, which had
not been fastened for years, flapped noisily on the station floor.
His happy and excited mood was echoed in his deep voice….
It seemed as if thousands of eyes were watching him when
we accompanied him to the car. He enjoyed his audience….
The first thing to do in Virginia was to outfit him in suitable
garb of the day, which he greatly appreciated. The transition
was amazing.[12]

Adney knew, of course, he would arrive at Grand Central Station in New
York City, a place with which he was thoroughly familiar but had not visited
for many years. His "happy and excited mood" was no doubt in response to
returning to where his artistic and scholarly careers had their beginnings, but
also because he was on the way to see his canoe collection in its new home.
From the amusing way he was dressed, he seems to have been playing to
the image of the wild man from the north woods. The old coat may have
been what he had for winter weather, but the coonskin cap was certainly
a backwoods affectation, *à la* the American folk hero Davy Crockett, and
deliberately calculated to catch attention. His grateful acceptance of later
being outfitted in "suitable garb" for his visit to The Mariners' Museum
confirms the point. When a *Time* magazine reporter took photographs of
Adney at his writing desk in his bungalow for an article on him in 1944,
Adney was dressed in a white shirt, plaid necktie, and sport coat. He had a
sense of dressing for the occasion.

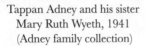

Tappan Adney and his sister
Mary Ruth Wyeth, 1941
(Adney family collection)

In July 1941, Adney wrote to Fred Hill about his progress on the canoe book, including details about the type of paper he was using for the background in making photographs of model canoe paddles. He ended the letter with a recitation of his recent activities:

> I stopped off Washington overnight (lucky got a room at the Bellevue), saw Smithsonian people and Congr. Library, and took night train for NY; called Glenn on the phone, then went over Sunday to see sister at Windsor, CT. Returned to NY, saw Clark Wissler at the Amer. Mus., took night train for Boston and East, turning off at Bangor for Passamaquoddy. The Indian Governor was off trapping muskrats and I waited there till he returned on Friday.[13]

In this same letter, he explained how he worked. Either he did something immediately, or else he put it out of his mind entirely. This meant he couldn't provide progress reports that required thinking about what he was going to do next. This way of working was frustrating for Hill and Ferguson, who expected he would finish one portion of the manuscript, submit it, and then go on to the next. Adney's position was that because he would be continually making revisions, he had to finish the entire manuscript before submitting anything. Anyone who has written a book can understand that his method of composition is the way writers typically work. Hill and Ferguson, who were eager to get the book published, didn't fully appreciate why this method was important.

After visiting Adney in September 1941, Hill reported that considerable work had been done:

Some fourteen sheets of models of canoe paddles have been
mounted with an average of six to eight paddles each, numbered,
and the data sheets compiled. About fifteen various models
showing bow interior construction, form and tying, with their
written material have also been done. The data sheets form part
of his book notations. Progress has also been made on his book.
Mr. Adney has apparently worked quite steadily since his return
in early April.[14]

The agreement between The Mariners' Museum and Adney was not
formalized with a written contract. It existed only as an oral agreement,
which came to be interpreted differently by each party. Differences of
understanding surfaced almost immediately. The museum saw the
monthly cheques as advance payment on the book. Adney saw them as
installment payments on the purchase of his models, since he considered
the loan-redemption payment to be a small fraction of their true value.
He wrote to Fred Hill saying the monthly cheques had nothing to do with
the book, since that was his alone and he had made no promises about a
completion date.

This led to frustration on both sides. Adney had wide-ranging interests
and numerous projects going simultaneously. As he explained in a letter
to Fred Hill, he rested his mind by periodically switching focus from one
project to another. Now, at his advanced age, he had a variety of projects
that commanded his interest and called on the employment of his research
skills. In particular, the language of his Wəlastəkwi friends was now a
renewed focus of study. And the issue of Indigenous rights was soon to
take centre stage.

In the past, when he had a project deadline, he would work with
maniacal concentration for weeks or even months, with little or no rest.
Assembling the nearly five-hundred-page *The Klondike Stampede* book in less
than a year is an example of his ability in this regard. But that approach
didn't work for the canoe book. It was simply too large a task. After eight
years of starts and stops, he had finished only chapter 1, with other chapters
in various stages of completion. Although he had made excellent sketches
for his own reference, detailed drawings for full-scale construction were
yet to be done.

Finally, in September 1947, after learning he had not worked on the
manuscript for nearly a year, the museum suspended monthly payments.

Adney explained he had been working full time to help his Wəlastəkwi friends with a legal battle involving treaty rights. In a letter to Fred Hill he explained: "The cessation [of payments] hasn't in the least hurried me. I can't explain it. It is just so. That has always been my way."[15] He was seventy-nine years old.

Although the relationship with The Mariners' Museum had its bones of contention, Adney was grateful for its recognition of his work and continued backing. And the museum was long-suffering in its support for Adney. Fred and Nola Hill placed a high value on the canoe collection and were determined to publish his canoe book to complete and anchor the full scope of his ethnographic project.

But there was another factor that likely played into their relationship with Adney. Nola was born in Halifax, Nova Scotia, and Fred was from Saint John, New Brunswick. Perhaps this heritage predisposed them to recognize the value of this unique cultural project that had blossomed from their home region. After their careers with The Mariners' Museum, of which Fred eventually became the director, they retired to Great Village, Nova Scotia.

The Mariners' Museum monthly stipend may seem meagre, but in 2024 valuation it would be $1,800 per month, $24,000 per year. During the nearly eight years they made payments to Adney, the total came to $10,000, which would be $200,900 in current dollars. In addition, the museum funded travel expenses for Adney's visits to the museum, paid for repairs and improvements to his house, and provided him with food and clothing. All this was a considerable investment, and if it did not produce the book in the way the Hills and Ferguson expected, it did help support Adney during the time he helped launch what has become one of the most significant legal battles in Canadian history.

He knew most of his model canoes were now secured in a museum that fully appreciated them and where they would be professionally curated. His concern for the Indigenous rights and legal status of the "St. John River Indians" took precedence over completing the canoe book. His lifelong attraction to the challenge of new research now had the prospect of directly benefitting the Wəlastəkokewiyik. Perhaps he expected his canoe book manuscript would find its way into the hands of those who would recognize its significance and prepare it for publication. If so, he was correct.

When Adney died in 1950, The Mariners' Museum had a substantial investment in the model canoes and the unfinished book. The models

Howard Chapelle with an
Adney model canoe, undated
(James W. Wheaton collection)

had become part of the museum's permanent collection, but their value as cultural artifacts could only be fully appreciated in the context of the background information and Indigenous knowledge documented in Adney's manuscript. After his father's death, Glenn made sure the manuscript and all papers and notes associated with the canoe project were deposited with The Mariners' Museum.

After Adney died, Fred Hill, with the manuscript in hand, contacted Howard I. Chapelle in 1951 and enlisted him in the task of completing and preparing Adney's canoe book for publication. Chapelle was a well-known naval architect and boat builder who had already written and published five highly regarded books on sailing ships and wooden boats. His career began in 1919, when, at the age of eighteen, he became an apprentice designer in the ship-building business on the coast of Maine. He eventually established his own boat-building business. He later served as the head of the New England section of the Historic American Merchant Marine Survey. During the Second World War, he served as an officer in the boat-building program of the US Army Transportation Corps. In 1950 he went to England on a Guggenheim fellowship to research colonial ship design. In 1951 he published *American Small Sailing Craft*, a book that has become a classic.

It's unlikely a better match could have been found. Chapelle had done research on the skin boats of the Inuit and written a chapter on them for the proposed *Encyclopedia Arctica*. Like Adney, Chapelle had no academic education beyond high school. And, again like Adney, he had become a master craftsman and a foremost expert on a body of knowledge by learning through direct experience.

The way this trajectory of connections lines up — Tappan Adney, Fred and Nola Hill, Howard Chapelle — is a stroke of amazing good fortune. Without the unique abilities and sensibilities of these four it's quite possible the birchbark canoe might have gone extinct — passed into oblivion with only a few museum specimens remaining as testimony to a high point in the evolutionary adaptation of human culture to Earth's natural environments.

In addition to sorting through Adney's papers to complete the manuscript, Fred Hill asked Chapelle to prepare detailed scale drawings that illustrated the construction of full-size canoes. Chapelle offered to do the job for the current equivalent $49,800 for the book and $8,300 for research expenses. Chapelle also stipulated that his name be added as the book's co-author. He estimated the task would take up to eighteen months. It would include making thirty detailed drawings, editing Adney's completed work, organizing and completing unfinished chapters, and doing the research and writing needed to fill in the gaps that remained.

Fred Hill wrote to the museum board that although Chapelle's fee seemed high, he could be relied upon to properly handle the Adney book. Hill recommended acceptance of Chapelle's terms, and the board approved. The fact that the museum was well-funded enabled the board to readily approve projects of high value. Archer Huntington, who had established The Mariners' Museum in 1930, was heir to his father's vast fortune from the coal and railroad business. A five-hundred-acre park in Newport News, Virginia, near the James River, was first created as a setting for the museum.

Chapelle found some of Adney's papers to be completed chapter manuscripts and others in a chaotic state. After struggling with this material for many months, he declared in a letter to Hill that he was now an expert on Adney's way of thinking. One of Chapelle's major tasks was to convert Adney's working sketches and measurements into detailed scale drawings accurate enough to serve as blueprints for full-size canoes. When he found gaps in documentation, Chapelle turned to the models for measurements and proportions, just as Adney had intended would be possible. His construction of the model canoes was so precise they served as three-dimensional blueprints. Chapelle finished his work in June 1954, more than two years after he began. The completed manuscript, which included 156 illustrations and 53 detailed scale drawings, was turned over to The Mariners' Museum for publication.

While Chapelle was working on the book, Hill was busy trying to secure a publisher. His goal was to find a commercial or university press to print the book at no cost to the museum, with publication expenses to be reimbursed from sales of the book. Hill received nothing but rejection from every publisher he approached. They all said the book would have high production costs and a limited market that would not generate enough sales revenue to cover costs.

At this point, even the board of the museum was reluctant to put more money into a book that might never pay for itself. In 1956 the decision was made to put publication on hold. The manuscript, drawings, photos, and illustrations were placed in storage to wait for a time when changed circumstances would favour publication. Once again, Adney's life's work lay hidden away.

Re-enter Howard Chapelle. In 1957 he was appointed curator of the Division of Transportation at the Smithsonian's National Museum of American History. In this position he oversaw an annual budget for publications, and he asked if the Smithsonian could publish the Adney-Chapelle manuscript. The board happily agreed on condition that the Smithsonian would not incur additional editorial costs.

In January 1958, the Smithsonian Institution formally accepted the manuscript for publication, but it became mired in the bureaucratic processes of the Government Printing Office, which led to a series of delays in the printing schedule. Meanwhile, Chapelle was busy with other projects. He had prepared a chapter-length manuscript on Inuit skin boats, including scale drawings, to be included in the proposed twenty-volume *Encyclopedia Arctica*. In April 1960 he was told the encyclopedia project had been cancelled; his skin boats manuscript would not be published. His first impulse was to have the manuscript published by the Smithsonian as a booklet. But his experience with printing delays on Adney's canoe book gave him second thoughts. He decided, with agreement from The Mariners' Museum board, to add his chapter on skin boats to the Adney book, which already had a publication schedule.

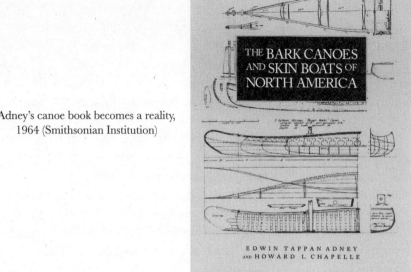

Adney's canoe book becomes a reality, 1964 (Smithsonian Institution)

This decision led to further delays for additional editing and layout work. Eventually, the canoe book was scheduled for printing sometime in the winter of 1962–63. But in July 1963, after more delays, Chapelle wrote to Fred Hill that the canoe book was now scheduled for December 1963. He added with characteristic understatement, "We have great difficulty with our publications here—inadequate staff and a very poor system of scheduling."[16]

Nearly a year later, Adney's book had still not been printed, but Chapelle remained optimistic. He again wrote to Hill, saying, "The canoe book is about ready to go to press—the final proofs passed through my hands this morning. I will be relieved to see it published. It has been an extraordinarily slow job."[17]

Finally, in late September 1964, *The Bark Canoes and Skin Boats of North America* rolled off the press at the US Government Printing Office. It was fourteen years since Adney's death, ten years since Chapelle had completed his work, and six years since it had been submitted to the Smithsonian for publication. Chapelle received a letter from The Mariners' Museum acknowledging the first shipment of the newly printed book had arrived. Harold Sniffen, assistant director, wrote: "There is rejoicing here that this work, started by Fred Hill and into which we have poured much time and investment, has finally come to fruition."[18]

The list price for the first hardcover edition was $3.25. Copies can be purchased today from rare and used book dealers for $50 to $100, depending on condition. As with most scholarly books, the initial print run was expected to recoup its printing costs over many years. By the early 1980s, continuing demand had depleted warehouse inventory. The book was reprinted in 1983. In 1993, the book was on the press again, this time in a paperback edition. The Smithsonian has kept it in print ever since.

In the nearly six decades since publication, *The Bark Canoes and Skin Boats of North America* has become the essential book for anyone interested in the cultural history of bark canoes and their construction. Its publication sparked a renaissance for Indigenous and non-Indigenous canoe builders that continues to the present. Its documentation of construction details saved numerous regional styles from extinction. And it has sparked interest in bark canoes among contemporary canoeists who knew little or nothing about them. The book is an enduring monument to Adney and to the bark canoes of North America he loved so much, and also to Fred and Nola Hill, who had the foresight to understand the full ethnographic significance and cultural value of Adney's canoe project, and Howard Chappelle, who had the technical knowledge and editing expertise to assemble Adney's manuscript into a book that has achieved classic status in ethnographic literature and serves as a canoe builder's bible.

Chapter Twelve

Maliseet (Wəlastəkwey) Linguistics and the Preservation of Culture*

I have no board of trustees hanging over me. I therefore say, to hell with pedantries. There is very little that is worthwhile that cannot be expressed in language that the non-technical student can understand. —Tappan Adney

Tappan Adney's formal education during the 1880s included Greek, Latin, and French. He apparently had an extraordinary talent for languages and rose to the challenge when he first heard Maliseet spoken. He saw it as a living, working language as he watched and listened to Peter Jo and others at his family's Upper Woodstock camp speaking a language that had passed generation to generation from ancient times.

When Adney was making the now famous sketches of Peter Jo building a birchbark canoe, the number of bird species around his camp also captivated him. After recording the names of all the parts of a canoe, he began recording the Maliseet words for the birds and animals around the camp. In the next few years, he compiled lists of the names of many birds, animals, fish, and plants and added their Indigenous meanings. This was the beginning of a lifelong interest in learning Maliseet, a language not yet thoroughly studied or well known outside the Maliseet communities.

Although Harvard professor Montague Chamberlain and Smith College professor W.F. Ganong had started to compile word lists in Maliseet using the English alphabet for their 1899 publication, *Maliseet Vocabulary*, they did not include translations of the meanings of the Indigenous terms nor their sources or dates.[1] There were no published instructions or dictionaries to check the spelling of the Maliseet language. In contrast, Adney's papers are well-documented, with the names of his informants and dates that the information was given.

---

* In composing this chapter, Nicholas N. Smith used the name *Maliseet* for the Indigenous language and People of the Wəlastəkw region of New Brunswick. This was common usage when Adney was studying the language.

By 1890, when he was twenty-two, Adney had a sufficient list of birds and animals with Maliseet names and meanings to present a lecture on his research at New York's Linnaean Society. In 1893 his compilation of eighty-nine bird and twenty-five mammal names in Maliseet, English, and Latin was published by The Linnaean Society. It is the first published Maliseet-language word list that includes the meanings of most words included.[2]

The Maliseet names fascinated Adney. He wondered if some of these words might go back in time to the first Maliseet utterances by people developing an oral communication system. He analyzed the plant, bird, animal, and fish names, learning that they were from one of four categories: a specific description of the animal, a unique typical action characteristic of it, a use for it, or an imitation of the sound it made. As he became secure in using Maliseet, he grew critical of Chamberlain and Ganong's 1890s renderings of the language.

Adney enjoyed ferreting out the old hunters, men who had become silent observers of the culture that was replacing theirs. In the early days of Adney's research, his mentors were Noël Polchies, William Neptune, and Peter Bear, who were representative of the traditional hunting culture and were familiar with its vocabulary. Later he found Tom Moulton and Noël Moulton, who came to the Woodstock area from Greenville, Maine, because it was easy to pick up farm jobs at harvest time. Their vocabulary included agricultural terms. Adney's work established the forms for writing the language using the English alphabet to form the sounds. The old language was the heart of Maliseet culture and their philosophy of life, a life of adaptation to the woodland and river environment of their home territory.

After Adney settled permanently in Upper Woodstock, he would often sit in his house pondering a Maliseet word or phrase with the door open and a supply of peanuts in hand, some of which he set out for the squirrels. They quickly arrived after he made a certain sound. He tested this many times. It was clear to him the sound he made was understood by the squirrels to mean *food*, and it drew them from the treetops into his house. It seemed logical to him that sounds made to indicate food must have been among the earliest words in the development of human languages.

He later began visiting the Woodstock Maliseet Reserve on Sunday afternoons, where he encouraged the Elders to meet with him to answer questions about their language. Some curious young people also joined

Peter Paul teaching Maliseet (Wəlastəkwey), undated
(UNB Archive MG H 151 Peter Paul Fonds)

the meetings, which became a Sunday afternoon routine. At one meeting, Adney asked what the Maliseet word was for a certain item. None of the Elders knew. A young man at the back of the group raised his hand and gave the answer. Adney responded, "How is it that you know this, but the Elders don't?" Peter Paul replied that he was raised by his grandparents (Noël and Susan Polchies) and grew up speaking their version of the language. The Polchies spoke only the old Maliseet hunter-gatherer language in their house and camp, and Peter said he did not really learn English until he was twenty-eight. Before that he knew only enough so he could shop in town for what he needed. Adney immediately saw this young man as a potential informant and teacher. The two formed a close working association and a friendship that lasted the rest of Adney's life.

Peter Paul considered the Maliseet spoken at Woodstock the most authentic version. He knew changes in the language had occurred at other Maliseet villages. He could usually tell if a person was from Oromocto, Kingsclear, or Tobique if he listened to them speak for a few minutes. Over the years, Paul regularly "corrected" the dialects Adney picked up from other villages.

In the early 1920s, many residents of the region saw an airplane that flew up the Saint John River valley. It was an interesting event and became a popular topic of conversation. Adney later heard this story and wanted to know if the Maliseet People who had seen the airplane had a name for it. He went to each reserve with his question. He found that the Elders of the different reserves used a different word for the airplane, but each one was a descriptive noun that all Maliseet speakers would understand.

In 1944 Adney wrote a new linguistic report, "Malecite Indian's Names for Native Berries and Fruits," that was published in the first volume of the *Acadian Naturalist*.[3] The topics of his research continued to expand, taking in geographical expressions and terms relating to other areas of natural history. Geographic terms were of great importance to those dependent on hunting, fishing, and trapping. For example, they customarily depended on the same springs for water in winter and summer, but their terms differed in the two seasons. In winter, spring water was called warm water because it rose with a little steam from an opening encircled by ice and snow; in summer, it was called cold water because it was cold and refreshing. Everything in the Maliseet world was either animate or inanimate. Some rocks were animate, but most were inanimate. By adding a suffix to the name of a material, like a roll of spruce bark, one knew whether it was flexible or stiff. Adney insisted, "Language is history, culture and traditions." The Saint John River is the primary geologic feature that had enabled the Maliseet People to establish and maintain settlements throughout the region that was their home terrain. French explorers had a habit of giving Christian names to places and geographic features of the landscape they "discovered." For example, when Champlain "discovered" a great river in this region on June 24, 1604, he named it the Saint John because it was the feast day of Saint John the Baptist.

The Maliseet, of course, had a much older name for their beloved river—Wəlastəkw. Adney learned their concept of the river could not be easily translated into English. Various writers used terms such as *good, pleasant,* or *beautiful.* Adney found that in Maliseet it was all these words wrapped together and combined with a great feeling for all the natural life of the region. He wrote that English describes the river by how it looks; Maliseet describes the river by how it feels. The entire environment of the region was included in the name Wəlastəkw.

Traditional campsites along the rivers of the region were named for the topography and direction of the prevailing winds, such as "over the hills winds" or "down river winds." Plant names indicated what was edible, medicinal, or otherwise useful—for example, for making rope. Adney's Maliseet friends instructed him in the language for each type of wood that identified their properties and how they were used for specific purposes. Animal, fish, and bird names gave him similar information. The language around deadfall traps and stretchers for curing pelts provided important information about Maliseet hunting traditions.

Adney had Indigenous friends from Tobique to Saint Andrews, where he engaged with the Passamaquoddy (Peskotomuhkati). He broadened his field of contacts to include the St. Francis Abenaki of Quebec and the Penobscot of Maine. He concluded that the Mahican and Pennacook dialects were the result of Indigenous refugees who fled their homelands and settled with the Abenaki in the Kennebec River valley and in Quebec. The Penobscot also took in western refugees, and their language changed as a result. The Maliseet did not allow those from other tribes to join them so their language remained unaltered by outside influence, as was also the case with the Passamaquoddy.

Tappan Adney lived at a time when researching and recording an Indigenous language was not a profession that provided a livelihood. Nonetheless, he remained devoted to his linguistic studies. His study of Maliseet provided him with knowledge of this community that probably no other non-Indigenous person possessed. He sometimes complained that living in Upper Woodstock did not allow him to associate with other linguists and or give him access to a good research library. His opportunity to develop a close association with other linguists changed when he heard about and contacted Fannie Eckstorm. She was familiar with the Penobscot language and had recently published a book about Indigenous place names on the Maine coast.

Fannie was the daughter of Manly Hardy, a fur trader living alongside the Penobscot River at Brewer, Maine. He operated a trading house for the Penobscot and Passamaquoddy. As a youngster, Fannie became accustomed to associating with the people who came to trade, often camping in her backyard. She liked to hear their stories. She invited them into the Eckstorm house, and they became her friends.

From a young age she accompanied her father on his trapping and fur-trade expeditions. They travelled by canoe with Penobscot guides deep into the waterways and forests of the region around Mount Katahdin. When she was in her teens, she took notebooks with her, filling them with the guides' fascinating stories. She included the Penobscot names of the plants and animals they saw as they paddled the lakes and streams of this wilderness area. She made a written record of the words fresh from the mouths of her guides. She, too, became fascinated by Indigenous place names, which became a favourite topic of conversation with the guides. She began submitting articles to *Forest and Stream* magazine that included notes on the guides' language. Fannie and her father became favourite authors for the publication. The University of Maine published Fannie's book, *Indian Place Names of the Penobscot Valley and the Maine Coast*, in 1941. It is an engrossing study and a primary resource that has been twice reprinted.[4]

Eckstorm and Adney became aware of one another's work. They were destined to meet. Eckstorm, like Adney, was emphatic about using the letters of the English alphabet instead of special symbols for specific sounds. She interpreted the meaning of the words just as he did.

When Adney wrote to her, hoping it would lead to a fruitful correspondence, Eckstorm still lived in the house where she grew up in Brewer, Maine. She had achieved a well-deserved reputation as a scholarly author who wrote about Maine Indigenous history and folklore. Adney's opening correspondence queried Eckstorm on examples of words that were sticklers, which showed he had a serious knowledge of the Indigenous regional language. Her reply is especially interesting for its astute recognition of Adney's approach.

> You may wonder at my offering to give away material to an
> entire stranger, when I have given nothing to Dr. Speck and
> Frank Siebert whom I have known for years. But in your first
> letter you gave me the "high sign." It was the sign of the woods,
> the old, old welcome of our woods where the invitation was,
> "Stranger, draw up and eat," and there was no asking of names
> or of the business in hand. You were willing to share your stuff.[5]

They soon made an appointment to meet. He asked his good friend Peter Paul to drive him to Brewer (Adney never owned or operated a car). Paul was also interested in meeting the woman who was said to have a deep knowledge of Indigenous languages and a real interest in local folklore. The meeting went well. They talked far into the night until Eckstorm was too tired to go on (she was seventy-nine, three years older than Adney).

Tappan and Peter left for the night but returned in the morning for more conversation. Before they returned to Woodstock, Fannie warned Tappan not to give information to the professionals. She told him the first time Frank Speck, a prominent anthropologist and professor at the University of Pennsylvania, visited her, she didn't hesitate to cooperate with him and answered all his questions. A little later she read one of his publications, in which he fully credited himself with discovering the information she had willingly provided. He made no mention of Fannie Eckstorm. Never again would she allow a professional anthropologist to interview her.

The situation with Adney was different. They respected and trusted each other. They used the same methodology. Adney's admiration for Eckstorm increased to the point where his thoughts turned to marriage. The two could make great strides as they worked together on Indigenous languages. Eckstorm hesitated. She was nearly eighty years old and not eager to jump into a marriage. Unfortunately, she died in 1946, soon after she and Adney became well acquainted. He felt her death as a great loss.[6]

In late 1950, there was a flurry of activity around the small bungalow Tappan Adney had built in 1913 on the Sharp property in Upper Woodstock. Cars with New Jersey, Massachusetts, and Maine license plates were parked nearby. Glenn Adney, Tappan's son, appeared to be the central figure. As a child he had lived with his parents in this small house but was now an actuary for Metropolitian Life Insurance. He lived in New Jersey, commuting daily across the George Washington Bridge to the company's headquarters in New York City. He was now the lone heir to his father's estate.

Glenn sat in the middle of the bungalow. This was Tappan's home where he lived and worked surrounded by boxes of his Maliseet linguistic papers, an unfinished manuscript on Indigenous canoes, models of birchbark canoes, books, and paintings. The residence was a storehouse of Adney's images of Indigenous culture, canoes, and hunting and trapping in New Brunswick forests. The papers on Maliseet linguistics included a file of correspondence from admirers of his research on Indigenous languages. Now Glenn and a small group of associates and professionals had to decide how Adney's papers and artifacts could best be allocated to libraries and museums for archival preservation.

Wendell Hadlock, acting as an agent for the Peabody Essex Museum at Salem, Massachusetts, stood by nervously eyeing the many boxes containing sixty years of papers and notes pertaining to the Maliseet language and a new system for learning it. Hadlock was the only person interested in the linguistic material that Adney had accumulated and worked with since he first visited New Brunswick in 1887. He was particularly interested in the linguistic papers because Adney was the first scholar to make a systematic study of the Maliseet language and culture. Notable among the papers was the beginning of a planned publication titled *The Language of the Malecite or Etchemin Indians: Illustrating a New Method of Analysis, with Words, Sentences and Texts*. It consisted of two parts: basis and principles of the particle or alphabetical methods of analysis explained and illustrated by Maliseet words, with their European correspondences; and Maliseet words, sentences, texts, classifications of words and ideas, and grammatical forms explained.[7]

It was a massive undertaking, never completed, but even so it would be useful for students of the language. The typewriter where the thousands of pages were typed was still on the desk where Adney worked.

The boxes of linguistic papers were loaded into Hadlock's vehicle for the long trip to Salem. Hadlock was elated to obtain Adney's work, and Glenn was happy to see a large part of what had to be distributed out the door and on its way to a secure home. He wondered who would be interested in a language that only a handful of people still spoke. The general feeling, commonly expressed at that time by Maliseet People, was: why would anyone want to continue speaking a language not understood in the shops of Woodstock or Fredericton and used by only a few Elders? If you wanted a job, you needed to know the primary language of the land.

The director of Peabody Essex Museum, Ernest Dodge, was delighted to add the Adney papers to his archival collections. It would be a companion collection to Frank Speck's generous donation of his Penobscot studies and be a primary resource for scholars interested in northeastern Indigenous languages and the history of the tribes in this region. New Brunswick researchers, however, found it inconvenient to travel to Salem, Massachusetts, to study the Adney papers. Vincent O. Erickson, professor of anthropology at the University of New Brunswick, was given permission to photograph a selection of the papers for the Harriet Irving Library Special Collections at UNB, which provided easy access for local researchers.

In late 1950, I [Nicholas Smith] had the opportunity to study some of Tappan Adney's linguistic research documents at the Peabody Essex Museum and found them extremely interesting, comprehensive, and detailed. Peter Paul is often acknowledged as the informant. In 1951, about a year after Adney died, I drove to the Woodstock First Nation Reserve in New Brunswick to meet Peter Paul. I told him it was Adney's work that brought me and that I wanted to learn the Maliseet language. Adney had learned more than a language. He acquired a substantial knowledge of their culture and philosophy of life declaring that the Maliseet had a "high standard of simplicity." This was a difference between Adney's method and that of the academically trained linguists. For Adney it was more than putting an identifying nametag on an object. Language was culture.

Peter Paul later invited me to accompany him to Adney's residence in Upper Woodstock. He needed birchbark and knew where some was stored under the building. It was a wonderful opportunity to see the small house Adney designed and built. It is sometimes described as a cabin, but it was a fully framed and appointed small house. The building was well hidden by a grove of majestic spruce trees between it and the highway. It stood on a knoll sheltered by the woods from the cold blasts of winter storms and from the noise of the nearby road.

When I got out of the truck, I immediately noticed the pleasant aroma of woodland that filled the air. The whole scene had the feeling of a secluded place where Adney worked undisturbed by the outside world. The tall spruce trees gave me the feeling of being in the deep woods of the far north. Civilization seemed miles away, although I was only two miles from Woodstock's business district. The setting was Thoreauvian, a perfect atmosphere for one who wished to save the Maliseet's vanishing language and culture. We walked to the door of the bungalow. Peter grasped the knob, turned it, and pushed as he had done many times in the past. The door was stuck. He pushed harder. It had not been used for over a year and groaned under the pressure to move it. It was swollen with moisture from the rains and had not had the benefit of warm fires within to keep it dry. Finally, it opened with a grumbling welcome, allowing us to enter.

Entering the empty house must have been emotional for Peter, who had visited his friend here for many years. During the last two weeks of Adney's life, Peter tended the fires, keeping the residence warm while Peter's wife, Minnie, cooked, cleaned, and did laundry. I stood at the entrance for several minutes trying to visualize Peter sitting beside Adney at his desk and typewriter, working on the Maliseet language. The bungalow was light and airy, what one would expect an artist to have. It was small enough to be easily heated yet large enough to comfortably accommodate Adney's activities. He had a wide range of interests that kept him busy. I tried to imagine the setting in the winter. His desk was at the north end. His bed was to the left of the entrance. The fieldstone fireplace, which served for cooking as well as heat, was located at the southern end. I imagined winter's snow piled up around the foundation. It was a simple but practical home for the artist and linguist dedicated to the preservation of Indigenous cultural heritage.

Adney was emphatic that only the letters of the English alphabet be used to represent the sounds of the Maliseet language. Academic linguists used special typewriters with specific symbols to represent sounds not found in English, but Adney was certain the English alphabet could be used to identify and communicate the sounds and meaning of Maliseet words. He argued that the meanings — what the speaker had in mind when speaking — were also a philosophy of Maliseet life. To understand the language, these meanings were much more important to know than the use of precise symbols to correctly represent the sounds. This was the heart of the matter. This was to be his battle until he died.

The new science of linguistics in the English-speaking academic world emphasized the proper sounds when recording the words of an Indigenous language. It used special symbols to indicate unique sounds that cannot be represented accurately from the twenty-six letters, or any combination of them, in the English alphabet. The professional linguists had little interest in the Indigenous meanings of the words.

In 1963 a professional linguist supported by a grant from the National Museum of Canada (now the Canadian Museum of History) came to New Brunswick to study Maliseet with the intention of preserving it. Harvard professor Karl V. Teeter arrived on Peter Paul's doorstep and offered money to work with him. Peter could set his own timetable. But he would have to forget Adney's system and work with Teeter's method. Teeter also said the research based on Adney's system had no value and could be thrown in the stove. Teeter's papers and recordings are stored in the Harvard University Archives. Those wishing to access them must receive permission from the archive staff. Most of Teeter's Maliseet files cannot be accessed for eighty years.

Will the recordings be in an obsolete form impossible to use in eighty years? Teeter came to save the Maliseet language from vanishing, but what use are recordings if they are hidden away? In contrast, Tappan's work has been saved for study at the Peabody Essex Museum in Salem, Massachusetts, and much is available today at the Harriet Irving Library Special Collections at the University of New Brunswick.

Linguist Dr. Philip S. LeSourd helped Teeter translate and edit forty-two of Teeter's recorded Maliseet tales. LeSourd continued this work after Teeter's death and published *Tales From Maliseet Country: The Maliseet Texts of Karl V. Teeter* in 2007. The book has no commentary to explain why these specific tales were important enough for the Maliseet to remember them in the middle of the twentieth century.

Laszlo Szabo, a Hungarian immigrant of the Second World War era, was a language and linguistics professor at the University of New Brunswick. He also received grants from the National Museum of Canada for his Maliseet linguistic studies. Unfortunately Teeter and Szabo, who were studying Maliseet at the same time, did not work together. Szabo said he didn't want to work with Peter Paul because Peter knew too much and had a lot of contact with the outside world. Szabo wanted to work with those who had little contact with the outside world. Toward the end of his career, however, he did contact and work with Paul. Much of Szabo's work was published in German, a language not user-friendly for Maliseet. All three of these linguists—Teeter, LeSourd, and Szabo—worked for their academic audience and their own reputations as professionals, not the Maliseet People and their culture.

Around 1975, a professor who did a significant study of the northern Cree made CDs for teaching their language. Cree is an Algonquian language similar to Maliseet. Professional linguists were impressed with this language-learning device and obtained the CDs. It seemed an easy way to teach and learn the language. I acquired a set and took it to Peter Paul, telling him that the professionals were raving about this language-teaching tool. He sat attentively while I put on the first disk. It began in English with "Good morning" followed by the Cree words for *good* and *morning*. It then followed with a question, "What did you have for breakfast?" and an answer, "An orange, cereal, and toast." Again, there were Cree words for these foods. "Turn it off, turn it off!" Peter yelled. He then explained:

"That's not Indian! We don't combine our words for good and morning to create a greeting. We have Kwe or qwe for people we see almost every day, and a special greeting term for those who were returning after a long stay in a winter hunting camp. They were met with Pehkwinakwsiyin, now shortened to Pehkwinakws, on their return, meaning, 'Looking at you opens up the past with all its pleasant memories.'" (What a fine greeting for two old friends to offer one another when they met after the long winter season.) "And," Peter continued, "We didn't have oranges or cereal or toast."

It was obvious to us this was not the authentic Cree language of northern hunting communities where the families depended on the forest for foods and furs. It was, instead, a version of the language developed for school and college students in an entirely different cultural setting.

Adney, like Peter Paul, was concerned with and concentrated on the authentic descriptive language used by the Maliseet hunters of the late nineteenth and early twentieth centuries. It was a language that had developed over countless years by those who were sustained by the natural life in the Saint John River [Wəlastəkw] Valley. Whatever type of vocabulary would replace the hunting style would include new forms based on traditional forms remolded to fit new situations. Such words can be compared to a diamond from an old ring that is placed in a new setting. Language is an inheritance tying together history, culture, and traditions.

Nicholas N. Smith, 2006 (photo: Daryl Hunter)

Frank Siebert spent many years working on the Penobscot language. He began his career as a medical doctor, but his real interest was linguistics. Eventually, he gave up medicine and moved to Old Town, Maine, where he could work closely with Penobscot speakers. His big project was a compilation of a Penobscot dictionary, which gained the respect of professional linguists. Like Adney's compilation of Maliseet, Siebert's life-long endeavour was unfinished when he died in 1998.

In his later years Siebert developed health problems. His medical training should have warned him that his symptoms indicated a serious condition, but he ignored them and continued working. He was a researcher first and organizer second. Siebert seldom felt he had tapped all the resources for information on a subject, so he never reached the point of publication. At the same time, however, he was afraid that someone else might publish on "his" topics first. A group of professional linguists with an interest in Siebert's unfinished work agreed on a plan to organize and save his Penobscot research papers. Siebert had worked for the most part alone, obtaining grants each year that enabled him to continue. There was an enormous backlog of material to be sorted and organized before publication could be considered. Conor McDonough Quinn, a Harvard graduate and talented linguist, was recruited to help Siebert organize his mountain of Penobscot material.

Quinn was entering the field of Penobscot linguistics at an exciting time. He met many of the top Wabanaki linguists. He had the opportunity to learn some of the Penobscot language and to see the development of teaching aids. Quinn arrived at Siebert's small house in 1997 to find boxes of linguistic materials filling up most of the space, even stacked on chairs. There was no place to sit. A two-man crew from an audio-visual service was there to make a video showing a picture of an object with its written Penobscot form while a Penobscot speaker pronounced its name. All the professional linguists working with Wabanaki linguistics were interested in this high-tech method of language learning.

Frank Siebert died within a year, as was expected. His research papers—a massive volume of material—are now preserved in the American Philosophical Society Library in Philadelphia. His death did not create a job opening for Conor Quinn. For several years he likewise depended on grants for his income, which enabled him to continue his Penobscot project and sent him to the Passamaquoddy and the Maliseet communities to work with linguistic programs on reserves. He hoped a full-time linguistic position would become available at a Maine or New Brunswick university, but nothing opened up. He eventually applied for a position in Saudi Arabia teaching English and was accepted. After two years he was tired of a place where the air always seemed to be full of sand and the wind sent it into the tiniest crevices everywhere. He was ready for another try at a Maine or New Brunswick job in Indigenous linguistics.

Each summer during the late 1990s, professional linguists arrived at different Penobscot reserves in Maine and Maliseet reserves in New Brunswick with a special program to help save the Wabanaki languages. I regularly asked the linguists what they thought of Tappan Adney's approach to linguistics. The answers were always very similar. They would say Adney worked alone, not having contact with a large academic library or professional linguists. He never had a course in linguistics. His resource people were older men who probably didn't fully understand his questions. Many people like him who live close to reserves learn Indigenous languages using their own methods of writing sounds not found in the English alphabet but not the alphabet accepted by professionals, who have a common linguistic alphabet that identifies all known sounds so everyone knows the proper word sounds and can pronounce words written on a page correctly. Each professional said essentially the same thing. I was sure that none of them had taken time to investigate the Adney papers before making their criticism. It was discouraging.[8]

Conor Quinn was glad to be back. He searched for an academic position in the United States and Canada but found no attractive openings. He then came to the attention of Ted Behne, who asked him for an assessment of the Adney linguistic papers. Quinn had time and was interested. He wanted to be working on linguistics, and investigating Adney's research might result in a conference paper. I suspect Conor Quinn was the first professional linguist to examine the Adney papers in the Peabody Essex Museum.

In the introduction to his evaluation he states:

Adney's outstanding work with the material culture of the Maliseets often overshadows the equally extensive record he left of non-material culture. I will discuss…his work with the Maliseet language, and offer a brief appraisal of it from the viewpoint of a contemporary field linguist who has worked for many years with Maliseet-Passamaquoddy language and its close relatives.

He continues with an assessment of the strengths of Adney's linguistic work:

Indeed, the more I look through Adney's Maliseet language work, the more impressed I am with the sheer depth and richness of its documentation.... The human knowledge base that Adney had access to and the depth and respectfulness with which he plumbed it, is nothing short of incomparable. Everywhere in Adney's documentation I find clues to solutions to old problems, unexpected discoveries, and vocabulary never to my knowledge recorded by anyone else. And all of this in great quantities not just a new word here and there.

He concludes:

To a fair degree then, Adney's "particle" model, weaknesses in transcription, and other idiosyncrasies may to a large part be attributable to his being a fairly isolated scholar, which, especially for his time was hardly any distinctive failing of his own.

By present standards, the value of Adney's linguistic work lies primarily in its richness of access to specialized vocabulary. Adney's intimate and detailed contact with a very early genera-tion of Maliseet speakers with extensive knowledge of traditional culture has left us with a nearly unparalleled documentation of many presently most-difficult to reach aspects of regional Indigenous knowledge.... Only time will tell if what looks ques-tionable now may turn out to have unknown value in the future.

Finally, I find particularly laudable Adney's demonstrated desire to make his linguistic work (and other) scholarship maximally accessible...to non-specialists.... In Adney, we find a serious scholar who is driven by his own very personal love for the people and their ways of life, but also does not fail to share well what he has learned. Adney's linguistic work is, in sum, another way in which we are lucky to have had him in this world.[9]

Supporters of Adney's linguistic work were elated with Conor Quinn's evaluation, which is titled *Adney's Linguistics Report.* Peter Paul would have been overjoyed to see the report and all the excellent comments made about Adney's linguistics as well as about the man who continued to stick stubbornly to his vocation. All those years working on the language with Peter Paul were not wasted. The report cites specific examples with references to box numbers, showing that Quinn spent considerable time investigating the Adney papers.

It was music to the ears of Maliseet preservationists to also hear that Adney's work included an immense vocabulary. And, of course, it was in researching vocabulary that he increased his knowledge of Maliseet life and culture. This impressed Quinn, who once expressed the observation that courses in Indigenous linguistics lacked training regarding material and cultural life. Students did not get a feeling for or understanding of lifestyle and culture from learning the language as taught in college courses.

We are fortunate to have had the services of Conor Quinn, a professional from a younger generation of linguists. He had established a reputation in his field and did not feel bound to the criticism of an older generation. He had the freedom to do what others felt they should shy away from. Those interested in this linguistic legacy are grateful to Conor for taking the time to make a valid and helpful assessment of Adney's Maliseet language papers. Tappan Adney was not the maverick linguist so many had made him out to be. Of all the linguists who were attracted to Maliseet, Adney's papers are the best records of the language.

The end of the Second World War was the beginning of great changes with a new vocabulary replacing much pre-war speech. Perhaps that is why so many professional linguists had a problem with Adney's work. His studies were concerned with language from before even the First World War—the language of the traditional Maliseet hunter-gatherer culture. But there are Maliseet who still speak about Adney with great respect and admiration, knowing that he has given them a valid source to help save their language, culture, and traditions. Theirs was a way of life centred on food gathering, hunting and fishing, tool-making, supplying families with shelter and clothing, and using all the resources of the forest for their hardy livelihood.

Although Tappan Adney's linguistic studies focused on a way of life long past, the relationships and values expressed in the language are the same ones required for sustaining families and communities in the present and in the future. Perhaps Adney's devotion to the Maliseet heritage and linguistic studies was driven by a sense of his work as a gift to the future. If so, he was correct.

Chapter Thirteen

At Home in Upper Woodstock: Research as a Way of Life

It is a wonderful place, a mingling of old orchard trees, a now great timber of spruce and a bungalow, which needs an infinite number of repairs. — Tappan Adney

When Tappan Adney returned to Upper Woodstock in 1933, he continued with the canoe project. His work on linguistics came into full focus, and his defence of Indigenous rights emerged in the latter part of his remaining years. From 1933 to 1950, there were a number of additional associations and circumstances that round out his life story and legacy. He had come home to Upper Woodstock, but not to retire. Research was his way of life, and it showed up in a variety of ways.

In the epigraph above, he mentions the bungalow, built some twenty years earlier, now needing "an infinite number of repairs." As a craftsman, he no doubt set about to make the residence livable. Minnie Bell was blind and in failing health. Adney was entirely responsible for her care until she died in 1937. This situation no doubt caused a slowdown in his scholarly work since she needed his assistance for many details of daily life.

When Fred and Nola Hill showed up in 1938–39, Adney's time and attention would have been focused, to a certain extent, on the arrangements for the transfer of his model canoe collection to The Mariners' Museum in Newport News, Virginia, where, at last, it would have a permanent home and be professionally curated. The monthly stipend provided by the museum covered his basic expenses. It must have been with a sense of relief and a resurgence of motivation for his research that he entered the 1940s. Living alone, he was free to determine his own schedule — whether to spend the morning at his desk typing up the results of his latest research or in the woods observing the behaviour of birds. Ornithology had been his first love, and it appears to have been one of his last as well.

During these years Adney earned the reputation of an eccentric old man. He wore sandals, which was enough for at least one neighbourhood mother to warn her children to stay away from this strange person. He was reported to talk to the birds, which to some was a sign of mental derangement. Fortunately, we have a first-person account of Adney's relationship with the birds of his woodland environment, as well as his own account of his communication with squirrels. Both stories, while strikingly unusual, illustrate the extent to which Adney became immersed in the study of the wildlife around his residence. *Study* is not the right word; in his method of research, he became a *participant* in the lives of the birds and animals. He applied the ethnographic method of participant-observer to the wildlife cultures of his woodland environment, and the results gave Adney a legendary place in local folklore.

The first account comes from Leon Thornton, a community college teacher, who on July 9, 1985, tape-recorded his boyhood experiences with Tappan Adney on a visit to the Adney cottage at Skiff Lake.

By 1934 or so, I had seen Tappan Adney quite a few times from a distance. I knew who he was, and I knew—I don't know whether it's exactly the right word—his reputation. I was just a little shaver. My grandfather used to run the potato shed in Upper Woodstock, and that's just literally down the hill from where they [Tappan and Minnie Bell] lived.... at that age, like all young people, throwing rocks or anything else was just as natural as falling off a log backwards. So I happened to look up on the top of the potato house, and here was this partridge sitting up there. So I picked up a small potato and I threw it at the partridge... didn't come close to the partridge as far as that's concerned, and I heard this very polite "ahem" behind me. I looked around and here was a pair of ragged old sneakers with the toes all out of them, and a pair of bare legs clear up to a sawed-off...pair of khaki shorts. And I looked on up again, and of course, he was just about the color of this wall [dark wood paneling], and I said to myself, this has got to be Tappan Adney.

And sitting on his shoulder was a squirrel. And he said to me, "Why, young man, did you throw the potato at that partridge?" Well, I was flabbergasted for a minute, of course, at a loss for words, and finally I said, "Well it was just something to do." And he said, "Did you ever think that they could be your friends?"

Again, I didn't exactly get what he was coming at, but when he made a slight whistle, the partridge turned his head, looked at him, and flew down off the roof and landed on the other shoulder—the squirrel on one side, the partridge on the other. And then he began to give me a lecture—in quite stern tones—about wildlife and how we should befriend it and help it out and so on and so forth. And then he turned around and politely asked me if sometime I had the time would I like to come up and visit?

...As I recall, I think it was the following spring, we used to have cows in the pasture there, just where Tappan's place would be, and I used to come up from Woodstock first thing in the morning on a bicycle, milk three cows in a great big container, hang it on my handlebars, and head on back down to Woodstock again, then take a bath, change my clothes, and go to school.

So this particular Saturday morning...I got the milking done and was pushing the bike—it was too steep to pedal—and when going up I passed the road going up into their cottage...and I could hear the piano...and I stopped and listened to it. And then I heard; "Young man, are you returning my call?"...Tappan put his hand on my shoulder and said, "Now, would you like to go around the outside of the building—I've got some nice trails down through the lot here."

I don't think there would have been any other place within miles where you would have seen as many birds that were totally fearless, as there were there. Absolutely fearless. And he seemed to be able to emit these queer little whistles and other sounds, and he had those birds literally twittering around his head, or land on the top of his head. He had the complete and utter trust of all wildlife. It seemed like that.

Another thing I was surprised at was that when they seemed to be timid of me, he would again repeat these little sounds, as if to say, well, don't be afraid of him. And the birds—they'd never land on me like they did him—but they'd flutter around me and twittering away and talk. I think that he was the instigator of my love of nature. I think that that was the first instilling that wildlife wasn't to be indiscriminately slaughtered or shot at or maimed or whatever, and that you should learn to appreciate it and live with it.

Adney's fanciful but exact drawing of twenty-five bird species
gathered for a meeting in the forest, undated (CCHS)

Beyond the experience with birds, Leon Thornton gives us a further
view of Adney's comprehensive knowledge of the natural environment in
which he is living.

> As he walked down through the woods…he named every tree,
> and every piece of moss, and every flower that was there. And
> first would come the Latin name, which didn't mean a thing to
> me—I didn't even know what Latin was—I thought it was just
> a jargon that he was saying, and then he would come out with
> the common name. He was an amazing man, there's no question
> about that.[1]

Of all the legacies that flow from the life and work of Tappan Adney,
his ethic of appreciation and care for wildlife is perhaps the most easily
shared. His work in Wəlastəkwey linguistics is highly specialized, and only
a few dedicated craftsmen will ever build birchbark canoes, but a sense of
respect and fellow-feeling for wildlife can be passed from parent to child

and from teacher to student in the same way Tappan Adney passed it on to young Leon Thornton.

The story of the Adney woods and its animals has a second coming—enter Aida (McAnn) Flemming, born in 1896 at Victoria Corner, just a few miles up the Wəlastəkw from Upper Woodstock. Her career in education included teaching at Mount Allison University and Dongan Hall, a private secondary school in New York City. She also worked as a journalist and eventually married Hugh John Flemming, New Brunswick's twenty-fourth premier.

Aida Flemming became an internationally known humanitarian when she founded the Kindness Club in 1959. The Kindness Club organization was established to help children in New Brunswick develop feelings of kindness and friendship with animals. The movement grew to be an international phenomenon with local chapters around the world and Albert Schweitzer as its honorary president. It is still an active organization.

In 1964, Aida Flemming purchased the Adney property with the goal of securing it for a wildlife preserve. The Town of Woodstock now holds the property on behalf of the Adney/Flemming Trust. The trails that Tappan Adney walked when he ventured from his scholar's desk are still there. This sixty-acre woodland on the edge of Woodstock is growing into an evermore flourishing nature preserve dedicated to non-intrusive recreational and educational use as prescribed by Aida Flemming—a circumstance we can be sure would please its former denizen.

Adney was an early practitioner of participant-observer ethnography. This radical approach to anthropological research was pioneered by Frank Hamilton Cushing in the late 1870s and early 1880s with his study of Zuni culture in the New Mexico Territory of the American southwest, but the approach wasn't yet codified as an acceptable ethnographic methodology. In fact, it was looked at askance by academically trained anthropologists who at the time were keen on conducting ethnographic research in what they imagined was a highly scientific way: strict objectivity in recording ethnographic data, and avoiding relationships that led to emotional attachment—the danger of "going native."

Adney was by nature a participant-observer. It was his spontaneous response to the challenges of ethnographic research and the moral requirement of political engagement in the battle for fairness and justice. In self-reflection on what made him tick, he credited excellent early training from his father and that he has had a keen enthusiasm for being a student ever since.

When he returned to live in his Upper Woodstock bungalow—now surrounded by a rapidly regenerating forest—his relationship with the woodland residents, as we have seen in Leon Thornton's vivid account, was that of a participant-observer. This approach also involved squirrels and has a surprising connection to his language research. Adney gives this account in a letter to Frank Speck at the University of Pennsylvania:

By the way, I am discovering "origins of language" through observation of some friendly red squirrels that I have been regularly feeding. I chose the subject of eating as one upon which I felt we could arrive at mutual understanding in spite of speech limitations on both sides. They give out a call when they hear my back screen door slam. If I answer back, one comes threading his way along limbs to the roof of a low woodshed and stops. I move my lips, giving at the same time a smacking sound. Sciurus [Latin for squirrel] instantly makes the same lips gesture, repeating it each time after me. Both understand, have come to understand, that the subject is eating, apple, butternut, etc.

I was in the rear room of my bungalow "suite" lying on a couch reading. I had lifted a small board in the floor so squirrels could enter. When I heard or saw them I gave the mouth signal, then gave them some apple or other food. This time I heard a squirrel enter, and gave the usual signal which meant eating (I had never lied to them), and went on reading. The squirrel, finding no apple anywhere, came up to the couch, at my shoulder, then he ran up and touched my lips with his, jumped back, and repeated the act. Now, he had not seen my lips moving. But he had heard the accompanying vocalization now clearly associated with eating, and plainly had said to me, in effect, "You just spoke of eating. What about it?"

What had occurred was the process which I call translation of visual terms into vocal terms, and the same process runs through all language, forms its very basis. First there is visible, tangible phenomena of one kind or another, then a concept. First a visible action or gesture of the mouth leading to the concept of eating,

given expression in the vocal field as an element of language.
I did not give the M sound, but another obvious "mouth-sound."
Our vocal organs are too dissimilar for each to imitate the sounds
made by the other. We stood on no common ground on that, but
we did so stand in the mental field....

My little Mi-ko ("eats cones") has shown me his ability to
observe, to make comparisons via what William James calls
his "storehouse of memory," his cerebellum, then to observe
differences in the nature of such phenomena as concern him, as
he is interested in, as well as resemblances. He has thus established
a basis in his little cosmos of classification, and the same faculty
and identical mental processes lie at the base of human language
and of every system of classification that can be said to be based
in nature. It is all matter of extent and degree, not of kind.

The Indian himself, after all the years of depression and
misunderstanding, has revealed a persistence in ways of thinking
that gives a certain validity to the Indian's tradition. I never ask
a Malecite about the meaning of anything, but "Did you ever
hear the old people say (such and such)?" Then I do not get
his guesswork, but true tradition. All the Indians' knowledge
was passed on by word of mouth. His speech most faithfully
passed on with exactness. It should be so with ideas that his
speech has expressed. It is only surprising that with change of
his native environment so much should have been preserved.
But, as in my conversation with little Mi-ko, one must establish a
basis of confidence and understanding, and that you must have
established. The white man has never understood, nor seemingly
cared to understand.[2]

Adney's account of this incident with a red squirrel is further evidence of his relationship with the wildlife around his bungalow. But the
concluding paragraph brings us back to what is essential for authentic
participant-observer research: "one must establish a basis of confidence
and understanding."

Adney was adept at this relationship building with his Indigenous friends,
as well as with birds and squirrels, but it was not always the case with his

George Frederick Clarke
and Peter Paul repairing a
canoe made by Peter Jo
in the 1890s,1961
(Clarke family collection)

non-Indigenous colleagues. An example of this can be seen in his relationship with George Frederick Clarke after Adney returned to Upper Woodstock.

Clarke and Adney first met in 1907. They became well acquainted over the following decade when Tappan and Minnie Bell were attempting to revive the Sharp orchard business. During the years Adney was in Montréal they corresponded about canoes and ethnology. Clarke shipped canoe-making materials to Adney for his models. When Adney returned to Woodstock in 1933, they continued their association. Clarke had been seriously researching the history of the region's Indigenous people since 1923. He had found his first arrowhead in 1902 when he was nineteen, and he was familiar with the use of birchbark canoes. He was best of friends with Noël Polchies from 1907 until the latter's death in 1927. Noël Moulton, another Wəlastəkwi friend, frequently accompanied Clarke on his archaeological digs once he began systematically working at this avocation.

In 1923, Clarke noticed fragments of stone tools in an area along the shore at the Forks of the Miramichi, close to his fishing camp. Each spring the freshet would rise and wash out a bit more of the riverbank, leaving behind heavier debris and exposing a new soil surface. It was here he began to dig and find stone tools. The implications were clear: this must have been a place where generations of Indigenous people had set up housekeeping and tool-making. They would have come here for the same reason he and his fellow anglers had built their camps along this stretch of the river: the abundance of salmon.

With this insight in mind, Clarke began systematically exploring the Wəlastəkw and Tobique shorelines for places of ancient, repeated, and prolonged encampment. He had an eye for likely sites and made numerous rewarding digs. He became so adept at walking into a new site and within minutes unearthing spearpoints, arrowheads, scrapers, and hand axes that his friends regarded him as having uncanny powers.

They were not wrong. As a young man Clarke had worked for a time as a touring magician and hypnotist, demonstrating apparently clairvoyant powers. He was successful at it but quit the business because he sensed a danger in the exercise of this uncanny talent. He later used hypnotism on his dental patients for painless tooth extraction when they were allergic to Novocaine. Clarke was, in his own way, as unusual a man as Adney. When Adney returned to Woodstock, their mutual interest in the archaeology of the Wəlastəkw region was at first cooperative, but later conflicted.

As an archaeologist, Clarke was a gifted amateur. He was not professionally trained in this area of cultural research nor did he attempt to capitalize monetarily on his growing collection of artifacts. He worked for the love of it, for the excitement of the search, and the reward of discovery. He was a pioneer in the archaeology of western and central New Brunswick. No work of this sort had previously been done in the region. He worked out his own system of record-keeping and classification of stone tools.

By the time Adney returned to Woodstock in 1933, Clarke had a well-developed routine of archaeological work with an impressive collection of hundreds of stone tools. Adney's longstanding interest in cultural preservation had previously focused on artifacts and technologies of the Wəlastəkokewiyik people that were still in use but fading fast. Research that recovered the stone tools of their ancestors was a natural corollary to his previous work.

Although Adney was no more professionally trained in archaeology than Clarke, he did have a sense of the scientific method for documentation. But Clarke, although fifteen years younger than Adney, was the veteran in the field. He continued working according to methods he had developed over the decades he had been doing this research and collecting artifacts.

Unfortunately, what might have continued as a cooperative association took a turn toward competition and distrust. At first, Adney was critical of the way Clarke conducted his digs and recorded the results, but the latter had for years been successful at spotting places that yielded stone tools, and he was not inclined to alter his method of conducting digs or his system of record-keeping.

But there was more to the conflict. Adney regarded himself as the foremost authority on the heritage and culture of the "St. John River Indians," yet Clarke clearly equalled him in certain areas of skill and knowledge as well as in friendship with Wəlastəkwey. We know proprietary competition is an occupational hazard among ethnographers and archaeologists; the desire to publish original material and receive credit for it prompts a fear of competitors who might "steal your stuff" and get away with it.

Clarke was not competitive about his archaeological work. The feeling of rivalry came into play from Adney's sense of professional superiority. In 1937, their relationship came to a falling out when Clarke showed him a dig where he had uncovered clear evidence of a firepit and possibly a sweat lodge site. Adney asked him not to dig any further because he wanted to make sketches of the site. Later, when Clarke returned, the circle of firepit stones and the soil around them had been removed.

Clarke confronted Adney, who reacted by breaking off communication. Later, a reconstruction of the firepit/sweat lodge site appeared in the New Brunswick Museum credited to Adney. Adney might have justified this expropriation as rescuing an important archaeological find from the hands of an amateur, but the incident remains troubling, especially in view of the high value Adney had always placed on honesty and fair dealing in professional relationships.

Clarke was offended by the betrayal but also regretted the loss of their association. He genuinely admired Adney and enjoyed his company. One evening, over a year later, he decided life was too short to let things go on like this. He picked up a bottle of gin and walked the mile to Adney's bungalow in Upper Woodstock. As Mary Bernard, Clarke's granddaughter and biographer tells it, Adney was glad to see him "even before he saw the bottle of gin."[3]

This gesture on Clarke's part did not, however, alter Adney's attitude toward his colleague's archaeological work. Adney was eventually appointed to the advisory board of the New Brunswick Museum. His correspondence with ethnographers, anthropologists, and museum curators in 1947 and

1948 contain references to Clarke's archaeology in derogatory terms clearly intended to prevent his work and his collection of artifacts from being taken seriously by professionals. During this same time, Clarke was working on a monograph detailing and summarizing his archaeological work. Then, out of the blue in 1948, Adney wrote to Clarke as follows:

> Fred, I understand you are seriously at work on a 'book' based
> on your archaeological material in expectation of its publication
> by the NB Museum. As you may or may not know, all matters
> 'Indian' that the Museum is associated with are referred to me.[4]

He goes on to say that Dr. Webster at the museum wants Adney to work with Clarke in the preparation of the manuscript. Clarke was an accomplished and disciplined writer who had already written and published five books, including novels and a volume of poetry. There was no doubt he could produce a respectable monograph documenting the archaeology of the "St. John River region" as he had developed it and of which he was the pioneering investigator.

Writing the letter was odd. Adney passed Clarke's house every time he walked to town. He could have stopped in for a chat on the matter of the monograph. The letter was not an offer or a request; it was a demand and a warning. Clarke was also a strong-minded person who did things his own way. He did not respond and kept working on the monograph. He had previously been in communication with Dr. Webster at the museum about the preparation of the book. But when he completed the manuscript, the museum refused to publish it.

Adney's role in influencing the museum to make this mistake is an ironic parallel to the way he was treated by the museum administrators at McGill. Even if Clarke's monograph did not reflect the methods and systems of professional archaeology, its value as a record of the work he had done should have been recognized and preserved. It was, after all, the only record of the principal work in the field up to that time. When the museum declined to publish the mongraph, it should have at least been filed in its archive.

Clarke was understandably disappointed at the museum's rejection of his book. The manuscript was laid aside but not found when his papers were deposited at the Harriet Irving Library at the University of New Brunswick some years after his death. During these years, a fire in the attic of the

Clarke house destroyed some of his papers. The monograph manuscript was among them.

Adney, having gained a level of professional status with the New Brunswick Museum, allowed his rivalry with Fred Clarke and the status of gatekeeper at the museum to eclipse good judgment. He of all people should have generously welcomed all serious contributions to the field of Indigenous cultural preservation. Clarke thought it was a simple case of jealousy: allowing the value of his work to be recognized by the museum would potentially put Adney's contribution in a lesser light.

By 1948 Adney's health was failing. He had lost his monthly income from The Mariners' Museum and was living in poverty, which meant he likely did not have the benefit of a nutritionally robust and well-balanced diet and may not have had for a long time.

We also know from Nola Hill's reports on the Hills' annual and sometimes semi-annual visits that they regularly replenished Adney's supply of canned food. Living alone, absorbed in his research interests, and providing assistance to his Indigenous friends, Adney's dependence on the convenience of canned food is easy to understand. The evidence of this dependence can still be seen in the midden at the bottom of the knoll behind the site of the bungalow.

Adney's contentiousness seemed to increase as he got older. He became confrontational — often for good reason — when circumstances riled him in certain ways. But it is uniquely odd that he behaved as he did toward Clarke, who was the only person close at hand with whom he could enjoy collaboration on regional archaeology and other cultural interests. Professional jealousy may be enough to account for it, but it seems out of character considering he had previously collaborated with others on various projects, always with attentiveness to honesty and fair dealing.

Clarke, being the writer he was, put pen to paper again and in 1968 published a major memoir of his archaeological explorations, generously laced with regional history, charming anecdotes, and character portraits of those who worked with him. *Someone Before Us* became one of Clarke's most popular books. Adney appears in the story, but no rancour remains on the part of the author.[5] Clarke avoids all mention of the monograph affair and includes this moving tribute to Adney in the book's dedication:

And lastly to the memory of Edwin Tappan Adney, who knew
more about the bark canoes of the North American Indian
than anyone else in the world, and in his many other activities
was the most remarkable genius I have ever known, this book is
affectionately dedicated.[6]

As Adney continued his research on a range of topics, he became
increasingly wary about not receiving credit for the work he was doing.
It was not just credit for tangible accomplishments that concerned him;
his recognition for those was firmly in place. It was also in the realm of
historical, cultural, and linguistic theory on which he had worked that he
wanted to make sure the credit due would be recognized and not stolen
by others. A synthesis of Wəlastəkwey cultural information into paths of
transmission and explanation are central to his research and scholarship
at this time.

Fannie Eckstorm gave him fair warning and he took it seriously. A
particularly revealing picture of his research and of his proprietary fear of
infringement comes up in a memo he wrote at the time of his association
with her.

October 18/45
The following are subjects for which the material is assembled
needing editing and condensation to be ready for publication—
under the auspices of the N.B. Historical Museum—all source
material on the Indians of New Brunswick.

1) The dragon myth of the eastern Algonkins, Wi-wil-a-
mehkw of the Malecites and the decorative-symbolic Horns of
Wi-wil-a-mehkw the 'Double-Curve Motive.' Its Norse origin.
Illustrated. Drawings of the latter to go with Canoe markings
and decoration of the Malecite birchbarks in the work on Bark
Canoes of the World.

2) Monograph on the Bark Canoes of the world—North
America, South America, Amur River, Japan, Australia and
New Zealand, Europe also. (Mariners' Museum publication)

3) Natural History of the Malecite Indians with analyses
of names, including mythical beings with corresponding earth
forms.

4) A Malecite (and Algonkian) Theogony revealing primitive astronomy and season cycles associated with animals composing the theogony, based in the tales of the Gluskap series; why Bear is the mother, Sable the younger brother, Groundhog the grandmother, Turtle the uncle of Gluskap who heads the Family as personification of Sun-Moon.

5) The L Particle in the Languages of the Algonkins showing an early Eastern Division of the Algonkins; its probable origin. Paper in advance of publication of full work on new method of language analysis.

6) A new method of language analysis illustrated by the Malecite dialect of Algonkian; explaining also European correspondences.

7) Chi-bel'-akw, the Malecite Charon, bearer of the souls of the departed to star-land. The middle one and leader of the Three Star-Hunters who pursue a Bear; Matapya of the Fox myth (name mistranslated by Dr. Wm. Jones); Chibiasbos of the Ojibways.

8) Indian place names of New Brunswick and adjacent areas with correction of mistranslations of some other place and tribal names.

9) The Dup-sko-di-gun-ul or personal markings (signatures) of the Malecites illustrated by Indian drawings on birchbark.

10) Old Malecite wooden traps now obsolete with drawings and photos, made period 1890–1900. Mink, Sable, Blackcat, Otter, Bear.

For information of Dr. F.G. Speck   Edwin Tappan Adney[7]

The last line indicates this memo was intended for Frank Speck at the University of Pennsylvania, but it is not clear it was ever sent. Adney had corresponded with Speck, but after Eckstorm's warning, this may have changed. In any event, it's an impressive list of research projects. Unfortunately, much of the "editing and condensation" process never occurred, and Adney's papers on these subjects remained as unpublished notes and drafts, with the exception of the bark-canoe book manuscript. In May 1945, five months before this list of projects was compiled, Adney did complete and publish his research study "The Malecite Indian's

Names for Native Berries and Fruits, and their Meanings" in the *Acadian Naturalist*.

The first item in Adney's list is worth pausing over because it is an example of the way his interest could be piqued and his broad cultural knowledge lead him on tangential investigations. When he noticed the dragon myth found in the Algonquin family of cultures was similar to that found in ancient Norse storytelling, he was led into a study of Old Norse. In addition, similar symbolic art forms associated with the dragon myth can be found in both cultures. Finally, Adney detected similar forms of language in Wəlastəkwey and Old Norse that made him wonder if the ancient Viking expeditions had travelled as far as the Wəlastəkw region of the continent and sustained a degree of interaction with the Indigenous population that would account for these similarities.

This whole framework of speculation was regarded as fanciful by the anthropological establishment at the time and dismissed out of hand, but that didn't deter Adney from delving into Old Norse to track down the research leads he found intriguing. One thing that can be said is that since 1963 we've known for a certainty there was a Viking settlement on the northern peninsula of Newfoundland. In addition, in 1956, an authentic eleventh-century Viking coin was found at a site on the coast of Maine that included a large collection of stone artifacts and pottery sherds, indicating Indigenous trade activity stretching from the eastern Great Lakes to Labrador (although some archaeologists have wondered whether the coin was planted at the site). Does this make Adney's speculation about Viking cultural influence on the Wəlastəkokewiyik less fanciful? Perhaps. All this is a long way from the primary contributions Adney made to the preservation of Indigenous culture and the defence of Indigenous rights, but it indicates the way his attention could be pulled into sidebar research while other more pertinent projects remained to be completed.

Devotion to research that borders on an obsession is a hazard of the ethnographic profession. There can sometimes grow a reluctance to call a halt, to say enough is enough, to bring a project to a conclusion. The unwillingness to forego an enticing research prospect that may yield yet another nugget of information can impinge on the time and energy needed to complete projects. When research becomes a way of life, its continuation can become more compelling than its completion. We see this playing out in Adney's latter years.

Clockwise from top left:
Sweat lodge model, birchbark and
hide (NBM 1944.374);
Birchbark wigwam model
(NBM 1944.493);
Birchbark and hide lean-to shelter
model (NBM 1943.121)

During the time Adney lived in Montréal, he built up a network of correspondence with some of the leading ethnologists, anthropologists, and museum professionals in Canada and the United States. They corresponded with him on a peer level, which at least provided a degree of professional recognition and satisfaction. Dr. J.C. Webster, a historian associated with the New Brunswick Museum in the city of Saint John, was among his correspondents. Once Adney resettled in the province, Webster became his link with this provincial institution of cultural preservation.

Adney cultivated his relationship with the New Brunswick Museum to the point where he was appointed to its advisory board. This, too, must have brought a degree of professional satisfaction to his later years, although it did not improve his livelihood. As noted earlier, Adney came to regard his role with the museum as the gatekeeper for all things relating to the history and culture of "the St. John River Indians."

In 1943, Adney received notice that two large crates from McGill University had been delivered to the New Brunswick Museum. He was advised that the Canadian military had taken over a large part of the museum's space and the crates wouldn't be unpacked until after the war was over. He was thanked for not being like Dr. Clarke who thought everything he donated should be immediately on display. Museum curators have their problems as well.

The crates contained the remainder of Adney's model recreations of Indigenous artifacts that had been stored at the McCord Museum. We tend to think of his contribution to the preservation of Indigenous material culture as resting primarily with the model canoes, but the collection includes models of shelters, toboggans, pelt stretchers, fish spears, animal traps, and a variety of canoe paddles. Stone tools recently collected and model canoes that had not gone to The Mariners' Museum or had been made since were also donated to the provincial museum at this time. In addition, Adney donated site maps of archaeological digs in the Wəlastəkw Valley region. Thanks to his foresight and generosity, some part of his model collection and manuscript files are now permanently secured in New Brunswick and are available for viewing and research.

Overall, however, Adney's papers and artifacts are now held at the following places:

- Harriet Irving Library, University of New Brunswick, Fredericton, New Brunswick
- Fredericton Region Museum (formerly York-Sunbury Museum), Fredericton, New Brunswick
- New Brunswick Provincial Archives, Fredericton, New Brunswick
- New Brunswick Museum, Saint John, New Brunswick
- Carleton County Historical Society, Woodstock, New Brunswick
- Peabody Essex Museum, Salem, Massachusetts
- Dartmouth College Library, Hanover, New Hampshire
- Cranbrook Institute of Science, Bloomfield Hills, Michigan
- The Mariners' Museum, Newport News, Virginia
- American Museum of Natural History, New York City, New York
- Franklin D. Roosevelt Museum and Presidential Library, Hyde Park, New York
- Canadian Museum of History, Gatineau, Quebec
- McCord Stewart Museum, Montréal, Quebec

All this takes the Adney researcher on a long and winding journey like the river voyages and the lure of the wilderness that first started the man himself on his research vocation. Adney never obtained the kind of steady, professional employment in the field of cultural preservation for which he was well qualified. As a field worker, he would have enhanced the program of any museum or university. An institutional research environment might

Tappan Adney at his writing desk in his bungalow, 1944 (*Time*)

have given him the resources and structure in which to complete the various manuscripts that remained unfinished at his death. But he did finish building the model canoes that make this collection complete, and, thanks to Howard Chapelle, the book to go with the collection was eventually published. Adney's research papers have found secure, professional placements, even if he did not.

But perhaps this lack of institutional employment is not to be regretted considering what he accomplished as an independent scholar, researcher, and activist. There is good evidence Adney held this assessment as well. In a letter to Dr. Webster on February 28, 1939, he wrote: "I refused Penfield's job as art editor at Harpers just because it would tie me down perhaps permanently."[8] His expectation of attachment to the Ethnological Museum at McGill was not simply so he could work for the institution but for the museum to take on his canoe preservation work as a program of its ethnographic division. Adney's contribution to heritage preservation and the defence of Indigenous rights flow from this freelance career and his multi-faceted vocational path.

In 1944, *Time* magazine assigned a reporter to write a story on Tappan Adney. It was a brief article but included a photograph of him at his writing desk with model canoes in the background. The story and photo prompted people who had known Adney but lost track of him to renew their contact. This must have pleased him, although the extra correspondence likely deflected his attention from his scholarly work. Adney enjoyed correspondence. He often sent multiple-page, single-space, typewritten letters to his friends and colleagues. The prospect of an attentive reader would often get his thoughts flowing in especially creative ways.

From this photo, we can envision the scholar at his desk in his bungalow in the woods. From the knoll on which his residence stood, paths led into the deeper reaches of the forest, along which we can imagine him frequently walking and enjoying the participant-observer role that was his natural bent and might otherwise be called communion. Nearby, the Wəlastəkw flows with its unceasing witness of abundance and continuity. We can think of him walking down to the shoreline at Lanes Creek and remembering the days of that summer long ago when he sat with Peter Jo, shaving ash ribs and getting the bend just right for the canoe they were building.

Chapter Fourteen

Friend of the Wəlastəkokewiyik and the Defence of Indigenous Rights

It is strange to think that...they merely gave the English permission to settle and trade in a country recognized as theirs, and...now it would seem to be the white man who gives the Indian permission to live here.
—Tappan Adney

In 2013, members of the Woodstock Wəlastəkwey community noticed the graves of Tappan and Minnie Bell in the Upper Woodstock Cemetery were marked only by small, flat, weather-worn stones. They took the initiative to place a new memorial monument at the gravesite. A music staff was engraved on the stone under Minnie Bell's name. A canoe was engraved under Tappan's name along with the inscription "Friend of the Maliseet" in English and Wəlastəkwey. We have now come to the part of the Adney story that gives him this enduring epitaph.

Before launching into this final chapter, it is fitting to pause and reflect on a factor in Adney's cultural background that was also present in his professional and social life. When he graduated from Trinity, Queen Victoria was still on the throne, and the colonizing force of the British Empire was still intact. He grew up in a time and a cultural milieu in which class and race distinctions were prominent and taken for granted as the way things were and were meant to be.

The theological worldview that such arrangements were divinely ordained was, however, losing its grip and a natural-history worldview was coming into prominence. Some interpreted a version of this worldview as supporting a similar ranking of ethnic groups and cultures. Herbert Spencer's doctrine of social Darwinism was widely influential at this time and provided intellectual support for this discriminatory line of reasoning. In this view, evolution was a progressive force that, for reasons of natural superiority, had elevated the culture of Great Britain and English-speaking people generally to the forefront of human development.

Adney's worldview was tinged with this kind of thinking when he came to New Brunswick, but something clearly began to change for him in this regard when he learned how to build a canoe under the guidance of Peter Jo. He may not have immediately abandoned all the stereotypes that come with race-category thinking, but he sustained a significant learning experience from his encounter with a culture other than his own. When this experience was followed by an immersion in the Wəlastəkwey language, his appreciation for their way of life developed to the point that he devoted much of the last decade of his life to the preservation of their culture and the battle for Indigenous rights.

Mary Bernard, the granddaughter of George Frederick Clarke and author of his biography, may have the most comprehensive perspective on Tappan Adney of anyone still alive. She did not know him personally, but through extensive conversations with her grandfather she accumulated information that helps further document Adney's social thinking and characteristic relationships.

Bernard writes that Adney was known to have an air of paternalistic superiority toward Indigenous people while at the same time having close working relationships and genuine friendships with individual Wəlastəkwi. She learned from conversations with her grandfather, however, that Adney's air of superiority was not simply a matter of cultural or ethnic bias. Adney, she notes, felt superior to everybody.[1] It was a habit of mind he consistently displayed. He had been an enrolled student at the University of North Carolina at the age of twelve and successfully completed two years of college-level courses. He published the results of his ornithological research in the American Ornithological Union newsletter at the age of sixteen. He had an uncanny knack for learning languages. He had been proficient in his learning Greek and Latin at Trinity, and he was now learning to speak Wəlastəkwey. Clearly, Adney possessed extraordinary intellectual capacities.

Bernard provides a key to understanding how Adney's sense of superiority and his cross-cultural relationships played out and came to a kind of resolution. While the sense of intellectual prowess with which he viewed the world was a fixed characteristic, she sees his relationship with Peter Paul — his linguistic mentor, colleague, and friend — as an experience that eroded residual racial bias. The degree to which he devoted his time and energy to the preservation of the Wəlastəkwey language and the battle for Indigenous rights in the last years of his life could only have come from a high valuation of the culture and a deep sense of solidarity. Friendship, reciprocity, and solidarity dissipate race-based categories of thought and feeling. Adney was explicit about how much had been given to him by his Wəlastəkwi friends. When they came to him for assistance, he could do no less than respond as fully as he was able.

December 7, 2006, was a landmark day for Indigenous rights in Canada. In the Sappier, Gray, and Polchies cases, the Supreme Court affirmed the inherent right of Mi'kmaq and Wəlastəkwey to harvest trees from Crown (public) land for subsistence use. The court's unanimous ruling grew out of appeals of the convictions of three Indigenous men, one Mi'kmaq and two Wəlastəkwi, for harvesting trees on Crown land in 1999 and 2001 without a license from the New Brunswick government. The high court ruled that harvesting wood for subsistence use had been integral to the culture of the Mi'kmaq and Wəlastəkwey before the arrival of Europeans and that right must be permitted to evolve and to take modern forms.

The spirits of Tappan Adney and his Wəlastəkwi friend Peter Paul must have been whispering in the ears of the judges as they deliberated. In 1946, Adney mounted a legal defence in a strikingly similar case. Paul, a prominent member of the Woodstock Wəlastəkwey community, was arrested for harvesting black ash saplings on private land. He was found guilty by a legal system that did not recognize the treaty that legally set up the conditions of European settlement in the region—in fact, it did not even know the treaty existed and did not recognize that the Wəlastəkwey and Mi'kmaq nations had never ceded either their land or access to its resources.

The first recognition that Indigenous people in the Maritimes legally retained access to their homeland territory and its resources came with the Supreme Court's decision in 1985 that Maritime treaties were true treaties. This reversed a 1929 lower court decision declaring that they were not true treaties since the Mi'kmaq and Wəlastokewiyik were not considered to be nations capable of making treaties. Then came the Marshall case in 1999 and the 2006 ruling on the Sappier, Gray, and Polchies cases added to a growing dossier of decisions by Canadian courts acknowledging the validity of two specific treaties from the eighteenth century. These treaties, between the Indigenous Peoples of the Maritime region and the British Crown, were agreements to maintain peace and friendship. They ceded neither land or resources.

However, the European invasion of the Wəlastəkw began almost immediately after the last treaty was signed in 1760, in spite of objections and resistance on the part of the Wəlastokewiyik. It also appears to have occurred in violation of the Royal Proclamation of 1763, which declared that no Indigenous lands could be taken or settled unless they were first ceded or sold to the Crown. Nevertheless, colonial representatives of the Crown acted as if they had a legal right to grant huge parcels of Indigenous lands in the Maritimes to colonial immigrants. Following the American Revolution as many as eleven thousand Loyalists were granted ownership rights to Wəlastəkwey lands the entire length of the Wəlastəkw from its mouth to above what is now Woodstock.

Although the colonial representatives of the Crown continued to dispose of land into private ownership as if they had the legal right to do so, the Indigenous people of the region never forgot that their traditional territory remained unceded. Since the Peace and Friendship Treaties were ignored by colonial administrators and subsequent regional governments, the inherent rights of Indigenous people of the region were routinely violated.

The illegality of this situation was exposed when Adney prepared his defence of Paul based on his discovery of one of several Peace and Friendship Treaties from the 1700s. (More about the Peter Paul case in due course.) He did not prevail in his defence, but he was correct in his legal interpretation of the treaties. The work of subsequent researchers and eventual Canadian Supreme Court decisions have vindicated the case he made. Legally, the 2006 Supreme Court ruling in the cases of Sappier, Gray, and Polchies applies only to the Wəlastəkokewiyik and Mi'kmaq of the Maritime provinces, but it may serve as a precedent for similar cases in other parts of Canada.

Adney's work on behalf of Paul was but one of four Indigenous rights initiatives that absorbed his time and energy from the mid-1940s until his death in 1950. The other three were revising the Indian Act, reconstituting the "St. John River Indians" as a tribal unit, and opposing the forced removal of people from several smaller Wəlastəkwey communities to a centralized relocation at Kingsclear, New Brunswick.[2]

He considered his Indigenous rights work in the final years of his life a compelling obligation to his Wəlastəkwi friends even if it meant he would not be able to complete his canoe book. His devotion to the cause of Indigenous rights was a repayment, willingly offered, for the debt he owed the Wǝlastǝkokewiyik who had inspired a central theme in his life's vocation when he first came to New Brunswick.

In the eighteenth and early nineteenth centuries, non-Indigenous landowners in the Maritimes routinely acknowledged Indigenous rights for hunting, fishing, and gathering. In the mid-1800s, both federal and provincial authorities began curtailing and abolishing Indigenous hunting and fishing rights in New Brunswick, thereby preventing Indigenous communities from engaging in traditional self-provisioning activities. Indigenous rights to access wood, however, were generally recognized by land owners as the result of an oral recollection of a 1778 agreement between the Wǝlastǝkokewiyik and representatives of the Crown.

On his first trip to New Brunswick in 1887, Adney recorded the complaint of a Wǝlastǝkwi woman he called Old Margaret.

Seems like that government down Fredericton try let Injun starve. He make law can't ketch no salmon up here. I think that government better send soldiers up here and shoot all the Injuns. Then we die quick. Now we die slow.[3]

To survive, many Indigenous people simply continued their traditional lifestyle, hunting, fishing, and gathering as they always had, but now away from the watchful eye of the game wardens. During the late 1800s, the traditional subsistence activities of hunting and fishing, once considered the birthright of the Wǝlastǝkokewiyik, came to be considered illegal. Although the old belief on the part of landowners in the Wǝlastǝkwey right to access wood seems to have lingered in certain places, by Adney's time it was generally forgotten. There was no mention of this orally transmitted tradition in the written account of the 1778 meeting. Adney's intervention in the Paul case challenged the legal basis for this judgment and opened the way to the now widespread movement for Indigenous rights to land and its resources.

During the Second World War, Adney became involved with the movement to rewrite the antiquated and ineffective Indian Act. The Peter Paul case and the revision of the Indian Act became so intertwined that their stories can best be told as a single narrative. For some years prior to Paul's 1946 arrest, Adney had been corresponding with a Conservative member of Parliament, John R. MacNicol, about the desperate state of the Indigenous people in New Brunswick. MacNicol was an important contact for Adney because he was a member of the House of Commons committee in Ottawa that dealt with "Indian affairs."

MacNicol became convinced the Indian Act needed a major revision. He resolved to push for legislative reform after the war to address land claims, citizenship, housing, education, health care, and a long list of other concerns vital to the well-being of Indigenous people in Canada. A special joint Senate-House committee of Parliament was formed in May 1946 to consider revisions to the Indian Act.

Adney drafted a brief on the history of the relationship between the Wəlastəkokewiyik and the Canadian government to provide the committee with a factual foundation for their hearings. It was one of six briefs on various topics Adney provided the committee during its deliberations, which extended to 1948.

The major issue in the Maritime provinces was the denial of treaty rights and the unlawful confiscation of land from Indigenous people. From research Adney had been conducting for a book he was writing on the history of the Wəlastəkokewiyik, he knew the long sad story of gradual dispossession of land and access to the land's resources. It was clear to him from his research that the Peace and Friendship Treaty between the British Crown and the Wabinaki tribes of the whole region, signed at Boston in 1725 and signed again specifically with the Wəlastəkokewiyik and the Mi'kmaq at Annapolis, Nova Scotia, in 1726, was still legally in force. No relinquishment of land or access to the resources of the land was called for in these treaties. By the logic of the only legal context that existed and was still in force, Adney reasoned that government land grants to white settlers in New Brunswick were illegal without the consent of the Indigenous community — the original holders of the land.

In December 1944, two years before Peter Paul was arrested, Adney was prepared when asked for advice. Paul wanted to know how to deal with a landowner who had threatened him with arrest for cutting ash saplings on his property.

Here is part of Adney's response:

The relationship of the Malecite Indians of the St. John...to
the English...is not the ordinary one of citizens, but of solemn
treaty rights. In the treaties with the English at Boston and later
at...Nova Scotia...the Indians were guaranteed of remaining
in possession of certain rights pertaining to a hunting people.
Among these was "the free liberty of hunting and fishing."

Your people were, in all treaties, considered as a sovereign
nation and as owners of the soil. But many of his rights have
been taken away. He has been made subject to the game and
fishing laws, and there have been violations of his treaty rights,
against which he has been powerless to protest effectively.

One of the most important of these violations of treaty rights
concerns the land. The British authorities, at the close of the
Revolutionary War, in 1783, were faced with the problem of
numerous Loyalist troops and their families. Without consulting
the Indians, and without their permission, they surveyed both
sides of the river...and allotted lands...to disbanded soldiers of
the Loyalist troops.

Now the law among nations is that the terms of a treaty cannot
be changed without the consent of both parties. The Indians
have never given their consent—except as forced by superior
pressure—to any change in the treaty. In the transfer of authority
to the Canadian government the Ottawa government undertook
to carry out the terms of the treaties made previously with King
George and has made of the Indians what it terms wards.

Now in some of the Provinces the Indians have formally
surrendered their lands to the Crown.... There is no record
that the Indians of the St. John have ever made such surrender.
Consequently, the issue between you, Peter Paul, and the man
who claims ownership of the land where you have been cutting
your barrel hoop poles, is one of right and title. Even if you are
arrested for theft or for trespass, no magistrate has powers to deal
with the case...the magistrate must either dismiss the case or let it
go to the next higher court, which is not the county court, but the
Supreme, or King's Bench, Court.

Go right ahead and if the matter comes to trial, I will see
you represented by counsel (whether the Indian Agent chooses
to act or not). The complainant will be asked to prove his title...

and that will raise the question…of the Crown's right to dispose
of the Indian's land and land-rights belonging to him by treaty.
In the event of a charge being laid, civil or criminal, against
the Indian Peter Paul…I will ask for dismissal with costs to the
complainant:

> (a) From a magistrate's court, on the ground of no
> jurisdiction in a case where title to land and land rights are
> involved;
> (b) From the Provincial Supreme Court…on the ground
> that it has no jurisdiction where interpretation of a treaty
> is involved. This being purely and solely a Federal matter
> outside of Provincial jurisdiction.[4]

With all the research Adney had done for his book and for the revision
of the Indian Act, he had his arsenal of historical evidence and legal
argument loaded and ready for battle when Peter Paul was arrested and
formally charged with theft on August 21, 1946. Paul's status as a ward of
the state meant the government was responsible for providing him with
legal representation. He was not free to hire his own lawyer. Legal defence
had to be arranged for him by Edward Whalen, the Indian agent for the
region, who was based in Fredericton. But when Paul was charged, Whalen
was travelling out of the area and could not be reached. Pending Whalen's
return, Adney stepped forward as a "friend of the prisoner" to represent
Paul. This was an irregular situation, but apparently Chief Magistrate
K.E. McLaughlin allowed Adney standing in the case.

Adney's strategy in defending Paul was to assert that Paul had an *absolute*
right to hunt and gather wherever and whenever he liked, regardless of
private "ownership" of the land. The absolute right, Adney maintained,
was guaranteed in the 1725 treaty, covering all tribes from Massachusetts
to Nova Scotia, including the Saint John River Indians.

The guarantee of Indigenous rights in old treaties was well known in
the oral history of the Wəlastəkokewiyik, but the actual documents had
long since been laid away in a distant archive. With the help of his friend
and ethnologist colleague Fannie Eckstorm, Adney located an original 1725
treaty in the Massachusetts State Archives in Boston. He had a photostatic
copy made, certified, and mailed to him, but it had not arrived by the time
Paul's case was to be heard. (What Adney never seems to have known
was that two treaties were signed in Boston in 1725.[5] Both claimed to be

LEGAL ARGUMENT FORESEEN IN CASE

Indian at Woodstock Uses Old Treaty in His Defence

WOODSTOCK, Sept. 6—(Special) —The case of Peter Paul, a Maliseet Indian, charged with stealing poles from Harold Rogers, was continued in police court here. The defence is raising the plea that Indians have an old treaty right to enter private property and remove ash for their handicraft.

Little progress was made today. Lea Cain of Fredericton, who appeared for the defendant, told the court he had only recently been retained and as a great amount of research would be necessary he requested an adjournment of two weeks. It was intimated that both sides would probably require an additional adjournment at the end of that time. September 19 was tentatively set for hearing.

D. R. Bishop appeared for the Crown. Edward Whalen of Fredericton, Indian agent, was in attendance as was E. Tappan Adney of Upper Woodstock, who had been acting as prisoner's friend pending the obtaining of counsel. Paul is at liberty on his own recognizance.

Saint John *Telegraph Journal* report on the Peter Paul case, September 6, 1946 (Adney fonds, UNB Archives)

negotiated on behalf of all Wabanakis, but the one he obtained was never signed by any Wəlastəkokewiyik. That it was actually signed by Boston representatives of the Crown rather than Nova Scotia representatives has meant it has never been recognized in Canada. The other treaty of 1725, consisting of two parts, also contains specific hunting and fishing rights, but only in the part containing English promises to the Wabanaki First Nations. The part containing First Nations promises to the English is the only part that seems to have survived, that is until 1983.)

Adney prepared a brief that asserted the 1725 treaty was still in force since it had never been abrogated and the Wəlastəkokewiyik had never sold the land. He further declared that since Paul's case involved treaty issues, it could only be heard in a federal court, since only the federal government had jurisdiction in treaty matters. He planned to ask for dismissal of all charges because the local court lacked jurisdiction. Adney maintained that Paul actually had a better claim to the land and its natural resources than the plaintiff, Harold Rogers, because the treaty predated Rogers's purchase of the land.

On the day of the trial, August 22, 1946, Adney began presenting his treaty entitlement defence. When Magistrate McLaughlin saw where he was headed with this defence, he recessed the trial. It was clear Adney was presenting a defence that went to the heart of the historic relationship of the Indigenous people and the Crown, which now meant the federal government, a context of jurisdiction beyond that of the Carleton County Court magistrate.[6]

A few days later, Whalen returned and hired Fredericton attorney Leo Cain to defend Paul. Even though Cain and Whalen were aware of Adney's treaty defence and could have used his research, they chose instead to use the "colour of right" defence. This defence is based on long-standing, common, and uncontested Indigenous usage of both private and public land for hunting and gathering and on the defendant's honest belief his action was legal and that it was his right to continue this practice.

When the trial resumed several weeks later, the color of right defence came as a surprise to Adney, as did Cain's decision not to consult with him on defence strategy. It was particularly grating to Adney that Cain refused to use the certified copy of the 1725 Peace and Friendship Treaty Adney had now received from the Massachusetts state archives in Boston.

Cain's defence did not work. On October 24, 1946, Magistrate McLaughlin ruled there is "but one law of theft for both Indians and whites." The court did not recognize any special privileges or rights for Indians people. Paul was found guilty of theft but, significantly, was not jailed or fined; he was not even required to return the "stolen" property or to pay restitution. The magistrate simply instructed Peter Paul to ask permission next time he wanted to cut a tree on private property.

Apparently, Adney was incensed by the verdict and caused some sort of disturbance in the court. No record has been found of what he said or did, but here is what Crown Prosecutor D.R. Bishop afterward wrote in a letter to Adney:

> I did not think that even a difference with your own counsel was a reason for showing contempt of the court and everyone in it.
> I must state that I did not like your statement that the District

Attorney must never lose a case as fitness for office may be
questioned.[7]

Bishop concluded with a respectful nod to Adney, however, saying,
"I might say that I am quite disappointed that you did not argue the case
or assist in doing so."

In a timely coincidence, a fact-finding Royal Commission from Ottawa,
made up of members of the larger special committee on Indian Affairs,
visited the Woodstock Reserve shortly after Paul's conviction. They were
touring the Maritimes, visiting reserves and gathering evidence and written
testimony regarding a revision of the Indian Act.

When the Wəlastəkwey communities were notified by the Indian agent
that the commission would be visiting them, preparations were made
for what they expected would be substantial face-to-face conversations
in which they could air their grievances with sympathetic members of
Parliament. But the commission scheduled only brief visits to each reserve.
The Woodstock visit lasted less than half a day and did not fulfill the
expectations of a substantial dialogue. Adney was invited to lunch with
the members of the commission. When he told them about the Peter Paul
conviction, they urged him to appeal it.

In November 1946, Adney wrote a detailed appeal and hired Perth
attorney C.R. Mercereau to represent Peter Paul. However, a month later
Adney notified District Attorney Bishop that the appeal had been dropped.
He said in his letter that, after consultation with Paul and Chief William
Saulis, they had decided that appealing the case would be too expensive
and time-consuming and would have little chance of success because of the
lack of a treaty precedent in Canadian law. Adney wrote, "The case was
presented in writing to the Royal Commission when they visited Woodstock
Reserve and again at Madawaska. This is, in effect, an appeal to a higher
court."[8]

Adney was speaking metaphorically when he wrote "higher court."
He would have known that in presenting the case to the Royal Commission
he was moving it to the political level where laws are changed and initiated.
In this sense he was appealing to a higher level of decision-making.

He followed up on March 6, 1947, by sending a copy of his appeal brief
to the special committee in Ottawa. He reasoned that changing the law
via the special committee and parliamentary action would have the same

effect as winning the appeal in court. The special committee continued to conduct formal hearings, inviting tribal representatives from throughout Canada to testify in Ottawa with travel and living expenses paid by the government. But invitations were not issued to tribal representatives from the Maritime provinces because the Royal Commission had already taken evidence and depositions there during its tour. Chief Saulis of the Tobique Reserve attended the special committee hearings at his own expense. He wanted Adney to accompany him to Ottawa, but since the government would not cover costs, he was unable to do so.

The Special Joint Committee on Indian Affairs reported its findings to Parliament on July 10, 1947, including the recommendation that a claims commission be established to resolve hundreds of treaty and land disputes, some of them dating back centuries. The committee's report and recommendations languished through the 1948, 1949, and 1950 sessions of Parliament, held up by incessant wrangling over amendments. Perhaps the biggest barrier, however, was the Liberal government's reluctance to open a national debate on incendiary issues such as treaty claims, citizenship, and the notorious residential school system.

Adney received regular reports on the lack of progress through copies of *Debates of House of Commons*, sent by his friends on the special committee. He was undoubtedly dismayed and frustrated. The special committee had worked for two years, held sixty-seven meetings, heard 102 witnesses, received 153 written briefs, and produced 2,500 pages of the minutes of proceedings and evidence. In its deliberations, the committee discovered appalling statistics: 40 per cent of "Indian" children were not attending school and only 1 per cent went beyond the eighth grade; tuberculosis death rates among "Indians" were seventeen times greater than among other Canadians; pneumonia death rates eight times higher; infant mortality rates three times higher; and there were also the perennially higher rates of alcoholism, domestic violence, and suicide.

In the end, the hearings, the testimony, the statistics, and the Parliamentary debates made almost no difference to Indigenous people in Canada. The new Indian Act of 1951 made administrative changes in the way "Indians" were governed but no change in the fundamental issue of their official status as wards of the state, living under authoritarian rule and without adequate access to basic resources and livelihood opportunities.

A national consensus at the political level to make meaningful changes to the Indian Act simply did not exist. The new Indian Act was passed May 17, 1951 — nearly six years after the committee began working and six months after Adney's death. Nobody was cheering, not the special committee members, not the Indigenous people, not the public, not the press. An editorial in the *Globe and Mail* said it all:

> Five years ago when a Parliamentary Committee went to work on Canada's Indian problem, there was high hope that after nearly a century this minority in our population would get a new deal. The decrepit old Indian Act of 1876...was generations out of date.
> Now that the Government's conception of...basic reform has passed...the Act is still in that condition. Certainly there is nothing in the Indian Bill they approved to afford anything but humiliation and exasperation. If the public of Canada were half as interested as it should be in minority justice this poor measure would never have gotten through Commons at all.[9]

Adney's hope for sweeping policy reforms died a year before the bill's passage, when it became apparent that the new Indian Act would produce no fundamental change. Indigenous people in Canada would still not be able to vote or hold public office without surrendering their "Indian" status. They would not control their tribal finances, operate their own courts, or govern themselves on their own reservations. The local Indian agent would remain the final authority on all questions. They could not appeal his decisions to a higher authority. And there would be no land claims commission to settle land disputes.

The failure to effectively overhaul the Indian Act with regard to land and resource rights meant Peter Paul's case could not be advanced within the Canadian legal system. Paul's conviction remained on the books, adding to the weight of similar convictions that until the late 1990s and early 2000s supported the notion that Indigenous people had no special rights for fishing, hunting, or resource gathering.

For nearly three hundred years, Indigenous people in the Maritime region of Canada have known through their oral history that a treaty with the British Crown guaranteed their inherent right to hunt, fish, and gather resources from the land. In fact, there were two very different treaties, both signed in Boston in 1725. One, called Dummer's Treaty, was later ratified by Penobscots and Abenakis in what is now Maine in 1726. The text of the other one was written by Major Paul Mascarene who had been sent to Boston with instructions from the royal governor of Nova Scotia to draw up a different treaty for Nova Scotia. Wəlastəkwi and Mi'kmaq chiefs had not been present in Boston for the 1725 negotiating and signing. Only four Penobscots were there to negotiate a treaty. Nevertheless, they initialled both treaties, but since there is no record of any negotiations over the different terms of Mascarene's Treaty, it is quite likely that the Penobscots were not aware of the differences between the two. It is also possible the Mi'kmaq and Wəlastəkokewiyik who ratified the treaty in Annapolis were not aware of the different terms, either. They likely believed it was the same Peace and Friendship Treaty that their Penobscot brothers had signed.

By Adney's time, only one part of the treaty ratified in Annapolis had survived. And since it was the only part containing promises made by the representatives of the Indigenous tribes, Adney had every reason to believe there had been double-dealing by the British. It contained no reciprocal English promises and with only a one-sided list of obligations for Indigenous people, it did not even qualify as a treaty. Since the discovery of the missing part of Mascarene's Treaty in 1983, it is now known that this treaty did in fact include the important promise not to molest Indigenous people in their hunting and fishing, along with other promises.

That the treaty seemed to lack reciprocal promises was not the only reason Adney considered it to be an intentional fraud and a scheme by British authorities to steal Indigenous land in the Maritimes. He noticed disturbing differences between the two treaties, even in the part that did survive and contained the Indian promises. For instance, where Dummer's Treaty promises to respect Indigenous title to lands not already conveyed or sold to the English, Mascarene's contains no such promise. Instead, it requires Indigenous peoples in Nova Scotia not to molest settlements "lawfully to be made." And where Dummer's Treaty required that Indigenous Peoples submit to King George, Mascarene's not only demanded a pledge of loyalty to the king, but also declared King George to be "the rightful possessor of Nova Scotia or Acadie..."

Immediately after the signing, the two parts of the treaty were sent to England, where they were deposited in the Public Record Office in London. In 1983, Wəlastəkwi scholar Andrea Bear Nicholas found photocopies of both parts of the treaty in the Library and Archives Canada. In 2001, she was able to view the original in London. The second part of the treaty, which came to be known as Mascarene's Promises, states that "the Indians shall not be molested in their persons, hunting, fishing and planting grounds.[10]

With the addition of the 1983 discovery of the promises portion of Mascarene's Treaty, the version signed in Nova Scotia suddenly became useful to the Wəlastəkokewiyik, since two of them were in court at that same time facing serious fines for hunting deer. They were subsequently exonerated. Over the next few years, the province unsuccessfully appealed the decision twice, once even after the 1985 Supreme Court decision declaring Maritime treaties to be true treaties. Since the Nova Scotia version had been signed and ratified in Canada by both British authorities and Wəlastəkwi delegates, there is no question about its validity under Canadian law.

Over the intervening decades, and from generation to generation, the promises attached to the treaty were told and retold within Wəlastəkwey communities, becoming part of oral history and engendering an unshakable belief in their treaty rights. Two years after Andrea Bear Nicholas's 1983 discovery of Mascarene's Promises, the Supreme Court of Canada formally recognized the legal validity of the 1752 Treaty between the Mi'kmaq and the Crown. In making this decision the Supreme Court effectively reversed a 1828 Nova Scotia court decision that declared the Maritime treaties not to be true treaties since the Mi'kmaq were not deemed to be a nation.[11] Taken together with the finding of the complete Mascarene's Treaty it has heralded the dawn of a new day for Indigenous rights in the Maritimes.

Adney's claim of an absolute right for Indigenous people to fish, hunt, and gather resources from the land has now been entrenched in Canadian law. Supreme Court rulings in recent times have regularly upheld these practices. However, instead of accepting this new reality and instituting new regulations to accommodate the changed situation, the provincial governments of New Brunswick and Nova Scotia continued to oppose Indigenous rights in court in the 1980s. They appealed the rulings that upheld the rights of the Wəlastəkwey and Mi'kmaq to hunt, fish, and access other resources of their traditional lands. The government of New Brunswick lost in its own Court of Appeal and gave up its opposition. Nova Scotia followed suit.

Adney never knew about the existence of the English promises in Mascarene's Treaty signed in Nova Scotia in 1726. If he had, he would have most certainly presented them to the court as key evidence in support of Indigenous rights in the Maritimes. Even though Adney's defence efforts failed and his arguments were never given a serious hearing by the Canadian government, the fact remains he understood the legal essence of the Peace and Friendship Treaties and foresaw the outcome of their recognition sixty years before Canadian courts took up the issue and confirmed the matter. In assembling the rationale for the Peter Paul case in 1946, Adney became the first person to present a well-documented treaty defence of Indigenous rights in a Maritime-region courtroom.[12] Like his wife, Minnie Bell, Tappan would have made a great lawyer had he chosen that profession.

Years before the special committee's recommendation for a land claims commission, Indian Affairs bureaucrats in Ottawa claimed that Maliseets (Wəlastəkokewiyik) had no treaty rights because the "Saint John River

Chief Would Reconstitute Old Indian Tribe

PERTH, Dec. 10—(Special)— William Saulis, chief of the Tobique Indian Reserve, has undertaken to reconstitute the old Indian tribe along the St. John River. Already Chief Saulis has interested the Woodstock and Madawaska Reserves in joining with Indians on the Tobique Reserve in the movement. He hopes to enlist the support of Indian groups in the lower part of the province in the effort to reconstitute the old St. John River tribe of Indians, "Wullastooks," to deal more effectively with the Canadian government in Indian matters. While each present group would retain its chief, Indians on the various reserves would be united under a common chief.

Saint John *Telegraph Journal* report on reestablishing the "Saint John River Indians" as a recognized "tribe," December 10, 1946 (Adney fonds, UNB Archives)

Indians" who signed the 1726 treaty no longer existed as a cohesive tribal unit.[13] This was a misperception. The Wəlastəkwey had always lived in every part of the Wəlastəkw watershed with Meductic as the main village.

To make their case in dealing with the federal government, Adney persuaded Chief William Saulis of the Tobique community to organize all the Wəlastəkwey communities under the tribal name Wulastooks. The objective of the name change, and the establishment of a tribal council, was to create a jurisdictional unit for land claim negotiations. In order to successfully assert that the 1725–26 Treaty applied to the "Saint John River Indians," they needed to reconstitute their tribal identity.

Maliseet was a nickname given to the Wəlastəkokewiyik by the Mi'kmaq. It means, as Pat Paul of Tobique First Nation has said, "slow or lazy speakers."[14] The name was picked up by subsequent mapmakers and visitors and became commonly used. When it became apparent the original name of the tribe would enhance prospects for the settlement of land claims, Adney drafted legal papers to officially change the name and to revive and reconstitute tribal government, uniting the six "St. John River Indian" communities into one tribal unit with representatives chosen from local bands.

Meanwhile, Chief Saulis, representing Tobique, worked with the chiefs of the bands at Devon (Saint Mary's), Oromocto, Madawaska, Woodstock, and Kingsclear to reconstitute a tribal government with Wulastook as the official name. Adney was careful to play a supporting role, under the leadership of Chief Saulis. In the fall of 1946, he addressed a gathering of Wəlastəkwi Elders:

> Friends, men of the Wulastooks of the River St. John: I have
> known your people for many years, hunted alongside your old
> hunters, learned your ways.... Those years were valuable to me.
> And the past ten years and more have been the happiest of my
> life as I came to learn more of your language and came to feel
> that no Indian was more welcome at your homes.... Now we are
> about to have change, and as I have advised you when you came
> to me in your troubles and know how to talk to the highest in the
> land, I am now trying to help, with no thought of reward but the
> happiness that comes from helping others...who deserve help and
> good counsel.

He went on to express surprise and gratitude that they have spontaneously donated funds to help with the expenses of his treaty research before concluding:

> It is pleasing to see the Indians working together, and I hope you
> will work with those of Tobique, and maybe we can rebuild the
> old nation of the Wulastooks, called the St. John River Indians,
> and present your troubles to the Government as a solid body
> united.[15]

Adney outlined the reconstitution plan and sent it to the lawyer C.R. Mercereau on November 8, 1946, along with a letter in which he wrote:

> I am enclosing a plan for reconstituting the old tribe of the St.
> John River Indians, looking forward to formal incorporation.
> I suggested this objective to Chief Saulis in a rough plan....
> Saulis is a mighty good man and he proceeded to get the
> different reservations together to defend the local right of
> hunting, fishing, material gathering.... But he needs help, of a
> kind that can only come from me. This documentary part for
> complete reorganization he cannot do alone and I don't want
> to have him miss the matter. I am giving Saulis full support
> and credit.[16]

In 1948, Chief William Saulis sent a letter to Adney in which he wrote the following:

> ...you have an Indian heart...I don't know where I would have
> got, or how far I would have gone without your guiding hand,
> and I only hope that you will be able to carry on for years to
> come...side by side we have treaded along with one thing in view,
> the real justice for the tribe....[17]

Later, Chief Saulis wrote again:

> ...you have come to know me truly in all my dealings and
> contacts with you, and I have foreseen from the first day we met
> three years ago that you were one man that could be trusted

because on the base of our talk that day, printed in my heart
the nature of the man you were. I continue to tell my band of
Indians the true friend you are to them.... I have always said that
no White Man could ever understand a Indian unless he had
Indian blood in his veins, but how greatly I made that mistake,
because you understood me thoroughly. You even knowed my
feelings. I never will forget my true friend.[18]

In late December 1948, the reconstitution of the tribe was complete.
But maintaining the new tribal government and gaining formal acceptance
in Ottawa proved to be more difficult. Adney expected the new Indian Act
to institute a broad range of reforms, including land claim negotiations,
for which the new tribal government would be an effective representative
for the Wəlastəkokewiyik.

The new Indian Act came into effect in 1951, shortly after Adney's
death. When it turned out to be little more than a continuation of the
previous act, the opportunity for a tribal government to negotiate with
the federal government did not open up. With this lack of negotiating
opportunity, a unified tribal voice lost its primary rationale and faded—but
only temporarily.

In 1942, the Department of Indian Affairs (DIA) of the government of
Canada began formulating a plan to simplify its administration by closing
down Indigenous reserves with small populations and moving residents
to larger reserves where schools, housing, and medical facilities could be
provided more efficiently and at lower cost.

In early 1946, this scheme was applied to New Brunswick. Three
Wəlastəkwey communities were targeted: Woodstock, Oromocto, and
Devon (Saint Mary's). These reserves were to be closed and their residents
moved to Kingsclear, located on the west bank of the Wəlastəkw twelve
miles upriver from Fredericton. The DIA did not consult with the people
involved. The local Indian agent simply made the announcement.

The DIA purchased a five-hundred-acre farm and woodland adjoining
the existing Kingsclear Reserve with the intention of partitioning it into
three-acre plots for subsistence farming. In addition to the threatened loss
of "Indian" status, positive incentives were offered. The people were told
that Kingsclear would have new houses, a school, a medical clinic, graded

roads, land to farm, farm buildings and equipment, chickens and pigs, and potatoes and turnips in the ground ready to harvest.

Those who refused to relocate were told they would not be compelled to do so, but if they chose to stay in their current locations they would have to "provide for themselves." This meant the government would take no further responsibility for them. They would lose their "Indian" status and no longer be eligible for government housing, welfare payments, and schools for their children.

The residents of the Oromocto, Saint Mary's, and Woodstock reserves were understandably alarmed and contacted Adney for help. By May 1, 1947, only a few months after he concluded work on the Peter Paul case, and while his efforts to reconstitute the tribe and revamp the Indian Act were still ongoing, Adney wrote that the centralization scheme "is taking my full attention." In characteristic fashion, he launched a barrage of letters to newspapers, DIA officials, and his friends on the special committee in Ottawa. He forcefully stated the case against the legitimacy of the DIA unilaterally exercising this autocratic decision-making power.

> If Indian Affairs can, under the excuse of a centralization plan…
> close a reserve and disown those who choose to remain, it has the
> power to close any other reserve, and, in effect, all the reserves
> in Canada. This manifestly is a power the Indian Department
> should not be allowed to exercise. If the government is a trustee
> and the Indian a ward, the trustee has no right to terminate
> that trusteeship. That part of the Indian Act must be amended.
> The Indian Affairs department should not be allowed the power
> to dispose of the Indian question and the Indians' status as a
> ward of government.

Adney further noted the residents at the three reserves opposed their removal to Kingsclear under any circumstances:

> None want to become either part time or full-time farmers. They
> believe the condition of the reserves can and should be improved
> without the…residents having to remove from where they are,
> and they insist that the Indian Affairs was being deceitful when
> it said "the Indians will not be removed without their consent."

Adney saw through the DIA's strategy, saying consent was not the issue.

> The point is whether such consent is voluntary and without
> threat. Threat has been made at Oromocto that unless they give
> their consent they will no longer be considered Indians and the
> government will have nothing more to do with them. [19]

In early June 1947, the centralization issue caught the attention of probate judge George Y. Jones, who volunteered his services to file suit in Exchequer Court to have the DIA cease its removal activities. Two weeks later Adney visited Judge Jones's office and found he had suddenly acquired a different attitude. Judge Jones was now advising delay and accommodation with the DIA. Adney concluded that since the judge was a Liberal, and Liberals controlled the government, some sort of political deal had been made to change his mind.

Meanwhile, some Indigenous veterans who had served in the Second World War and others from Oromocto reluctantly consented to be resettled at Kingsclear as farmers, fearing that if they did not, they would lose assistance from the government. But by the following spring in 1948, nearly all those who had moved to Kingsclear had returned to Oromocto.

A letter from Chief John Paul of Oromocto to Chief Saulis of Tobique, then also acting secretary of the Wulastook tribe, describes what happened:

> ...we were told last spring that if we move to Kingsclear...we'd
> be well looked after. But things turn out just the opposite way.
> There isn't one thing we got we were promised. We supposed to
> get chickens and pigs...also good warm houses. Those houses
> weren't finished inside. They were very cold. Mr. Whalen our
> Indian Agent...told us he was planting potatoes and turnips for
> us. Well...each family received one bag of turnips...and that's
> all we got out of the whole racket.
>
> So now we are all back to Oromocto again, except three
> family which stranded at Kingsclear. Oh yes, Indian Agent went
> to work and dismantle houses while we were up Kingsclear. Also,
> there about 18–20 children running around every day, no school
> to go to. Our school was rented to white people. Looks very grim
> for us people down here in Oromocto. [20]

Unveiling ceremony of new Adney grave marker. Organizer Eric Paul, grandson of Peter Paul, stands to the left with paper in hand. Tappan and Minnie Bell's granddaughter Joan Adney Dragon and her two daughters, Lois and Kimber, are present. Upper Woodstock Cemetery, 2013 (photo: Daryl Hunter)

A year later, D.S. Harkness, a member of Parliament, a member of the special committee, and a supporter of Indigenous rights, brought the issue before Parliament in public debate on the floor of the House of Commons. Harkness also wrote to DIA officials demanding an explanation of their centralization policy.

DIA director Robert Hoey replied: "I cannot but regret your decision to make this matter the subject of a protest to the Indian Affairs Committee and the House against the action of this Branch and its officers...." Adney celebrated this small victory, saying, "I will have to practice up on the War Dance!"[21]

The last Adney paper found on the relocation plan is dated June 19, 1949, when he was approaching his eighty-first birthday. It restates all the previous arguments, but ends with a new plea:

> These...centralization plans have got to be stopped before more
> serious damage is done, and more important, to the feelings of
> the Indian toward the government and its officials.
>
>   Indian Affairs can no longer go ahead and give orders, but
> they don't seem to have learned that.[22]

No other documents, correspondence, or newspaper clippings have been found on the DIA centralization scheme, but the fact that all six Wəlastəkwey

New grave marker for Edwin Tappan Adney and Minnie Bell Sharp Adney.
Upper Woodstock Cemetery, 2013 (photo: Daryl Hunter)

communities are still functioning and stronger than ever testifies to the success of Adney's campaign. Perhaps the Wəlastəkokewiyik could have won the battle on their own, but certainly Adney's efforts raised awareness and support in Ottawa and in New Brunswick for the campaign to stop the DIA's forced removal scheme.

There is yet another poignant aspect to these four initiatives by Adney to help his Indigenous friends. While he was working to defend Peter Paul, to support the overhaul of the Indian Act, to reconstitute the tribal status of the "St. John River Indians," and to oppose the DIA centralization scheme, he was sacrificing work on his canoe book. His manuscript preparation was supported by a $100 monthly stipend from The Mariners' Museum. When the museum discovered in September 1947 that Adney had not worked on the canoe book for more than a year, the stipend was suspended in the hope it would induce him to resume work. Adney's reply says it all about the internal compass that had always oriented his work: "the cessation hasn't in the least hurried me. I can't explain it. It is just so. That has always been my way. I didn't like your approach. This is not New York."[23]

In a letter to Frank Speck, he identified his priorities and explained himself more fully: "The Indians from all over have been coming to me with their troubles, and I simply couldn't let them down, no matter what the cost."[24] In effect, Adney sacrificed the completion of an important part of his life's work to help his friends. And he did it deliberately. He knew his health was failing and his time was limited. Nevertheless, he could not turn his back on his friends when he knew he could be of critical assistance in advancing the recognition of Indigenous rights.

Preservation of cultural heritage was central to Adney's lifelong vocation, but finally it was service to his Indigenous friends and their contemporary communities to which he freely and fiercely gave his last measure of time and energy. Adney was not a religious man, and he was not a saint or a martyr, but there was something in him that prompted this ethic of solidarity and service. Even though at various times and in various ways he engaged the prospects of professional and commercial success, his work ethic was always that of the gift economy. He was, along with all the vocational skills he possessed and exercised, primarily an artist, and the ethic of the gift, of creating something of value as a service to the world, is at the heart of the artistic vocation.

Adney fell in love with the birchbark canoe and was devoted to its preservation. This was a gift of incalculable value. In the same way, his turn to legal and political activism in service to his Wəlastəkwi friends and their communities was a gift his sense of reciprocity and loyalty compelled him to offer. The legacy of Tappan Adney is a gift that keeps on giving as the cultural, legal, and political reality of Indigenous life draws Canada into a more fully developed expression of respect, equity, and justice.

Epilogue

A Legacy of Cultural Preservation

When Tappan Adney died in 1950, the legacy of his canoe project rested primarily with The Mariners' Museum in Newport News, Virginia, which had earlier acquired most of his model canoes. Seven models that Adney donated to the New Brunswick Museum in Saint John remained in the province. As of 2022, three of these models are on display in the Adney Room at Connell House Museum in Woodstock, New Brunswick.

After Adney's death, his son, Glenn, made sure the manuscript of the yet-to-be-completed canoe book was deposited with The Mariners' Museum as well. Adney always insisted the book was an integral part of the project. Models and book were both needed to fully preserve the heritage of North American Indigenous canoes. Through a series of fortuitous circumstances, the book was eventually completed by Howard Chapelle and published fourteen years after Adney's death. Once *The Bark Canoes and Skin Boats of North America* appeared in 1964, awareness of Adney's legacy began a steady ascent.

At first, the awareness spread among canoe enthusiasts, a small number of whom were eager to build this Indigenous craft with traditional materials and techniques. Adney's book made this accomplishment possible. As these newly built canoes began to appear, the awareness spread to an increasingly wider community of interest that included Indigenous and non-Indigenous people devoted to the recreation and preservation of the birchbark canoe.

In 1965, at the age of fifteen, Henri Vaillancourt, then living in Greenville, New Hampshire, set out to build a birchbark canoe. He was not yet aware of Adney's book. He collected as much information as he could find, but his first canoe was not a success by the standards to which he aspired. When he found *The Bark Canoes and Skin Boats of North America* it became, as John McPhee puts it, his "college." By 1975, when McPhee published *The Survival of the Bark Canoe*, Henri Vaillancourt had built thirty-three birchbark canoes and, by his exacting standards, had achieved near perfection in art and craft. As of 2022 he has built more than 120.

Left to right: Nicholas Smith, Steve Cayard, Darrell Paul, and Edyth Smith at
a Woodstock Wəlastəkwey First Nation canoe building workshop, 2012.
The Longhouse workshop and the canoe stand in the background. (photo: Daryl Hunter)

McPhee's account of Vaillancourt's canoe building skill and their
canoeing adventures appeared in the *New Yorker* before becoming a book
that included thirty-one pages of illustrations and photographs from *The
Bark Canoes and Skin Boats of North America*. John McPhee was already a well-
known non-fiction writer. *The Survival of the Bark Canoe* sold well and is still
in print. It provided a significant boost to the growing awareness of Adney's
contribution to the ethnography of North American Indigenous material
culture. It also called attention to the fact that *The Bark Canoes and Skin
Boats of North America* was a guidebook and manual from which traditional
Indigenous canoes could be replicated.

The ranks of birchbark canoe builders—Indigenous and non-
Indigenous—began to grow. In 1995, Steve Cayard, of Wellington, Maine,
following the instructions in Adney's book, began his canoe building career.
Cayard has since become a master craftsman of the art and an emissary for
the cultural revival and preservation of the birchbark canoe. Through his
close relationships with Wabanaki peoples, he has been recruited to guide
canoe building workshops in Penobscot and Passamaquoddy communities
in Maine and in Wəlastəkokwey communities in New Brunswick.

Darrell Paul, organizer of the Woodstock Wəlastəkwey First Nation canoe building
workshop, speaking at the launch day celebration, September 22, 2012
(photo: Daryl Hunter)

In the summer of 2012, Darrell Paul organized a canoe building
workshop with Steve Cayard on the shore of the Wəlastəkw at the
Woodstock Wəlastəkwey First Nation, which was of special significance for
the Adney legacy. Paul and his sister, Carol Polchies, the children of Peter
and Minnie Paul, remember Tappan Adeny, who was a frequent visitor
to their home as he worked with their father learning and transcribing
traditional Wəlastəkwey.

In organizing this workshop, Paul brought the canoe building heritage
of his People back to the place where Adney was inspired to begin his
lifelong work of preservation. Although he was still building his model
canoes into the 1940s, it had been over a century since a full-sized craft had
been built on the shores of the Wəlastəkw at Woodstock.

A Longhouse workshop was constructed by setting up two lines of birch
saplings that were curved and secured where they met at the top of the
structure. Tarps that could be rolled up to allow for ventilation were used
to cover the Longhouse, making it a secure and comfortable workshop.
Over the course of a month, people from the Wəlastəkwey community
joined in the construction of a canoe similar to the one Adney and Peter Jo

built in 1888 a mile or so upriver. Interested parties from up and down the valley came to observe and participate. Daryl Hunter, ever the archivist, photographed and videoed the whole project. As the canoe took shape, participation deepened. When the construction was complete and the graceful craft was ready for launching, a woman who had joined in the work was moved to say she could *feel the spirit of the ancestors in the canoe.*

A few years later, Eric Paul, Darrell's son and Peter Paul's grandson, built another birchbark canoe at his home workshop near Woodstock. When he learned his great grandmother, Sarah Paul, had participated in a canoe race when she was pregnant with his grandfather, Eric inscribed her name on the headboard of his canoe.

At last count, a dozen birchbark canoes have recently been constructed in the Wəlastəkwey communities stretching along the valley of the Wəlastəkw from Madawaska to Fredericton. Perhaps the spirit of *descendants* to come as well as *ancestors* of the past can be felt in the beauty of these canoes.

Tappan Adney's first focus on cultural preservation was strikingly similar to his last. He responded to requests for assistance in dealing with the legal system and Indigenous rights. He discovered and invoked the 1725 Peace and Friendship Treaty when defending Peter Paul in court on the charge of cutting ash saplings on private land. Adney lost the case but pressed the argument for Indigenous rights that is now recognized as legally valid.

He spared no effort in assisting William Saulis, chief of the Tobique community, in his dealing with the government of Canada. Adney mounted a campaign for the reform of the Indian Act that addressed issues of Indigenous rights. As we have seen, it gained some support within the federal government but was defeated shortly after Adney's death, and the momentum for nation-to-nation status lapsed.

In due course, and with the coming of a new generation, the Wəlastəkwey identity that William Saulis and Tappan Adney envisioned has emerged and is now a cultural, political, legal, and economic force embodied in three organizations: the Wolastoqey/ Wəlastəkwey Nation, the Wolastoqey/ Wəlastəkwey Tribal Council, and the Wolastoqey/ Wəlastəkwey Grand Council. The first two are service organizations with linked but distinct mandates. The third is a collective of traditional Elders that has taken on the responsibility of protecting the land and waters sacred to the Wəlastəkokewiyik and defending them against industrial and commercial exploitation. The Grandmothers of the Grand Council are informally organized to conduct direct action to stop the exploitation and despoliation of sacred land and waters.

In addition, the band council chiefs of the six Wəlastəkwey communities have joined in collective legal action and filed a comprehensive land claim on behalf of the whole Wəlastəkwey Nation, the primary focus of which is access to Crown land and its management for the common good as distinct from the current practice of maximizing corporate profits.

The cultural resurgence within the Wəlastəkokewiyik now includes a growing emphasis on learning and preserving Wəlastəkwey — the mother tongue of the Wəlastəkokewiyik. As Adney came to a deeper understanding of Wəlastəkwey, he insisted that "language is culture and culture is language." He was among the first non-Indigenous scholars to learn the language and start the compilation of a "Maliseet" (Wəlastəkwey) vocabulary.

In transcribing the language, he developed a system that was oriented toward its continued use by contemporaries. The study of Wəlastəkwey on going today follows in the tradition Adney laid out. He knew that if language is lost, culture is lost. He was evermore determined as the years piled up and his health began to fail to do what he could for the preservation of the Indigenous culture that had given so much to him. The gifts Adney was given through his engagement with his Wəlastəkwi friends, and that he endeavoured to pass on, are still vital and are growing stronger in their cultural resurgence.

"An Anthropology of Belonging"

A striking parallel to the life and legacy of Tappan Adney has recently come into full view with the publication a new book by historian Wendy Wickwire, *At the Bridge: James Teit and an Anthropology of Belonging.*[1]

James Teit was born in 1864 in the Shetland Islands of Scotland. He came to Canada at the age of nineteen to work on his uncle's ranch at Spences Bridge on the interior plateau of British Columbia, where he became acquainted with the Nlaka'pamux People. Acquaintance grew into friendships and a deep interest in the culture and traditions of his friends and neighbours. He began to collect and systematically record ethnographic information. He also worked as a hunting guide. Both occupations required travelling by horseback over wide areas. He married Lucy Antko, a Nlaka'pamux woman, with whom he had a family. He learned the Nlaka'pamux language.

In 1894, Franz Boas, who was working to position himself as what he thought of as the founder of "scientific anthropology" in North America, came to Spences Bridge to meet James Teit. Boas had been doing work on Indigenous cultures in British Columbia and heard about Teit and his reputation as a collector of ethnographic material. Boas seems to have been a man short on patience and not well suited to slow travel in rugged country or sitting still for elliptical storytelling around smoky campfires. After two days with Teit, Boas hired him for field research and relied on him to collect ethnographic data and furnish him with reports for many years thereafter.

Teit's reports were so well written Boas was able to edit and publish them to an admiring academic world as his own work. Boas clearly failed to give credit where it was due. It would have been embarrassing since Teit was not an academically trained ethnographer. He mentions Teit only as an "informant." Perhaps because he was paying Teit, Boas considered it his privilege to claim credit for the work.

As Wickwire makes clear in her investigation of the case, Teit was a first-class ethnographer whose work Boas appropriated. This recalls Fannie Eckstorm's experience with Frank Speck, who took the information she shared and published it without crediting her. Appropriation of the work of non-credentialed ethnographers appears to be an occupational temptation of academic anthropologists.

James Teit was an easygoing person, loved and admired by all who knew him. Like Adney, his anthropology was not separate from his friendships with the people whose culture he was studying. Wickwire calls it "an anthropology of belonging." This evocative expression could also characterize the ethnography of Tappan Adney. His, too, was an anthropology of belonging, a level of friendship and reciprocity that informed his research and his work for Indigenous rights.

Teit, like Adney, responded to the entreaties of his Indigenous friends for assistance in dealing with government and took up the work of defending their rights to land and resources. The Nlaka'pamux leaders made him their advocate in presentations to the British Columbia government and to the government of Canada. At this time, even though over 90 per cent of British Columbia land was yet to be covered by treaties with First Nations, logging and mining were rapidly despoiling unceded Indigenous territory.

From the forested valley of the Wəlastəkw in New Brunswick to the interior plateau of British Columbia, from Tappan Adney to James Teit, the anthropology of belonging moved two outliers in the ethnographic pantheon to spend the last years of their lives battling for Indigenous rights and the land claims that are central to equity and justice in Canada today.

Acknowledgements

The first acknowledgement must go to Jim Wheaton, the original author of this biography, and to Ted Behne who picked up the project when, for health reasons, Jim was no longer able to work on it. Their extensive research and unstinting devotion to this project is the foundation on which this telling of the Tappan Adney story has been assembled. In addition, Ted's wife, Elizabeth Behne, played a key role in keeping the project alive and advancing it toward publication.

The journey this book has taken in its long preparation calls for a list of acknowledgements beyond the scope of those who have brought it to publication. The research conducted by Jim Wheaton from the mid-1980s to 2005 investigated all the institutions where Tappan Adney's papers and artifacts are archived. In addition, he contacted, visited, and corresponded with numerous organizations and individuals that had a connection with or interest in the Adney story. Ted Behne picked up this encyclopaedic research when he took over the project after Jim died in 2005 and continued it until his death in 2014. Had these authors lived to see their work published, there would be a long list of persons to acknowledge for having assisted their research and writing in important ways.

We do not have the benefit of Jim and Ted's inventory of archivists, colleagues, associates, and friends who helped them, but we can honour them if not name then in these acknowledgements. They know who they are, and we trust they will note our recognition and gratitude for their assistance to Jim and Ted.

Joan Adney Dragon — Tappan Adney's granddaughter and Jim Wheaton's wife — along with her daughter Kimber Hawkey have been part of this project's support from the beginning. They generously donated their collection of Tappan Adney documents to the Carleton County Historical Society (CCHS) in Woodstock, New Brunswick, for archiving in the Connell House Museum and display in its Tappan Adney room.

John and Lois Thompson — key figures in CCHS and close friends of Joan and Jim — have been steadfast in their promotion of the Adney story and efforts to keep the biography project alive. Their cottage at Skiff Lake is adjacent to the Adney cottage, to which Joan and Jim returned each summer for many years. John and Lois have been particularly effective in facilitating communication about the Adney biography and associated legacy projects. In addition, they have provided generous financial assistance that helped cover the production costs of this book.

Joanne Barrett, executive director of CCHS and the Connell House Museum, and her temporary assistant, Tanya Daigle, have been instrumental in professionally archiving the collection of Adney material at Connell House, which greatly facilitated the final research and access to key documents.

As noted, Elizabeth Behne took up the custody of the Adney biography manuscript. She was as determined as Ted to carry the project forward. She revised parts of the manuscript and added new text. She kept in touch with and relied on the assistance of Daryl Hunter. She continued Jim and Ted's communication with Goose Lane Editions. Thanks to Liz, the Adney biography project did not fall by the wayside.

Daryl Hunter, with his extensive Adney archive and research skills, became an invaluable consultant for Jim and Ted. He prepared PowerPoint presentations for their use in giving talks about Tappan Adney, contributed chapter 8, and has remained engaged through the final preparation of the manuscript with unflagging enthusiasm. His particular expertise has been in noting details of information and their sources, along with supplying access to and curating the graphics—photos, paintings, drawings, and maps—that illustrate this book.

Nicholas Smith composed chapter 12 with Daryl Hunter's assistance. Nick's ethnographic expertise, his personal familiarity with Adney's papers on linguistics, and his association with Peter Paul—Adney's primary linguistic informant—filled in this part of the story in a way no one else could have provided.

Mary Bernard played an important role in the Adney biography project. As George Frederick Clarke's granddaughter and the Clarke family archivist, she assisted Jim Wheaton, at his request, from the beginning of his work on the biography. In addition to being a source of Adney related documents, Mary's association with her grandfather gives her personal knowledge of the Tappan Adney story. In addition, her close reading and edits of this biography corrected several factual errors and improved the text at numerous points, for which we are most grateful.

Clarissa Hurley applied her editing expertise to the final manuscript in a way that improved the logic of its structure, sharpened its presentation, and polished phrasing to good effect. Alan Sheppard, managing editor at Goose Lane Editions, likewise added helpful advice at this stage.

Nicole O'Bryne, Faculty of Law professor at the University of New Brunswick and scholar of law with respect to Indigenous rights, kindly scrutinized chapter 14, correcting word choice, phrasing, and conceptual characterization where required. This important work improved our presentation of Adney's engagement with Indigenous rights and the Canadian legal system.

Andrea Bear Nicholas, professor emerita at St. Thomas University and former chair of Indigenous Studies, reviewed the entire manuscript, providing scrutiny and correction on many details of Indigenous language usage. In addition, she provided significant editing of chapter 12 on Wəlastəkwey linguistics and chapter 14 on Adney's battle for Indigenous rights. We are particularly grateful for her generous assistance in this regard.

Carole Polchies, a teacher of Wəlastəkwey, likewise, served as an adviser on language issues. Carole and Andrea's consultation with each other on behalf of the project was instrumental in our decision to use the schwa orthography in the spelling of Wəlastəkwey names.

Carol Polchies and Darrell Paul, daughter and son of Peter and Minnie Paul, have been supporters with a strong interest in the Tappan Adney story. They both remember Tappan Adney from his frequent visits to their home for language research with their father. Eric Paul, Darrell's son, who recently built a birchbark canoe following the instructions in Adney's book, has also, along with his wife, Ramona, brought support to the wider dimenions of the Adney project as it continues to develop in the Woodstock area. This family line and its significant relationship with Tappan Adney is an important local grounding for the story this book endeavours to unfold.

Our thanks to copy editor, Jill Ainsley and proof reader, Kristen Chew, who applied their expertise to the final polishing of the text. A special thanks and recognition of critical assistance go to Susanne Alexander, publisher at Goose Lane Editions, along with her colleagues, Julie Scriver, creative director, and Alan Sheppard, managing editor, for their enthusiastic response to an arrangement for co-publication. The expertise of the Goose Lane team in handling certain details in the final stages of production helped smooth out the complexity of the project and bring it to fruition. In addition, Goose Lane's capacity for promotion, marketing, and distribution far exceeds that of Chapel Street Editions and will give the Adney biography the launch needed to reach the audience waiting for this story to be more fully told.

Finally, from Chapel Street Editions, a heartfelt drumroll of gratitude for the financial support of the Tappan Adney biography by the Town of Woodstock, the Carleton County Historical Society, and Woodstock/ Wolastoqiyik First Nation.

Funding from the Historical Society was made possible by donations from John and Lois Thompson, Dwight and Fay Fraser, Melissa and Ed Barrett, Patrick and Carolyn Goguen, Barry Craig and Sara MacDonald, Greg and Sarah McPherson, Wes and Cindy Corey, and Stuart Kinney and Gloria Yachyshen.

Funding from the Woodstock First Nation commemorates the important relationship between Tappan Adney and the renowned Wəlastəkwi Elder, Dr. Peter Paul, CM.

It has taken over three years of active engagement with the manuscript of this biography to produce the book it has become. We are immensely grateful to all those who have made this outcome possible.

Keith Helmuth
Publisher and Managing Editor
Chapel Street Editions

Appendix One

The Tomah Joseph 1898 Canoe Model

In the late 1920s, Adney continued to build models and add them to his collection on loan to the Ethnological Museum at McGill University while he searched for a buyer. He had approached the Ethnological Museum and many other museums in both the US and Canada without success.

At this time, Henry Ford was developing a museum of transportation in Dearborn, Michigan. Adney thought his models might fill a niche in the museum's plan, since canoes were important modes of transportation in North America throughout the period of exploration and colonization by Europeans. Adney knew his former Klondike cabin mate, Leroy Pelletier, had worked closely with Ford, having been his private secretary and advertising manager for many years.

In 1929, Adney visited Pelletier, then retired and living near Detroit, Michigan. The visit was to renew their friendship, which Pelletier had previously encouraged, and to explore the possibility that the new Henry Ford Museum might be interested in purchasing the model canoe collection. It's not clear whether Ford ever saw the sample Adney brought with him. He returned home without a commitment from Ford, despite a written recommendation from Pelletier urging Ford to buy the collection.

Adney's model of a full-size 1898 Tomah Joseph canoe, Franklin Delano Roosevelt Library, Hyde Park, NY (photo: Behne family collection)

Nearly two years later, in 1931, Adney sent Pelletier a model he hoped would spark Ford's interest and clinch a purchase decision for the collection. The model canoe was a particularly fine specimen, with distinctive etched artwork from a full-size canoe built by Tomah Joseph, a Peskotomuhkati builder who worked for the Roosevelt family at their residence on Campobello Island—a part of New Brunswick just off the coast in the Bay of Fundy.

Adney had measured, photographed, and repaired the full-size Tomah Joseph canoe several years earlier for its owner, T. J. Newbold, at Upper Saranac Lake, New York. Newbold was a close friend of Franklin Delano Roosevelt. Joseph had built the canoe for the Roosevelt family at Campobello in 1898, where he worked as a handyman and hunting and fishing guide. He was skilled in Indigenous handcrafts and his work was later much sought after by collectors. Many examples of his fine work are on display in the Roosevelt home on Campobello Island. Joseph was a contemporary of Peter Jo, who mentored Adney through his first canoe building project. Both were born within a year of each other in the 1840s and grew up together in the Peskotomuhkati community near Princeton, Maine.

Apparently, Ford's interest did not include a canoe collection for his museum but Pelletier retained the model, hoping Ford might take another look at it and change his mind. Pelletier died of a heart attack in 1938, still in possession of the model canoe. Adney tried to contact Pelletier's family to recover his canoe, but without success. Pelletier's widow was acquainted with FDR's cousin, Hall Roosevelt, comptroller of the City of Detroit, who along with FDR had used the full-size Tomah Joseph canoe at Campobello when they both summered there as teenagers. With Roosevelt's help, and assuming that Adney had given the model to her husband, Mrs. Pelletier donated it to the Roosevelt Library in Hyde Park, NY, along with an extensive dissertation Adney had written for Henry Ford explaining its significance and which Leroy Pelletier had retained.

Adney eventually tracked down his model at the Roosevelt Library but, following FDR's death in April 1945, it became government property and a permanent part of the FDR Library collection. Adney never saw his model again, but he continued to press for recognition as its donor. In 1946 he wrote to Eleanor Roosevelt, appealing to her to help set the record straight.

Mrs. Roosevelt forwarded the letter to the director of the library, who agreed to credit the donation to Adney, instead of Mrs. Pelletier.

Appendix Two

Model Canoe Locations

The following list provides the location and design type of twenty-three Adney model canoes not part of The Mariners' Museum collection. Some are duplicated in the museum collection but others are unique.

**The Franklin Delano Roosevelt Presidential Library,
Hyde Park, New York**

1. Peskotomuhkati (Passamaquoddy) ocean canoe, one-fifth scale, built 1930, decorated, after original by Tomah Joseph.

The New Brunswick Museum, Saint John, New Brunswick

2. Wəlastəkwey (Maliseet) canvas canoe, one-fifth scale, built 1930 after original by Peter Bear.
3. Mi'kmaq rough water canoe, one-fifth scale, built 1930 after original in use on the Restigouche River, NB.
4. Iroquois elm bark canoe, one-fifth scale, built 1935 after 25-foot original, formerly in the NY State Museum, Albany, NY.
5. Peskotomuhkati (Passamaquoddy) ocean canoe, one-fifth scale, built 1927 after original by Frank Atwin.
6. Peskotomuhkati (Passamaquoddy) canoe, one-fifth scale, built 1930 after a smaller, similar canoe now in The Mariners' Museum, Newport News, VA.
7. Wəlastəkwey (Maliseet) spruce bark canoe, one-fifth scale, built 1935 after original by Peter Bear.
8. Wəlastəkwey (Maliseet) moosehide canoe, one-fifth scale, built 1935–38 after original by Peter Bear.

The American Museum of Natural History, New York, New York

9. Wəlastəkwey (Maliseet) river canoe, one-fifth scale, built 1888 after original in use on the Wəlastəkw (Saint John River).
10. Wəlastəkw (Saint John River) log driver's batteau, one-eighth scale, built 1888 after original in use on the Wəlastəkw (Saint John River).

Cranbrook Institute of Science, Bloomfield Hills, Michigan

11. Wəlastəkwey (Maliseet) spruce bark canoe, one-fifth scale, built 1935–38 after original by Peter Bear.
12. Mi'kmaq woods canoe with single rectangular gunwale and continuous lashings, one-fifth scale, build date unknown.

Canadian Museum of History, Hull, Quebec

13. Algonquin old-style canoe with miniature paddle and salmon spear, 41" long, one-fifth scale, build date unknown.
14. Fur trade canoe with etched winter bark decorations, one-fifth scale, 70" long, build date unknown.
15. Kootenay canoe, 33" long, one-fifth scale, build date unknown, one of several sturgeon-nose canoes Adney made.
16. Moosehide temporary canoe, 43" long, one-fifth scale, build date unknown, one end severely damaged.
17. Beothuk ocean canoe, one fifth-scale, build date unknown, with unusual sharp midpoint in humped gunwale, likely an experimental model to test the feasibility of such a gunwale. Since the Beothuk People are now extinct, Adney had to experiment to recreate models of their canoes from drawings and grave excavation models.

Château Ramezay, Montréal, Quebec

18. Abenaki hunter's canoe, 25 ½" long, one-fifth scale, built 1929, copy of an identical model in The Mariners' Museum collection.

Fredericton Region Museum, Fredericton, New Brunswick

19. Wəlastəkwey (Maliseet) spruce bark canoe, 36" long, one-fifth scale, build date unknown, after original by Peter Bear.

Peabody Museum at Harvard University, Cambridge, Massachusetts

20. Wəlastəkwey (Maliseet) spruce bark canoe, one-fifth scale, build date before 1927, donated by Adney in 1927.

Adney Family

21. Wəlastəkwey (Maliseet) spruce bark canoe, one-fifth scale, built 1933 after original by Peter Bear. Bark on one side damaged and repaired by Adney with a birchbark patch.

Unknown Locations

22. Wəlastəkwey (Maliseet) birchbark canoe, one-fifth scale, built 1888, loaned to Allison Connell for safekeeping, returned to Adney and later stolen.

23. Fur trade canoe, estimated length 57″, from photo in *La Presse*, Montréal, Quebec, November 14, 1925.

Appendix Three

Winter Wildlife around Adney's Bungalow
From a letter to Frank Chapman, March 16, 1945

The Mongolian Pheasant has also been introduced here and elsewhere in the Province, protected against the time when they will become established and shootable. The pheasant is becoming common locally. There are flocks about, they are coming into barnyards and associating with the chickens and the farmers are feeding them. I have a bunch at my place here on the edge of the village (a tract of 11 acres with groves of spruce and other trees now grown up wild). They have even nested in a secluded corner. I notice them feeding on seed tops of grasses, and I hear they even eat burdock burrs. Now the snow has covered the ground this is all up but an occasional burdock. The birds are naturally wary and wild, but hunger overcomes their shyness. I am feeding a flock of two females and three or four cocks right in my backyard putting oats inside a little shed only 20 feet from my back door to prevent a covering up with snow. Because of the deep snows covering their natural foods it seems to me they will never become acclimatized. Even the native ruffed grouse have a hard time of it. They dive into the deep snow for the night, a precaution against predatory animals and birds. But if a thaw comes with a crust they cannot get out. I am sometimes reminded of an old Hindoo tale illustrating how disastrous well-meant intentions can be sometimes. A tender-hearted elephant accidently stepped on a nest of young partridges and killed the mother. The elephant was very, very, much grieved, so said to the young partridges, 'I will be a mother to you'—and sat down on the nest....

... we may yet discover that the wild animals and birds have a value, in these times, above that of food. Some have made that discovery, but until the democratic majority discovers it, it will be hard to give full protection to even our native species. The Indian only killed what he needed, safeguarded the future, as by leaving some breeding beavers in house or pond. But we the Superior Race must kill for amusement only...

I could run on about the birds as I see them around my place. I see tiny chickadees in the coldest weather of this North, hunting in little flocks, keeping track of each other, cheerfully singing as they hunt, and I often think of what courage the little things have, surely an example for us in periods of trial and anxiety. The wild birds measurably control their destiny, their lives, given any kind of chance. We in the artificial conditions that civilization has created, are obsessed by fears, because the individual can no longer control his destiny. Mental troubles consequently exist that did not formerly in remote times.

... There seems to be a mania for searching out and naming the littlest new thing, as if naming were the end and purpose of natural history study...Study of Nature, of the birds and other animals, the restfulness of nature, is one outstanding curative agency right at hand.

Sincerely as ever, Tappan Adney.

Abbreviations for Image and Reference Sources

CCHS – Carleton County Historical Society

UNB – Harriet Irving Library Archive, University of New Brunswick

MM – Mariners' Museum

NBM – New Brunswick Museum

PANB – Provincial Archives of New Brunswick

PEM – Peabody Essex Museum

Notes

Chapter One: Family and Early Education

1. Edwin Tappan Adney, "Biography of W.T.G. Adney," *Ohio University Bulletin*, 1908.
2. *Annual Catalog of the Ohio University, 1865–1866*.
3. Adney, "Biography of W.T.G. Adney."
4. Letter from Thomas G. Wilde to Rutherford B. Hayes, July 29, 1872, Rutherford B. Hayes Presidential Center, Fremont, OH.
5. Margaret Mead, *Blackberry Winter* (New York: William Morrow, 1972), 71.
6. Letter from Tappan Adney to R.P. Gorham, July [?] 1944. Adney papers, PEM.
7. University of North Carolina catalogues 1880–1881 and 1881–1882, Chapel Hill, NC.
8. *Chatham Record*, October 27, 1881; *Raleigh News and Observer*, October 15, 1881.

Chapter Two: Trinity School and the Art Students League

1. The founding of the Art Students League and its program of study and training is an early example of progressive education, a movement underway in the late nineteenth century. John Dewey articulated the theory and practice of experiential education at this time, although his classic book in the field, *Experience and Education*, was not published until 1938. Having been homeschooled by his father in an environment that included experiential learning, Adney was well primed to take his continuing education into his own hands.
2. *Art Students League Catalog, 2003-2004*.
3. Georgia O'Keeffe and Ella Condie Lamb quoted at www.theartstudentsleague.org.
4. Attendance register 1886, Art Students League.
5. Letter from Tappan Adney to Mary B. Reinmuth, Fraser Companies Ltd., September 22, 1948. Adney papers, Phillips Library, PEM, Salem, MA.
6. Nola Hill, "Museum Pieces," Hill papers, MM.
7. Letter from Spencer F. Baird to Tappan Adney, October 10, 1885. Adney family archives, Charlottesville, VA.
8. Edwin Tappan Adney, "The Cardinal Grosbeak Breeding in Brooklyn, NY," *Auk* 1, no. 4 (October 1, 1884), 390.
9. Edwin Tappan Adney, "Naturalization of the European Goldfinch in New York City and Vicinity," *Auk* 3, no. 3 (July 1, 1886), 409–10.

Chapter Three: A Fateful Decision and First Encounter with the Birchbark Canoe

1. C. Ted Behne, ed., *The Travel Journals of Tappan Adney, Volume 1: 1887–1890*, rev. ed. (Fredericton, NB: Goose Lane Editions, 2016), 19 and 20.
2. Behne, *Travel Journals*, vol. 1, 20.
3. Behne, *Travel Journals*, vol. 1, 23.
4. Behne, *Travel Journals*, vol. 1, 67.
5. Edwin Tappan Adney, "Milicet Indian Natural History," *Abstract of the Proceedings of the Linnaean Society of New York for the Year Ending March 1, 1893*. Adney read his paper at a meeting of the society in 1889.
6. Edwin Tappan Adney, "How an Indian Birchbark Canoe is Made," *Harper's Young People*, July 29, 1890.
7. Behne, *Travel Journals*, vol. 1, 19 and 23.

Chapter Four: Tobique Expeditions and Natural History Journalism

1. C. Ted Behne, ed., *The Travel Journals of Tappan Adney: Volume 2, 1891–1896* (Fredericton, NB: Goose Lane Editions, 2014), 301.
2. Large herds of caribou once lived in New Brunswick. In the late 1800s and into the early twentieth century overhunting, especially by sport hunters from the United States, greatly reduced the population. The reduced caribou population and heavy logging of New Brunswick's forestland created the opportunity for white-tailed deer to move in from New England. The deer carried a brain parasite that also affected caribou and increased the mortality of the stressed herds. By 1930, caribou were virtually extinct in New Brunswick. The provincial archive has a photograph labelled "The last caribou shot in New Brunswick."
3. Behne, *Travel Journals*, vol. 2, 21.
4. Behne, *Travel Journals*, vol. 2, 22.
5. Behne, *Travel Journals*, vol. 2, 23.
6. Behne, *Travel Journals*, vol. 2, 43.
7. Behne, *Travel Journals*, vol. 2, 45.
8. Behne, *Travel Journals*, vol. 2, 46.
9. Behne, *Travel Journals*, vol. 2, 93.
10. Behne, *Travel Journals*, vol. 2, 107.
11. Behne, *Travel Journals*, vol. 2, 117.
12. Behne, *Travel Journals*, vol. 2, 161.
13. Behne, *Travel Journals*, vol. 2, 160.
14. Behne, *Travel Journals*, vol. 2, 160–61.
15. Behne, *Travel Journals*, vol. 2, 168.
16. Behne, *Travel Journals*, vol. 2, 195.
17. Behne, *Travel Journals*, vol. 2, 207.
18. Behne, *Travel Journals*, vol. 2, 216.
19. Behne, *Travel Journals*, vol. 2, 217–18.
20. Behne, *Travel Journals*, vol. 2, 229.
21. Behne, *Travel Journals*, vol. 2, 229.

22. Behne, *Travel Journals*, vol. 2, 221.
23. Behne, *Travel Journals*, vol. 2, 279.
24. Behne, *Travel Journals*, vol. 2, 252.
25. Behne, *Travel Journals*, vol. 2, 253–54.
26. Behne, *Travel Journals*, vol. 2, 254.
27. Copies of Adney's articles written for a variety of New York–based publications between 1889 and 1897 are collected in his scrapbooks, now held by the Carleton County Historical Society in Woodstock, NB.

Chapter Five: To the Klondike: A Perilous Journey

1. Letter from Henry L. Nelson to Tappan Adney, July 28, 1897. Adney papers, Rauner Library, Dartmouth College, Hanover, NH.
2. No information has been found on the balance of *Harper's* payment, but considering the amount of the advance, it was likely substantial.
3. Edwin Tappan Adney, *The Klondike Stampede* (Vancouver: UBC Press, 1984), 14. Narrative structure, observational details, and quotations for this chapter are drawn from this source.
4. Minnie Bell Sharp's diary, Adney family archives, Charlottesville, VA.
5. William R. Morrison, *Showing the Flag: The Mounted Police and Canadian Sovereignty in the North, 1894–1925* (Vancouver: UBC Press, 1985), 40.
6. Adney, *Klondike Stampede*, 74.
7. Adney, *Klondike Stampede*, 71.
8. Adney, *Klondike Stampede*, 72–73.
9. Adney, *Klondike Stampede*, 74.
10. Adney, *Klondike Stampede*, 103.
11. Adney, *Klondike Stampede*, 108.
12. Adney, *Klondike Stampede*, 109.
13. Adney, *Klondike Stampede*, 110.
14. Adney, *Klondike Stampede*, 110.
15. Adney, *Klondike Stampede*, 119.
16. John B. Burnham, "Headwaters of the Yukon," *Forest and Stream*, July 16, 1898.
17. Adney, *Klondike Stampede*, 137.
18. By the following year, 1898, the North West Mounted Police required would-be miners who overwintered at Lindeman Lake hire an experienced pilot and register the occupants of each boat so next of kin could be notified if they drowned.
19. Adney, *Klondike Stampede*, 142.
20. Adney, *Klondike Stampede*, 145.
21. Adney, *Klondike Stampede*, 150.
22. Adney, *Klondike Stampede*, 163–64.
23. Adney, *Klondike Stampede*, 164.
24. Adney, *Klondike Stampede*, 165.
25. Adney, *Klondike Stampede*, 166.
26. Adney, *Klondike Stampede*, 170.

27. Adney, *Klondike Stampede*, 174.

28. Adney, *Klondike Stampede*, 175.

Chapter Six: On the Ground in the Gold Rush: From Reporter to Ethnographer

1. "William Judge," https://en.wikipedia.org/wiki/William_Judge

2. Edwin Tappan Adney, *The Klondike Stampede* (Vancouver: UBC Press, 1984), 182.

3. Adney, *Klondike Stampede*, footnote, 188.

4. Adney, *Klondike Stampede*, 258.

5. Adney, *Klondike Stampede*, 207.

6. Edwin Tappan Adney, *Map of the Indian River and Klondike Goldfields*, https://explorenorth.com/klondike/klondike_goldfields_map-tappan_adney-1898.html.

7. Adney, *Klondike Stampede*, 358.

8. Adney, *Klondike Stampede*, 212.

9. Adney did not include the Tr'ondëk Hwëch'in hunting expedition in his dispatches to *Harper's Weekly* or in his book *The Klondike Stampede*. His account was published in *Harper's New Monthly Magazine* with numerous paintings and sketches. An expanded version was published in the March 1902 issue of *Outing* magazine, illustrated with a different set of paintings and sketches. Edwin Tappan Adney, "Moose Hunting with the Tro-chu-tin," *Harper's New Monthly Magazine* (March 1900).

10. Adney, "Moose Hunting." The article is also available at http://chiefisaac.com/moose_hunting.html.

11. For an account of Jack London's experience with scurvy in the Klondike, see Charlotte Gray, *Gold Diggers: Striking it Rich in the Klondike* (Toronto: HarperCollins, 2010), 169–70 and 187–88.

12. Adney, *Klondike Stampede*, 359.

13. Adney, *Klondike Stampede*, 365.

14. Adney, *Klondike Stampede*, 377.

15. Adney, *Klondike Stampede*, 455.

Chapter Seven: Minnie Bell Sharp and the Last Years in New York

1. D.G. Bell, "Sharp, Minnie Bell (Adney)," *Dictionary of Canadian Biography*, vol. XVI (1931–1940), http://www.biographi.ca/en/bio/sharp_minnie_bell_16E.html.

2. D.G. Bell, "Sharp, Minnie Bell (Adney)."

3. David Bell, "The Lady Music Teacher as Entrepreneur: Minnie Sharp and the Victoria Conservatory of Music in the 1890s," *BC Studies* 191 (Autumn 2016), 85–110.

4. David Bell, "By Their Fruits Ye Shall Know Them: The Strange Career of Minnie Bell Sharp Adney" (paper presented to the Carleton County Historical Society, Upper Woodstock, NB, March 22, 2002).

5. Bell, "By Their Fruits."

6. "Minnie Bell Adney: An Autobiography," *Carleton Sentinel*, October 24, 1919.
7. Dispatches from Nome Gold Rush. Adney papers, Rauner Library, Dartmouth College, Hanover, NH.
8. Principal information on the railroad-tunnel scheme obtained from Gordon E. Tolton, "Healy's West: The Life and Times of John J. Healy," unpublished manuscript.
9. Letter from Tappan Adney to Minnie Bell, May 3, 1906. Adney papers, PEM.

Chapter Eight: The Orchard Business in New Brunswick

At the time this book went to press in July 2024, the New Brunswick Museum archive was closed pending relocation making it impossible to verify the full dates of documents in the Sharp fonds.

1. Letter from Tappan Adney to W.T. Macoun, date unknown. F.P. Sharp fonds, NBM.
2. *Dispatch* (Woodstock, NB), October 2, 1895.
3. Obituary of Francis Peabody Sharp, date unknown. F.P. Sharp fonds, NBM.
4. Letter to W.T. Macoun, date unknown. F.P. Sharp fonds, NBM.
5. F.P. Sharp letter to Minnie Bell, April 10, 1890. F.P. Sharp fonds, NBM.
6. F.P. Sharp letter to Minnie Bell, [May 1983]. F.P. Sharp fonds, NBM.
7. Adney on orchard loss, date unknown. F.P. Sharp fonds, NBM.
8. The New Brunswick Museum holds a typewritten document with a cover page and header, in pencil, titled "A Scientific Study by E.T. Adney, 1910." It covers such topics as "Sharp's Law of Antagonism of Stalk and Root" and his examination of the flow of sap in plants and how he applied this knowledge to control fruiting. Adney wrote, "It was this study and experiment with the sap that led to his discovery of his LAW OF ANTAGONISM BETWEEN THE STALK AND PLANT which provided him with the MEANS for a CERTAIN CONTROL OF WOOD GROWTH OR FRUIT, AT WILL. He regarded this as the one discovery of his which would eventually have the most far-reaching effect upon apple culture." F.P. Sharp fonds, NBM.
9. Edwin Tappan Adney, "A Scientific Study by E.T. Adney," 1910. F.P. Sharp fonds, NBM.
10. Letter from Tappan Adney to the Department of Agriculture, date unknown. F.P. Sharp fonds, NBM.
11. Letter from A.G. Turney to Tappan Adney, [1910]. F.P. Sharp fonds, NBM.
12. A.G. Turney, *Maritime Farmer*, January 24, 1911. F.P. Sharp fonds, NBM.
13. Tappan Adney's reply to A.G. Turney's article, *Carleton Sentinel*, date unknown. F.P. Sharp fonds, NBM.
14. Letter from Tappan Adney to F.B. Carvell, date unknown. F.P. Sharp fonds, NBM.
15. Letter from F.B. Carvell to Tappan Adney, date unknown. F.P. Sharp fonds, NBM.
16. F.P. Sharp's response to the question "Can New Brunswick Grow Apples?" had been written many years earlier and was supposed to be read at the provincial

Fruit Growers Exhibition in Saint John in 1911 but was omitted. F.P. Sharp fonds, NBM.

17. Adney's comment. F.P. Sharp fonds, NBM.

18. "Carleton County Fruit Growers Meet and Organize: Neglect of the Hazen Government Causes the Present Action," *Woodstock Press*, February 3, 1911.

19. "Carleton County Fruit Growers Meet," *Woodstock Press*, February 3, 1911.

20. Durwood Jones, "History of the Apple Industry in New Brunswick and Outlook" (paper presented to the New Brunswick Apple Growers Association, 1988, provided by the author).

21. "Minnie Bell Adney: An Autobiography," *Carleton Sentinel*, October 24, 1919.

22. Edwin Tappan Adney, "New Brunswicker or Duchess," *Woodstock Press*, August 2, 1921. The F.P. Sharp fonds also include the *Report on Horticulture for the Province of New Brunswick for the Year 1911*, to which Adney contributed a seventeen-page report titled "Francis Peabody Sharp: His Work in Horticulture."

Chapter Nine: An Interlude of Military Service

1. Letter from Tappan Adney to Diamond Jenness, April 26, 1941. Adney papers, PEM

Chapter Ten: Art and Ethnography: The Montréal Years

1. Letter from Tappan Adney to Mrs. W.J. Hornaday, November 29, 1922. A transcript of this letter is part of James Wheaton's research database. The original appears to be privately held, perhaps by a descendant of Mrs. Hornaday.

2. Letter from Tappan Adney to Diamond Jenness, April 26, 1941. Adney papers, PEM

3. Letter from Tappan Adney to Edward Sapir, July 28, 1925. Adney papers, MM.

4. Edwin Tappan Adney description of heraldic art, Carleton County Historical Society, Woodstock, NB.

5. *La Presse*, August 20, 1927.

6. Letter from Tappan Adney to George Frederick Clarke, September 2, 1930. PEM.

7. Edwin Tappan Adney, *McGill University Expedition to Lake Missinabi—Indian Rock Painting 1930*, McCord Museum, Montréal, PQ.

8. Memo from Tappan Adney to McGill University. December 5, 1932. Adney papers, MM.

9. Letter from J.C. Simpson to A.P.S. Glassco, December 28, 1932. Adney papers, MM.

10. Cyril Fox, *A Survey of McGill University Museums*. Montréal: McGill University, 1932.

11. Letter from Tappan Adney to Lionel Judah, May 14, 1933. Adney papers, MM.

12. Letter from Tappan Adney to George Frederick Clarke, August 18, 1926. PEM.

13. Letter from Minnie Bell Adney to Susan True, March 16, 1931. Adney papers, PEM.

14. Letter from Glenn Adney to Tappan Adney, May 8, 1931. Adney papers, PEM

15. Letter from Glenn Adney to Tappan Adney, May 22,1931. Adney papers, PEM.
16. Adney's notes on Minnie Bell's condition, September 16–November 20, 1931. Adney papers, PEM.
17. Letter from Peggy Adney to Tappan Adney, [February 1932]. Adney papers, PEM.
18. Letter from Tappan Adney to Cleveland Morgan, February 16, 1933. Adney papers, MM.
19. Letter from Tappan Adney to Lionel Judah, September 11, 1933. Adney papers, MM.

Chapter Eleven: A Legacy of Canoes

1. The full-size canoe Adney built with Peter Jo is preserved in the Canadian Museum of History in Hull, Quebec. It was donated in the fall of 2006 by the estate of George Frederick Clarke. At the time of the donation, the Adney connection was unknown. It was later established by the discovery of an interview with Clarke included in an article on canoes by Robert Thomas Allen published in the August 30, 1958, issue of *Maclean's* magazine:

   > Several years ago [1946] there was a sixteen foot birchbark canoe made by Adney and Peter Jo in the Exhibition Building in Woodstock. A heavy snow storm caved in the roof of the building. Clarke waded through the snow to the building and saw that the cave in had broken off about five feet of the bow of the canoe. "I saw one of the Exhibition members. He agreed to give it to me. I contacted Adney. We got a horse and sled and took it to Adney's bungalow in Upper Woodstock."
   >
   > Clarke and Adney went about rebuilding the canoe following the same methods used by the Indians. In early spring they found a suitable birch tree, one in which the sap had not yet ascended, and stripped off a piece [of bark] seven or eight feet long. In mid-May Adney scooped out a flat depression in the ground, put the canoe in it with the broken portions in place, and drove stakes into the ground for a form. He then laid in the new birchbark, the thin strips of cedar sheathing, and reset the ribs. "It was as good as new," Clarke says.

   In 2008, Ted Behne recounted his examination of the canoe in a letter to Mary Bernard, Clarke's granddaughter, who along with her brother, Ian Bernard, had donated the canoe.

   > When I visited the CMH [Canadian Museum of History] last fall and examined the canoe, I looked for the repairs described by GFC [George Frederick Clarke]. I knew about the repair work from reading a second hand account of the *MacLean's* article in Roger MacGregor's book, *When the Chestnut was in Flower*. It describes the canoe and the repair, and asserts that Adney and Peter Jo made the canoe, but doesn't quote GFC, so I didn't believe it. It wasn't

until Greg Campbell in the Woodstock Library got me a copy of the original article that I discovered that GFC was the one who said that ETA [Edwin Tappan Adney] and Peter Jo had built the canoe. The only way GFC could have known, was if ETA had told him.

At the CMH, I looked for the repairs described by GFC. At first I couldn't find them, they were done so well. But, on closer inspection, it became clear that about five feet of bark at one end had been completely replaced, just as GFC had said.

2. Tappan Adney, quoted in James W. Wheaton, "Tappan Adney's Maliseet Studies: More Than Canoes," (paper presented at 34th Algonquian Conference, Language, and Linguistics, Queen's University, October 24–27, 2002), 2002. Adney papers, UNB.

3. Edward S. Morse published *Japanese Homes and Their Surroundings* (New York: Harper & Brothers, 1895), an unprecedented study of traditional, pre-modern Japanese material culture, the year before Adney came to New Brunswick. This four-hundred-page book with three hundred illustrations by the author was widely reviewed and highly praised as an eye-opening contribution to the study of culture. Adney's understanding of the "high standard of simplicity" found in traditional Japanese material culture was quite possibly prompted, or at least enhanced, by the attention this book garnered in New York's artistic and intellectual circles.

4. Letter from Tappan Adney to Diamond Jenness, January 7, 1939. Courtesy of Mary Bernard, Clarke family archive, Cambridge, UK.

5. Letter from Tappan Adney to George Frederick Clarke, March 23, 1925. Courtesy of Mary Bernard, Clarke family archive, Cambridge, UK.

6. The "astonishing output" assessment comes from Ted Behne's experience building replicas of Adney's models. He reported that it took him approximately 125 hours to complete a one-fifth-scale model canoe.

7. Fred and Nola Hill. In-house museum notes [n.d.]. Hill papers, MM.

8. Letter from Tappan Adney to Diamond Jenness, January 7, 1939. Courtesy of Mary Bernard, Clarke family archive, Cambridge, UK.

9. Hill papers, MM.

10. Letter from Diamond Jenness to Tappan Adney, January 12, 1939. Adney papers, MM. Keith Helmuth visited the museum in 2002. After viewing the Adney model canoes on display, he suggested to a staff person that some of the collection might be repatriated to Canada. The response was a broad smile and "Good luck with that."

11. Hill papers, MM. The typewriter replaced the one Adney had used since before his Klondike days and which he'd used on that assignment. The letters on some of its keys were worn down to illegibility.

12. Hill papers, MM.

13. Hill papers, MM.

14. Hill papers, MM.

15. Hill papers, MM.
16. Hill papers, MM.
17. Hill papers, MM.
18. Hill papers, MM.

Chapter Twelve: Wəlastəkwey (Maliseet) Linguistics and the Preservation of a Culture

1. Montague Chamberlain, *Maliseet Vocabulary*, introduction by William F. Ganong (Cambridge, MA; Harvard Cooperative Society, 1899).
2. Edwin Tappan Adney, "Milicite Indian Natural History: A List of Bird Names Together with a Supplementary List of Names of Other Animals," *Abstract of the Proceedings of the Linnaean Society of New York City for the Official Year 1888–89.* Adney's commentary is at times playful and poetic, and his sense of humour is evident in his description of the Saw-Whet Owl (Kupkamis):

   > Kup, pitched in a high key, is the sound uttered by the owl. It is "whetting" the sound that sometimes, as we read, leads travelers, lost at night in the forest, to hunt for the saw-mill and the workmen, who in filing their saws make the sounds that come with such suggestiveness out of the gloom of the lonely woods.... No Indian hunter, if he is sane, thinks of injuring or mocking Kupkamis. Nor should anyone imitate that diminutive sorcerer, or something about your camp will get a good scorching.... if anyone kills him he will as certainly get hurt himself.

3. Edwin Tappan Adney, "The Malecite Indian's Names for Native Berries and Fruits, and Their Meanings," *Acadian Naturalist* 1, no. 3 (1944), 103–10.
4. Fannie Eckstorm, *Indian Place Names of the Penobscot Valley and the Maine Coast* (Orono, ME: University of Maine Press, 1941; 1978).
5. Letter from Fannie Eckstorm to Tappan Adney, November 28, 1945. Fannie Eckstorm Collection, Raymond H. Fogler Library, University of Maine, Orono, ME.
6. Nicholas Smith, the author of this chapter, likely learned about Adney's thoughts of marriage and Eckstorm's hesitation from Peter Paul. Paul was a friend of Adney, accompanied him when he met Eckstorm, and was closely associated with him during the time he was communicating with her. Nicholas Smith died in 2022.
7. Edwin Tappan Adney, *The Language of the Malecite or Etchemin Indians: Illustrating a New Method of Analysis, with Words, Sentences and Texts.* Adney papers, PEM.
8. Nicholas Smith is commenting on his own research and his conversations with professionally trained linguists.
9. Conor Quinn correspondence with Daryl Hunter, August 2015.

Chapter Thirteen: At Home in Upper Woodstock: Research as a Way of Life

1. Leon Thornton, interview, 1985, transcribed by James Wheaton, Carleton County Historical Society, Woodstock, NB.
2. Letter from Tappan Adney to Frank Speck, January 15, 1944. Speck papers, PEM.
3. Mary Bernard, *The Last Romantic: The Life of George Frederick Clarke, Master Storyteller of New Brunswick* (Woodstock, NB: Chapel Street Editions, 2015), 265.
4. Letter from Tappan Adney to George Frederick Clarke, August 18, 1948. PEM.
5. For a detailed account of the Adney–Clarke relationship, see Bernard, *The Last Romantic*, 283–88.
6. George Frederick Clarke, *Someone Before Us: Buried History in Central New Brunswick* (Woodstock, NB: Chapel Street Editions, 1968; expanded edition, 2016). The expanded edition includes colour photos of stone tools from Clarke's collection and an essay by David Black, professor of archaeology and anthropology at the University of New Brunswick, on the significance of Clarke's pioneering archaeology.
7. Tappan Adney, research subjects memo, October 18, 1945. Adney papers, PEM.
8. Letter from Tappan Adney to J.C. Webster, February 28, 1939. Webster papers, NBM.

Chapter Fourteen: Friend of the Wəlastəkokewiyik and the Battle for Indigenous Rights

1. Mary Bernard, *The Last Romantic: The Life of George Frederick Clarke, Master Storyteller of New Brunswick* (Woodstock, NB: Chapel Street Editions, 2015), 287.
2. Martha Walls, "Countering the 'Kingsclear Blunder': Maliseet Resistance to the Kingsclear Relocation Plan, 1945–1949," *Acadiensis* 37, no. 1 (Winter 2008), 3–30.
3. C. Ted Behne, ed., *The Travel Journals of Tappan Adney, Volume 1: 1887–1890*, rev. ed. (Fredericton, NB: Goose Lane Editions, 2010), 37.
4. Letter from Tappan Adney to Peter Paul, December 1944. Adney papers, UNB.
5. Andrea Bear Nicholas, "Maliseet Aboriginal Rights and Mascarene's Treaty, Not Dummer's Treaty," in *Papers of the Sixteenth Algonquian Conference*, ed. William Cowan (Ottawa: Carleton University Press, 1986), 215–29. See also Andrea Bear Nicholas, "Mascarene's Treaty of 1725," *University of New Brunswick Law Journal* 43 (1994): 3–18.
6. At the time Magistrate McLaughlin was confronted with Adney's treaty defence of Peter Paul's Indigenous rights, he lived at 150 Chapel Street in Woodstock, NB. In 2006, Keith and Ellen Helmuth purchased this heritage residence. The dining room is now the office of Chapel Street Editions, where the final assembly and editing of this book took place. It is likely where Magistrate McLaughlin took his evening meal on August 22, 1946, as he pondered what to do about Adney's treaty defence.

7. Letter from D.R. Bishop to Tappan Adney, October 29, 1946. Adney papers, UNB.

8. Letter from Tappan Adney to D.R. Bishop, December 16, 1946, Peter Paul family archive, Woodstock, NB.

9. *Globe and Mail*, May 19, 1951.

10. Bear Nicholas, "Maliseet Aboriginal Rights," see also Bear Nicholas, "Mascarene's Treaty."

11. Heather Conn, "Marshall Case." www.thecanadianencyclopedia.ca/en/article /marshall-case.

12. D.G. Bell, "A Commercial Harvesting Prosecution in Context: The Peter Paul Case, 1946," *University of New Brunswick Law Journal* 55 (2006), 86–104.

13. Letter from Tappan Adney to Norman Lickers, July 5, 1947. Adney papers, UNB.

14. Letter from Pat Paul to Ted Behne, September 7, 2007.

15. Tappan Adney's address to Wəlastəkwi Elders, fall 1946. Adney papers, UNB.

16. Letter from Tappan Adney to C.R. Mercereau, November 8, 1946. Adney papers, UNB.

17. Letter from William Saulis to Tappan Adney, 1948. Adney papers, UNB.

18. Letter from William Saulis to Tappan Adney, 1949. Adney papers, UNB.

19. Letter from Tappan Adney to J.R. MacNicol, June 20, 1947. Adney papers, UNB.

20. Letter from Chief Paul to Chief Saulis, undated but likely written in the spring of 1948. Adney papers, PEM.

21. Adney noted this on his copy of a letter from Robert Hoey responding to the parliamentary debate, April 11, 1948. Adney papers, UNB.

22. Letter from Tappan Adney to J.R. MacNicol, June 19, 1949. Adney papers, UNB.

23. Tappan Adney quoted in a memo from Fred Hill to Homer Ferguson, September 8, 1947. Ferguson papers, MM.

24. Letter from Tappan Adney to Frank Speck, February 26, 1947. Adney papers, PEM.

Epilogue

1. Wendy Wickwire, *At the Bridge: James Teit and the Anthropology of Belonging* (Vancouver: UBC Press, 2019).

Selected Bibliography

Adney, Edwin Tappan. *The Klondike Stampede*. New York: Harper & Brothers, 1900. Reprint, Vancouver: University of British Columbia Press, 1994.

Adney, Edwin Tappan and Howard Chapelle. *The Bark Canoes and Skin Boats of North America*. Washington D.C.: Smithsonian Institution, 1964.

Adney, Edwin Tappan. *The Travel Journals of Tappan Adney: 1887–1890, Vol. 1*. Edited by C. Ted Behne. Fredericton. New Brunswick: Goose Lane Editions, 2016.

Adney, Edwin Tappan. *The Travel Journals of Tappan Adney: 1891–1896, Vol. 2*. Edited by C. Ted Behne. Fredericton, New Brunswick: Goose Lane Editions, 2014.

Helmuth, Keith. *Tappan Adney and the Heritage of the St. John River Valley*. Woodstock, New Brunswick: Chapel Street Edition, 2017.

Jennings, John. *Bark Canoes: The Art and Obsession of Tappan Adney*. Richmond Hill, Ontario: Firefly Books, 2004.

McPhee, John. *The Survival of the Bark Canoe*. New York: Farrar, Straus and Giroux, 1975.

Index

Page numbers in **bold** denote illustrative material.
Page numbers in *italics* denote references in notes.

About the Authors

James W. Wheaton (1933–2005) was an electrical engineer by training but spent much of his time and great energy on his passions—genealogy, history, writing, sailing, and playing trombone in Dixieland bands in the Boston and Clearwater, Florida, areas. During his long engineering career—which notably involved measuring the strain on the hulls of enormous ore carriers in the Great Lakes and instrumenting and testing the strength of materials used in nuclear power plants—he found time to develop an extensive genealogical record of ancestors on both sides of his family.

Jim Wheaton was president of the Hingham Historical Society, Hingham, Massachussetts, in the 1970s and led the organization with enthusiasm and energy. During this time he shepherded the development and publication of *When I Think of Hingham*, a view of Hingham's history told through photographs and text. He corresponded widely with genealogical sources throughout the United States and England and, through these efforts, came into possession of the original letters and journals of Dr. Charles Brackett, his great-great-grandfather, who served in the Union Army during the Civil War. Jim transcribed and annotated these letters and published them in the book, *Surgeon on Horseback: The Missouri and Arkansas Journal and Letters of Dr. Charles Brackett of Rochester, Indiana 1861–1863*.

Jim then became interested in the life and legacy of Tappan Adney, the grandfather of his wife, Joan Adney Dragon. He began an extensive research and writing project aimed at producing the first biography and full account of Adney's accomplishments. By 2003, Jim had completed the first draft of a fourteen-chapter Tappan Adney biography, which he passed on to Ted Behne for completion.

C. Ted Behne (1943–2014) retired in 1998 after a thirty-year career in communications management with AT&T. He was previously an information officer with the US Air Force. After retirement, he combined his skill as a writer with his passion for canoes, snowshoes, and other handcrafts of North American Indigenous cultures. He wrote and published many magazine articles based on his research. Using his extensive knowledge of Indigenous history and culture and his collection of handcrafts, he made numerous school presentations in New Jersey, where he lived. He was also able to share his knowledge by becoming a substitute teacher in local middle and high schools.

After working with James Wheaton on the biography of Tappan Adney, Ted took on its completion when Jim became ill. He expanded his research and continued to revise and develop the manuscript. During this time, he also transcribed and edited Adney's travel journals from 1887 to 1896. Ted built a full-size canoe as well as scale models of birchbark canoes of the type built by Adney. He died before the biography was fully prepared for publication, and his wife, Elizabeth, picked up the work, added to the development of the manuscript, and kept the project alive.

Daryl Hunter retired twenty-two years ago from a government career in geographic information systems. His job required travel throughout the Maritime provinces, which enabled him to also collect historic varieties of apples from abandoned home-steads and farms and establish a heritage orchard at his home on Keswick Ridge in New Brunswick. As he researched heirloom apple varieties and studied the history of the fruit growing industry in New Brunswick, he discovered Francis Peabody Sharp. Daryl was appointed to the board of Kings Landing Historical Settlement, where he led a project that established a heritage orchard and nursery commemorating Sharp's pioneer achievements in apple hybridization.

In researching Francis Peabody Sharp, Daryl discovered Tappan Adney, Sharp's son-in-law. In 1998 James Wheaton was introduced to Daryl as a source on Francis Sharp, and Daryl's interest and research diverted from Sharp to Adney. His subsequent Adney research has assembled a major archive on his life and legacy. Jim asked Daryl to interview the Elders of the Wəlastəkwey communities who remembered Adney. This led him to writing monthly historical articles for the *Tobique Wulustuk Times*, an Indigenous newspaper published for over a decade. Adney's "Malecite Natural History" papers inspired many of Daryl's articles. As he says, "Adney's spirit is still alive today, and his work continues on."

Daryl Hunter is an adviser and consultant to the Carleton County Historical Society for the management of its Adney archive and the development of the Tappan Adney Room at Connell House Museum. He is also an adviser to the board of trustees of the Adney-Flemming Trust and the Town of Woodstock on the development of the Adney-Flemming Nature Preserve, as well as a property management volunteer.

Nicholas N. Smith's (1926–2022) career as an ethnographer was devoted to the study and preservation of Wabanaki cultures and languages. As a young scholar in the early 1950s he was asked to sort and organize the Tappan Adney papers on Wəlastəkwey linguistics that had been deposited with the Phillips Library at Peabody Essex Museum in Salem, Massachusetts. He became a close friend of Peter Paul of Woodstock First Nation and worked with him on the preservation of Wəlastəkwey language and culture.

From 1954 to 2018 Nick published many papers and book chapters on his Wabanaki research. He created an extensive computer-based bibliography for the study of Wabanaki history and culture, which is now administered by the University of Maine. In the 1970s and 1980s he lived and worked with the Cree in northern Quebec. The University of Maine awarded him a honorary doctor of humane letters in 2007. He was the author of two books: *Three Hundred Years in Thirty: Memoir of*

Transition with the Cree Indians of Lake Mistassini and *Penobscot Traditions with Little Devil Fish.*

Keith Helmuth's career in the book business includes managing independent, academic bookstores serving the University of Iowa, Syracuse University, Columbia University, and the University of Pennsylvania. In addition, he spent two decades as the co-editor of the book publishing program of Quaker Institute for the Future, of which he was a founding board member. Keith was the library manager and on the environmental studies faculty at Friends World College and also served as a bibliographic consultant to Metanexus Institute. He is now the publisher and managing editor of Chapel Street Editions in Woodstock, New Brunswick.

The Helmuth family operated North Hill Farm at Speerville, New Brunswick, for almost thirty years, during which time they initiated the founding of the Woodstock Farm Market. Keith has served in the public participation program of the Saint John River Basin Board and as a local representative on the Western Valley Region Solid Waste Commission. He has written for publication for more than fifty years on environmental issues. He is the author of numerous books, including *Tracking Down Ecological Guidance, Tappan Adney and the Heritage of the St. John River Valley*, and *Working in the Commonwealth Books: A Cultural Memoir* (forthcoming in 2025).